HOW TO WRITE LAW EXAMS

IRAC Perfected

SECOND EDITION

<hr style="width:30%" />

S.I. Strong

ASSOCIATE PROFESSOR
UNIVERSITY OF SYDNEY LAW SCHOOL
ADJUNCT PROFESSOR OF LAW
GEORGETOWN UNIVERSITY LAW CENTER

<hr style="width:30%" />

WEST
ACADEMIC
PUBLISHING

© 2016 LEG, Inc. d/b/a West Academic
© 2020 LEG, Inc. d/b/a West Academic
    444 Cedar Street, Suite 700
    St. Paul, MN 55101
    1-877-888-1330

West, West Academic Publishing, and West Academic are trademarks of West Publishing Corporation, used under license.

Printed in the United States of America

ISBN: 978-1-64708-099-0

Dedication

For Peter and Zachary

Preface

This is a book for law students, so it is only appropriate to begin by thanking the many research assistants who provided invaluable assistance on both the first and second editions of this text. In particular, I would like to thank Steve Cady, Jared Guemmer, Claire Hawley, Brittney Herron, Kayla Kemp, Katherine Kolisch, Kayla Meine, Laura Petkovich, Taylor Rakes, Allyson Vasilopulos, and Niya Young for their contributions to this text.

I would also like to thank my former colleagues at the University of Missouri, particularly Brad Desnoyer and Amy Schmitz, for insights into how they evaluate law school essays. I also owe a debt of gratitude to colleagues at the Universities of Cambridge, Oxford, Sydney, and Georgetown for similarly instructive conversations.

Legal writing is deeply influenced by the demands of legal practice, and I want to acknowledge the advice and guidance I received in practice. In particular, I would like to thank former colleagues in the New York and London offices of Weil, Gotshal & Manges LLP and the Chicago office of Baker & McKenzie LLP.

Summary of Contents

Table of Contents

HOW TO WRITE LAW EXAMS

IRAC Perfected

SECOND EDITION

CHAPTER 1

An Introduction to Writing Law Exams

A. Excelling on Law School Exams

Law students' number-one concern in law school is how to excel on their exams. Rumors abound about the difficulty of law school exams, and in many ways these rumors are true. Law school exams are qualitatively different than any other type of exam and require students to present information in a unique and challenging manner. In fact, most students' biggest difficulty in law school is not mastering the substantive material; it is demonstrating their knowledge to their professors in a way that the professors recognize and reward.

Rather than focusing on study skills, time management, and the like, this book provides detailed and comprehensive information about the exam itself. Although study skills are important, they are secondary to the more critical question of how to write a good law school exam essay.

This book shows you how to master the specific techniques needed to excel on law school exams. The chapters of this book also show you how law school exams are linked to the work of a practicing attorney, thereby preparing you not only for your exams but also for life as a lawyer. However, there are several other ways in which this text is special.

1. Focus on the Finish Line

As a law student, you already know about setting goals. If you didn't, you wouldn't be a law student, let alone a law student who cares enough to read a book about mastering exams. You know that, like a long-distance runner, you must focus on the finish line. Every step counts, but only if you are on the right path. Too many law students sprint aimlessly when it comes to exams. This book helps you avoid that and other errors.

The best way to achieve a goal is to break it down into individual elements and then set out to master each of those constituent parts. As a

1

law student, you must achieve two things if you are to do well on your law school exams: (1) learn the material properly and (2) present your knowledge in the best possible light. Most students focus on the first of these elements and ignore the second. However, a better understanding of the end product (namely, what a good law exam essay looks like) will not only help you present your knowledge of the law in the best possible light, it will help you learn the underlying material properly.

Most law students, particularly those in their first year and those at the bottom of the second- and third-year classes, believe that it is critically important to memorize every fact of every case, including the procedural posture. If the goal of a law student is only to know the material discussed in class or in the course materials, then that type of information might seem important. However, professors do not assign cases hoping that you will absorb the minutiae of all the various decisions. Instead, the professor wants you to understand the legal rule associated with each case and how that rule operates under a different set of facts, particularly the facts that are presented in the final examination. Law school is all about expanding from the specific to the general. Only after you have learned to recognize the universal principles reflected in the specific features of the cases read in class and apply those principles in other contexts can you do well on a law school exam and get the grade you want.

TIP

Many of the details of a particular case are irrelevant when it comes to the final exam.

This book teaches you how to take the substantive material that you learn during each of your courses and apply that material to new fact patterns in an exam scenario. In so doing, the book makes you a better law student and a better lawyer by focusing on the finish line.

2. In-Depth Discussion

This book is not short. There is a lot of detail, and some law students might feel that their time is better spent with a short guide with simple bullet points. However, short cuts seldom provide good results, particularly in the law. If you are to truly understand how to master a law school exam, you need more than a few pithy aphorisms—you need real content.

TIP

Doing well on a law school exam requires a considerable amount of preparation, including prep on exam skills.

This book provides you with meaty, in-depth information about each step of the exam process. While it may take you a bit more time to digest the information, the result will likely be a higher grade in your classes.

3. Real Exam Answers

Students who are hoping to improve their grades always want to see a model answer. However, not all sample essays are created equal. For example, a model response that has been written by a professor may identify the substantive issues that the professor wants to see but typically does not explain how to present that information. As a result, students don't learn how to get from where they are to where they need to be.

This book helps students with this particular skill. If you look at the last chapter, you will see numerous essays written by actual students. However, these essays are not included as a means of helping you learn the content of the law. Instead, these essays are used as teaching tools to show you how actual students have approached actual law exam questions. Including multiple examples helps you understand how the various writing techniques and suggestions contained in this book are put into practice.

This book does more than simply provide actual student essays. Instead, each student essay is subject to a detailed, line-by-line critique that describes how well the student authors implemented various exam-writing techniques discussed elsewhere in the book. Because the commentary focuses on writing rather than substance, readers can learn certain universal rules about how to write a good law exam essay. These principles apply across all subject matters, which makes this book useful to you in all your classes, regardless of the substantive content.

B. What Makes Law School Exams Particularly Difficult?

Most people who choose to study law are smart, motivated, and hardworking. They know that law is a very competitive field, and they are prepared to do whatever it takes to do well. Why, then, do so many intelligent students fail to achieve the grades they want? The answer is simple: law students are never taught how to demonstrate their legal knowledge in an exam scenario.

The differences between law school and undergraduate exams are striking. Most undergraduate tests ask simple, straightforward questions, either in multiple-choice or short-answer form, and seek equally simple and straightforward answers. The key to doing well on these types of exams involves memorizing the necessary information and repeating it back in virtually the same form.

Undergraduate essay examinations follow the same general pattern. Students who want a good grade simply regurgitate information found in the teaching materials accurately and comprehensively. Questions that ask for independent analysis can usually be answered with the students' own opinion, even if that opinion is largely unsubstantiated.

TIP ✓

A good law school grade is based on effectively answering a question, not just knowing the underlying information.

Law students face an entirely different task. Knowing the underlying information is important, but it is not enough. To do well, students must learn how to manipulate various cases and statutes and apply the information contained in those materials to new and unique fact patterns. Students must also learn how to structure their essays in a manner that is responsive to the question and explain the legal analysis in a precise and understandable manner.

You might wonder why, if writing and analysis are so important, they are seldom taught outside of your first-year legal writing course. Quite simply, few doctrinal professors feel that it's their job to teach these particular skills. In fact, most professors believe that law students should already be proficient in writing and analysis before they come to law school and that the purpose of law school is to teach substantive legal principles.

However, there is a second and much more problematic issue. Quite simply, most law professors don't know how to teach legal writing. As a result, most of the feedback that law professors give on written work tends to focus on either substance (i.e., missed legal issues) or on grammar (i.e., misplaced commas, passive voice, etc.). As useful as these sorts of comments may be, they don't help students learn how to structure an argument or to present information effectively.

NOTE 🔍

Contrary to popular belief, the ability to write well is not a genetic trait. It is a learned skill.

The one writing tip that is commonly offered by law professors is that students should utilize a technique known as IRAC, which stands for Issue, Rules, Application, Conclusion. However, very few law schools provide any advice on how to understand and apply the IRAC method. This book fills that gap in your legal education and helps you write strong, effective, well-structured exam essays.

C. Getting Inside the Professor's Mind

It's hard to write an excellent essay if you don't know what criteria professors are using when they grade your work. Unfortunately, there is no standardized rule about what constitutes a good exam response. To some extent, every law professor has his or her own idea about what a good essay looks like. As a result, it is imperative that you ask your professor to describe his or her views about grading before you take the exam. You can also talk to other students who have taken classes with that particular professor to try to glean any additional insights, although law students are not always the best source of exam information.

Although law professors differ somewhat in what they say they are looking for, there are nevertheless some qualities that are universally recognized as reflecting a top exam response. For example, to achieve one of the top grades in your class, your answer must:

- pay close attention to the question asked;

- contain detailed knowledge of the topic addressed as well as a deeper understanding of the context in which that topic exists;

Do your research. Identify what your particular professors are looking for in their exams.

- reflect excellent coverage of the question, including both breadth and accuracy, with no or almost no significant errors or omissions relating to the law at issue;

- identify at least some of the less obvious points of law;

- reflect outstanding structure, argument, and writing;

- demonstrate excellent use of supporting information and ideas;

- identify a number of counter-arguments; and

- present theoretical or policy-based arguments concerning the subject as well as significant critical analysis and a thoughtful personal perspective on the debate.

It may seem impossible to demonstrate all of these qualities within a single answer, particularly in a timed exam situation, and the standard is indeed high. However, experience shows that students can write essays of this nature, particularly if they know what the relevant standard is.

An above-average essay is not quite as good in each of these regards, although the student nevertheless covers most major points. Therefore, responses falling into this category can be said to:

- pay attention to the question as it is asked;

- provide a relatively detailed knowledge of the topic addressed as well as a good understanding of the context in which that topic exists;

- contain good coverage of the question in terms of breadth and accuracy, with few significant errors or omissions relating to the law at issue;

- reflect strong organization, argument, and writing;

- demonstrate good use of supporting information and ideas;

- identify a few counter-arguments; and

- reflect some degree of familiarity with theoretical or policy-based arguments concerning the subject as well as a significant degree of critical analysis.

An average essay (meaning one that falls around the median grade at your law school) conveys some understanding and analytic skill but lacks detail and overall insight into the problem. Thus, an average answer:

- provides information about the general subject matter of the question does but not precisely address the question asked;

NOTE

An average exam answer conveys some understanding and analytic skill but lacks detail and insight.

- demonstrates average knowledge of the topic addressed as well as an average understanding of the context in which that topic exists;

- reflects acceptable coverage of the question, with reasonable breadth and accuracy, though with some substantial errors or omissions relating to the law at issue;

- reflects average organization, argument, and writing; and

- uses supporting information and ideas, but with a weak theoretical, policy-based, or critical approach.

Finally, a below-average exam answer demonstrates a minimal understanding of the question and issues as well as significant organizational shortcomings. These essays therefore:

- discuss the basic subject matter of the question, albeit with a lack of attention to the question as it is asked;

- demonstrate some knowledge of the topic at issue as well as some understanding of the general context, although the answer may not be entirely accurate and could include significant errors and omissions in the law;

- reflect a poor organizational structure, lack analytical focus, and demonstrate a poor ability to express oneself; and

- reflect only a limited ability to use supporting information and ideas and offer little theoretical, policy-based, or critical analysis.

YOUR TURN

Make a list of all the qualities of an "A" exam answer. Compare this list with your practice exam answers or ask a friend to review your draft responses. Have you fulfilled the criteria necessary to earn a high grade? Where can you improve?

_____

_____

_____

_____

_____

As these lists show, law school exams are graded very differently than exams given at the undergraduate level. Furthermore, the emphasis in law school exams is entirely different than that in undergraduate courses.

The focus at the undergraduate level quite often appears to be solely on the outcome of a particular inquiry. Students are typically provided with a list of questions to answer and given points depending on whether the student gave a correct or incorrect answer. Although undergraduates occasionally win points by "showing the math" (i.e., showing the underlying analysis), the emphasis in most programs is on providing an objectively correct response.

Law school is not like that. In law school, professors typically provide you with a fact pattern and ask you to discuss all potential legal issues and form a conclusion about which party or parties will prevail. Most importantly, your professors want to know why you reached your conclusion.

The "why" of a response is important in a law school setting because there are very few times in either law school or the practice of law where one argument is completely right and the other completely wrong. Law is all about persuasion and "showing the math." A law school essay that simply states a conclusion—the equivalent of "the answer is seven"—does not win points and does not earn a top grade.

Instead, to do well, you have to demonstrate each step of your analysis in order to persuade your reader that you are right. Often there is no objectively "right" answer.

Law students who want to achieve top grades therefore must learn how to "spot" each issue, intelligently discuss the relevant law, correctly analyze the facts by correlating the relevant facts with the law previously discussed, and then enunciate a conclusion. The more correct and relevant things you say, the more points you get. Although you do not earn extra points for good organization, an essay that follows a logical sequence and describes each point clearly and concisely is more persuasive than an essay riddled with grammatical errors and organizational flaws. Such essays therefore deserve a top grade.

The IRAC method outlined in this book helps you with each of these elements by showing you how to identify relevant issues, present supporting legal authority, and craft sophisticated arguments containing detail, insight, and relevance to the question asked. IRAC also allows you to present your ideas quickly and efficiently, thereby giving you more time to write your answers and increasing the breadth and depth of your discussion.

YOUR TURN

How does a law essay differ from an undergraduate essay?

_____

_____

_____

_____

_____

D. What Is IRAC?

Although IRAC is mentioned constantly throughout law school, the concept of an IRAC essay can be confusing to those who have never seen the system put into practice. In fact, IRAC is a simple, four-step method of legal analysis and writing that provides students with a practical and proven method of answering law school exams. Each of the four steps requires you to demonstrate a different kind of analytical skill. If you implement the IRAC method in your exams, your grades should improve dramatically, since you will be showing your professors precisely the qualities that are required of a practicing lawyer.

The first step of an IRAC analysis identifies the legal **issue(s)** raised by the exam problem. Here, you show your professor that you can spot legal controversies, construct multiple lines of argument, and respond to questions as they are asked.

Answering the question as asked is the same as responding to the cause of action asserted in a lawsuit. What happens if the defense lawyer fails to address the legal questions as presented by the plaintiff or prosecution? A malpractice suit, among other things. Don't commit law school malpractice— answer the question as asked!

The second step in the IRAC system involves the presentation of the applicable **rules** of law and relevant cases. In this section, you identify and analyze the relevant legal authorities regarding each of the legal issues discussed in the first step of your essay, thereby demonstrating your grasp of the materials discussed in class on a deep, rather than superficial, level.

The "A" step of IRAC requires you to demonstrate your legal reasoning skills by **applying** the facts in the question to the legal rules you have presented in the "R" section of your essay. Some students are confused about how to distinguish between the "A" and "R" steps, since the two elements are closely linked. However, it is easy to appreciate the difference if you remember that the first step focuses on identifying the relevant legal standard while the second considers whether that standard has been met under the facts presented.

IRAC's fourth step requires you to identify the **conclusion** of your argument. In so doing, you weigh up the different arguments, decide which arguments are most compelling, and introduce any relevant theoretical or policy points that may bear on the issues at stake.

This book is organized to provide you with a good understanding of how to use the IRAC system in your own essays. For example, chapters three through six provide you with detailed discussion of each of the four elements of IRAC. Chapter seven shows you how to adapt IRAC to various types of policy or "discuss" questions, while chapter ten provides numerous student-authored essays to show IRAC in action.

Although the IRAC system is useful, it will do little to help your grades if you cannot express yourself clearly. Poor writing does more than slow down the reader—it actually obscures the meaning of your arguments. Chapter eight therefore outlines the fundamentals of grammar and good writing to make sure that you are aware of certain basic rules that may never have been taught to you in all your years of schooling. Not only will these suggestions improve your grades in law school, they will also help you once you get out in practice.

There are other ways that this book can help you after you leave law school. For example, the IRAC methodology is actually used by practicing lawyers, as discussed in chapter nine.

Those who don't believe that grammar matters should compare the phrase "Let's eat, Mom" with "Let's eat Mom." Which would your mother prefer?

A good law school exam cannot exist without good content.

As useful as IRAC is, it is not a magic bullet. Good organization cannot overcome a lack of understanding of the building blocks of a legal essay (i.e., the law itself). Therefore, the following chapter briefly discusses how to read, understand, and summarize the legal materials that form the bedrock of a good IRAC essay.

YOUR TURN

How can IRAC help you?

_____

_____

_____

_____

_____

CHAPTER 2

Building the Necessary Foundation: Reading and Understanding Legal Materials

The IRAC method acts like a blueprint to writing law school exams, since it provides you with a framework for analyzing and answering legal questions. However, IRAC, by itself, is not enough. To produce a worthwhile essay, you have to combine the blueprint—IRAC—with more concrete elements, namely the relevant principles of substantive law. You may have a great structure and flawless prose, but if you don't say anything of substance, then you will not receive a good grade. The best organization and writing style in the world cannot overcome a lack of knowledge.

Good writers know another secret: the more substance an essay has, the better the organization and writing naturally become. People who don't quite know what they want to say usually end up repeating themselves or focusing on vague generalities. Although each statement may be true in and of itself, these types of wandering, unfocused essays typically do not respond to the question the professor has asked in any useful way. Tight, narrowly focused essays are what earn the highest grades in law school.

NOTE

Good content leads to good structure.

EXAM

Students who don't know the material try to answer the question they wish had been asked rather than the question that was asked.

Students who don't know the underlying legal material also spend a lot of time qualifying their remarks, creating elaborate hypotheticals that are not part of the question, and resorting to "legalese" to hide their lack of knowledge. Some students even think that they can bluff their way into a good grade by extensive use of various terms of art and high-sounding language. In fact, law professors see right through that technique. Quite simply, you have to know the material if you are to do well.

11

Learning the law is hard work. However, simply spending a lot of time with your books does not always guarantee a good grade. In fact, research has shown that the students who work the hardest often do not get the highest grades.[1] While this phenomenon leads some people to conclude that an aptitude for law is genetic and that "you either have it or you don't," the ability to grasp the nuances of the law is in fact a learned skill.

The difference between students at the top of the class and those at the middle or bottom of the class is that the top students have figured out (1) how to present their knowledge in a way that the professor can appreciate (typically through the IRAC system) and (2) how to study and outline in a way that maximizes their exam scores. Most of this book focuses on the first of these two skills. This chapter focuses on the second.

There are three types of legal materials that you use in law school: (1) cases, (2) statutes, and (3) secondary sources, which includes legal encyclopedias, casebooks, law review articles, and treatises. Each of the three types of authority is discussed separately below, since each requires a different study approach.

A. Case Law

As you already know, most of your time in law school is spent reading and analyzing case law. Law schools in the United States focus on case law for three reasons. First, statutes cannot, and are not intended to, cover every possible situation. Instead, statutes are supplemented by case law that describes how a particular piece of legislation is to be applied in particular circumstances. You must know and describe relevant clarifying cases whenever you think a statute governs the issue at hand.

Second, statutes sometimes incorporate common law definitions or principles by reference. Discussing a statute without the accompanying case law gives the court—and your professor—an incomplete and thereby incorrect description of the law.

Finally, there are times when no statute applies. Instead, the law is embodied in the various cases that have developed over time, and your job is to identify and discuss the various cases that establish the relevant legal standard.

As you will see in chapter four, there will seldom if ever be only one case relevant to your analysis, regardless of which of these three scenarios appear on an exam. However, you cannot (and should not) try to discuss every case that has been mentioned in class. Instead, you must

---

[1]   *See* Jennifer M. Cooper, *Smarter Law Learning: Using Cognitive Science to Maximize Law Learning*, 44 Cap. U. L. Rev. 551 (2016).

demonstrate good legal judgment when introducing different cases into your essay.

Too often, laptop users transcribe class discussion nearly word for word. Don't fall into that trap. Practice discretion in your note-taking.

The key to developing good legal judgment lies in good note-taking and study habits. Students who receive average or low grades in law school usually fall into one of two possible traps. For example, one type of student worries about his or her ability to distinguish between relevant and irrelevant facts and ends up taking notes that are too voluminous to be helpful at the revision stage. Research has shown that students who take notes on laptops are more prone to this particular problem.[2] These people are also less than discriminating when it comes to highlighting their casebooks and cover their books in fluorescent yellow ink.

This kind of behavior is understandable if the assumption is that law school exams are based on the retention of one critically important detail. However, once you understand that your ability to analyze a question and construct a strong legal argument is not based entirely on your ability to remember minute details about every case that has been decided since 1776, then you will be less prone to excessive note-taking. Good lawyers demonstrate their judgment as much by what they don't say as by what they do say, a point that will be discussed further in chapter four. Note-taking is all about cutting down the information you've been given to a manageable quantity. If, at the end of a class or reading period, you still have too much information to process easily, you are not exercising enough discretion at the initial stage.

TIP ✓

Note-taking is all about cutting down the material to a manageable size. Be ruthless.

Other students have the opposite problem. These are the students who have relied on excellent short-term memories to get by in the past or who overestimate their understanding of the materials and therefore fail to take sufficiently detailed notes during the semester. When it comes time to prepare for finals, these students find they can't remember as much as they thought they could, which means they have to go back and re-read the original materials when they should be focusing on organization and memorization of facts. People who fall into this category also worry about doing too much work before they understand the entirety of the course and thus wasting time on less-than-fruitful

---

2   *See* Association for Psychological Science, *Take Notes by Hand for Better Long-Term Comprehension* (Apr. 24, 2014), *available at* http://www.psychological science.org/index.php/news/releases/take-notes-by-hand-for-better-long-term-comprehension.html (last visited May 17, 2020).

inquiries. In fact, the process of figuring out what the important points are and why, is what learning law is all about.

People who worry that they are unable to identify the key points during the term can rely on several techniques to help improve their understanding of the larger picture. For example, it is possible for students to contextualize their learning by checking the chapter headings in their casebooks or by reviewing the topic headings of their syllabi. This technique helps place a particular case into the course as a whole.

1.   Reading and Understanding Cases

The first thing you need to do is learn how to read a case. Judicial opinions are very different than anything you read during your undergraduate years, and students often come to the conclusion that many if not all judges intentionally mean to make their decisions unclear. Not only is it difficult to identify which aspects of an opinion are truly important, but many cases involve dissenting and concurring opinions that further complicate the analysis. Happily, there are techniques that can help you.

The first thing you must do is learn the language of the law, typically known as "terms of art." Terms of art include phrases that are unique to the law (for example, *ex post facto* or "fee simple") as well as language that is used in ordinary conversation but that has a special meaning when used in legal contexts (for example, when a layperson uses the term "offer," he or she does not necessarily mean to confer upon another person the power to form a contract).

While it is easy in some instances to work out the meaning of a particular phrase in the context of a judicial opinion, it is equally easy to forget the meaning of the term as soon as you see it out of context. Therefore, you should start a vocabulary list for each subject at the beginning of each semester. Doing this will solidify your learning and help you when exam time comes.

Start a vocabulary list for each subject.

Learning vocabulary is relatively simple. What is more difficult is parsing out the important aspects of a

(Over)using commercial outlines and friends' notes hinders your ability to learn legal analysis and excel on exams and in legal practice.

judicial opinion. Here, the key is not to memorize every fact of the case but to understand why the court decided as it did. However, to really appreciate the court's decision, you must read every sentence with a critical eye and ask yourself why the judge wrote what he or she did.

This kind of analysis takes time, and you may think that it is easier and better to rely on various shortcuts such as commercially prepared case briefs or recycled outlines from other students. While these techniques may seem to be both efficient (since you can get through more cases in fewer hours) and effective (since you seem to be assured of identifying the "right" answer), relying on other people's materials actually hurts you in the long run, since you are not learning how to parse through judicial decisions for yourself. These types of shortcuts actually make learning the law less interesting, since you are missing out on the nuances and intricacies of argument that make the study of law so intellectually challenging. These shortcuts also make the transition to life after law school that much harder. Practicing lawyers have to work with original materials, and if you don't learn how to read case law now, you will have a painfully steep learning curve once you start your first job. Since the consequences of underperformance are more severe at that stage, your best option is to do the hard work now, in law school.

TIP

The catchphrase in legal education is "learning to think like a lawyer." The emphasis is not on knowing facts or even legal holdings—the key is learning a method of analysis that requires the ability to deal with legal authorities in their original form.

Students who rely extensively on prepared case briefs and old outlines are also reflecting an undergraduate approach to law school. An undergraduate mentality assumes that to do well in law school, you only need to know the facts and the outcome of a particular decision. In fact, law school is all about learning how to construct an argument based on legal authorities, which is a skill that can only come from reading and understanding the cases in their entirety.

Perhaps the most important reason to read legal opinions in their entirety is because it is the best way to learn how to distinguish and harmonize cases. "Distinguishing" a case requires you to identify how and why a previously published decision does not apply to the question you are facing. Sometimes you can distinguish a case on the facts, which means that the factual circumstances of the two disputes aren't similar enough to warrant extending the legal rule from the earlier case to your situation. However, the more sophisticated approach involves a distinction as a matter of law. Here, you need to explain why the legal principles used in the first case cannot logically or fairly be applied to your fact pattern.

TIP

Distinguishing a case shows why it is not relevant to your fact pattern.

TIP

Harmonizing cases requires you to identify a general rule that comes out of a series of decisions.

Harmonizing a line of cases is a very different skill and requires you to look at a number of different decisions and explain the direction in which the law is moving. While distinguishing cases usually focuses on individual precedents, harmonizing cases usually focuses on a sequence of cases. Very often professors will pose questions that require you to distinguish and/or harmonize cases because that (1) invites you to introduce more than one case into your exam answer (an invitation many people decline, to their detriment) and (2) allows you to demonstrate a sophisticated understanding of the intricacies of the cases as you argue why the precedents should or should not be followed. Therefore, when your professors or casebooks indicate a split in authority on a certain matter, make a note of it as an issue that will likely appear on your final exam.

Reading cases in the original—meaning the edited version found in your casebook—does carry some risk. For example, not every judicial opinion is a model of good legal writing. Some judges rely heavily on the passive voice, while others use verbose, flowery language. Judges may also spend several paragraphs, or even pages, on a point that turns out to be irrelevant to the outcome of the case. Don't fall into these traps. Only discuss those matters that are determinative of the issue at hand. Straightforward, concise writing is your goal.

> **TIP** ✓
>
> Highlight splits in authority as ripe issues for exam questions.

Why read cases in the original (casebook-edited) form?

- It teaches you how to undertake legal reasoning.

- It teaches you how to distinguish and harmonize cases.

- It teaches you how to manipulate cases to suit your purposes.

- It reinforces your learning by repeating important points.

- It indicates the relative weight of precedent.

- It makes the study of law more interesting, since you are learning to argue creatively rather than merely memorizing facts.

2. Briefing Cases

Once you have read and understood a case, you need to "brief" it. When you brief a case, you are describing its legally relevant attributes in a concise and standardized form. Be careful about relying too much on class discussion to help you identify the important issues, since some professors ask you to discuss certain matters (such as the procedural posture of the case) that are in fact largely unimportant to the holding of the case.

Briefing is all about cutting down the information you've been given to a manageable quantity. If, at the end of the day, you still have too much information to process easily, you are not exercising enough discretion. Briefs allow you to cut down the volume of material that you have to review so that when it comes time to finalize your exam outline, you can focus on cross-referencing the material and organizing it in a useful manner rather than doing what should have been done during the first stage of the note-taking process: cutting down the material to a manageable amount.

TIP

Continually asking "why?" when briefing cases forces active reading rather than the passive highlighting of terms. "Why" is more important than "what."

A good case brief gives you a snapshot of the case and why it is important. Therefore, your briefs should be limited to the following information:

- Case name (i.e., *Smith v. Jones*)

- Full citation (i.e., 276 F. 245 (8th Cir. 1921))[3]

- Facts (one to two sentences at most)

- Issue (the legal question to be decided)

- Rule (the legal principle that justifies the outcome and that is applicable to future cases)

- Holding (the outcome of the dispute)

- Reasoning (the "why" behind the rule and the holding)

- Comments (any additional material that you think may be important, ranging from questions for yourself or your professor to *dicta* that might be persuasive in later cases)

A brief does not include all points of fact or law. Focus on the important legal issue relating to your course. If you don't exclude some material, you diminish the value of the brief. At first, briefing may slow you down slightly, but you will save time in the long run, since you will not be forced to re-read entire cases and reconstruct your analyses of the relevant issues when revising for exams.

---

[3]   You can delete the full citation in your notes if the citation appears on your syllabus or in the case index of your textbook. If you delete the citation, however, be sure to note when the case was handed down, since the timing of a decision can affect its precedential value.

Examples of Case Briefs

Following are some examples of case briefs in the area of torts. Look at the original decisions and see which elements have been noted and which elements have been discarded. Note that there is no right or wrong when it comes to case briefs; there is only what is helpful to you and what is not helpful to you.

Fisher v. Carrousel Motor Hotel, Inc., **424 S.W. 627 (Tex. 1967)**	
FACTS:	Manager of restaurant snatched a plate out of a potential customer's hand but never actually touched him. Manager shouted that the potential customer could not be served because that person was African-American.
ISSUE:	Can battery exist without an actual touching of the plaintiff?
RULE:	A defendant can make "contact" by touching an object that is "intimately connected" to the plaintiff's person, making the object part of that person.
HOLDING:	The manager made contact because the plate was intimately connected to the guest.
REASONING:	• Battery can be by indirect contact because our "person" extends to our clothes and objects we are holding. • Battery considers whether the act was offensive. Here, a reasonable person would be offended because of the context.
COMMENTS:	• Was the racially-charged language dispositive to the decision? No, not as long as the manager still acted in an offensive matter. However, words often show intent. • An exam question might arise where the issue is whether an object was part of the person. . .

Wallace v. Rosen, **765 N.E.2d 192 (Ind. Ct. App. 2002)**	
FACTS:	During a school fire drill, a teacher touched a parent on the back and turned her to get her attention. Parent alleged she fell down a staircase.
ISSUE:	Did the teacher intentionally make offensive contact?
RULE:	Because we consent to some personal contact in a "crowded world," a defendant does not

	intentionally make an offensive contact if the contact is "customary and reasonably necessary."
HOLDING:	The teacher did not intentionally make an offensive contact because she was merely getting the parent's attention.
REASONING:	• The teacher acted to protect, not "invade" the parent's "interests." • Just because a defendant may be offended does not mean there is a battery. Inevitably, people will touch each other. • Context matters. Did the parties know each other? Why was contact made? How was it made?
COMMENTS:	How to harmonize with *Vosburg v. Putney*? Both defendants did not intend the resulting harm. Is the difference that if you intend to commit a tort (i.e., harm or offend), you pay for whatever result that happens?

These are just some suggestions on how to brief these cases. You might emphasize different details and could use your own shorthand—whatever is necessary to jog your memory. For example, some people might refer to *Fisher* as the "plate case." Whatever abbreviations you use for the facts, you need to be precise when writing down the legal standards. Use the court's exact words, including terms of art, to the extent possible. Thus, in *Fisher* it is important to indicate that the standard relates to an object that is "intimately connected" with the plaintiff.

YOUR TURN

What is the most important one-word question to ask when reading and briefing a case, and why?

_____

_____

_____

_____

You should aim to brief the cases from the day's reading before class so that can spend your time in class refining your briefs to emphasize your professor's most important points. You should also use class time to listen for answers to all the questions you wrote in the "Comments" section of your brief. If at the end of the lecture you still do not have your answer, talk to your classmates and professor to try to figure out how to answer your question.

B. Statutory Law

Although law school seems to focus primarily on case law, statutes are also a key feature of U.S. state and federal law. However, the way statutes are presented in most courses—in short, excerpted form, sandwiched between numerous judicial decisions—often downplays the importance of legislation in the U.S. legal system.

Although casebooks do not always provide you with an entire piece of legislation, you need to understand the purpose of a particular enactment if you are to grasp it and its applicability to a particular legal question. Therefore, you must look at any legislation discussed in your reading or in class and should, at the very least, skim the section headings to see how the statute works together as a whole.

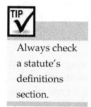

Always check a statute's definitions section.

Pay particular attention to the definitions contained within a statute, since a word in common usage may be given a technical definition in the statute. Consider whether and to what extent a defined term may differ between two different statutes. Note also how one statute may define a term by reference to a definition in another enactment.

You know from the previous discussion that case briefs should quote important judicial language precisely so that any subsequent analysis will be accurate. The same is true with statutory language: quote the relevant language in your notes and in your essays if you want to get top grades. While paraphrasing may sound more elegant at times, you must apply the correct legal standard, as it is written in the statute.

TIP Use the precise language of the statute in your notes and your essay, so long as the quote is not unduly long.

C. Encyclopedias, Casebooks, Articles, and Treatises

Many people find their first—and possibly only—introduction to law through the use of non-binding legal materials such as legal encyclopedias, casebooks, articles, and treatises. Although you will likely have used a number of these "secondary sources" in your legal research and writing course, these tools are useful study aides for other courses.

1. Legal Encyclopedias and *American Law Reports*

A legal encyclopedia, much like a traditional encyclopedia, provides general background information about a particular subject. Popular legal encyclopedias include *American Jurisprudence, Second* (Am. Jur. 2d) and *Corpus Juris Secundum* (C.J.S.). These encyclopedias give a broad perspective on a wide variety of subjects and use language that is easily understood by the student reader. They are an excellent place to start your research or to understand the basics of a topic.

When trying to get a general overview of a set of cases, look to legal encyclopedias and A.L.R. annotations. This step will save you time in the end.

The *American Law Reports* (A.L.R.) is another introductory resource made up of numerous individual "annotations." Like legal encyclopedias, annotations provide background information. However, annotations give more detail and focus on more exact areas of law. A.L.R.s also contain a Table of Jurisdictions, which give you case citations relevant to every applicable jurisdiction.

2. Casebooks

Law students typically use casebooks as their primary texts for class. A casebook provides heavily edited versions of various legal authorities, including cases, statutes, and law review articles. Although you would never want to cite to the excerpted materials contained in a casebook as binding legal authority (instead, you would refer to the case, statute, or article in its original form), casebooks also include varying amounts of original text before or after the excerpted legal authorities. These sections can be very useful in helping put the excerpted materials in context.

Reading this additional material is an excellent way to prepare for the final exam. Students who want to do well should pay particular attention to any hypothetical fact patterns that are included in this reading. Not only do these hypotheticals act as useful mini-exams, where you can test your ability to analyze and apply the cases and statutes discussed in that section, they also help you identify what types of issues might appear on an exam. Although students often feel as if final exam questions come out of nowhere, in reality professors are pretty limited in what they might test. Fact patterns and outcomes might change, but the legally relevant material stays the same. Running through a casebook hypothetical helps you learn how to apply the substantive law to a new fact pattern. That technique captures the essence of thinking like a lawyer and provides you with the substantive skills needed to write a good final exam answer.

Your professor may have only assigned the cases for reading, but you should always read the notes and hypotheticals that follow.

YOUR TURN

Why should you read the notes and hypotheticals in your casebook?

_____

_____

_____

_____

_____

3. Law Review Articles

Casebooks occasionally include excerpts from extremely well-known and highly-influential law review articles. However, some professors also require their students to read articles in the original. These materials can be challenging for students because law review authors are writing for practitioners and scholars who are already well versed in the subject matter under discussion.

However, reading law review articles in the original has its benefits, despite the associated difficulties. For example, law review articles are often much more timely than casebooks and provide a tightly focused analysis on a single subject. Law review articles also suggest how the law might evolve in the future and can therefore be helpful to students who need to answer questions about potential reforms in the law.

> **EXAM**
>
> Law review articles are helpful in answering "discuss" questions and in developing sophisticated analytical techniques.

If your professor assigns you an article, you can be sure that it contains some relevance to your course. However, you may need to parse out the pertinent points from a sea of detail. To ease your understanding, focus on the introductory and concluding paragraphs of the article and of each internal sub-section. Those paragraphs should give you some idea of the basic argument. You can then focus on those issues that are of primary relevance to your course, while skimming the rest of the piece. In so doing, you will not only be learning about the substantive law, you will be learning how to develop your legal judgment as you decide which aspects of the article are most worthy of your attention.

YOUR TURN

Why should you read secondary sources in law school?

_____

_____

_____

_____

_____

4. Treatises and Hornbooks

Treatises are books or series of books that resemble law review articles in that they are aimed at academics and practitioners, rather than students. As a result, treatises are often highly detailed, with a great deal of technical language, since they presuppose a certain level of familiarity with the subject.

Treatises differ from law review articles in that they cover a wide range of issues relating to a specific area of law. Thus, *Nimmer on Copyright* covers all aspects of copyright law and is the go-to source for experts in that field.

Hornbooks are similar to treatises in that they address a wide range of issues within a particular area of law. However, hornbooks are written with slightly less detail and are often aimed at both students and junior practitioners. As a result, hornbooks may be a better introduction for students to a particular legal issue. One well-known hornbook is *Weinstein's Evidence Manual, Student Edition.* Unlike casebooks, which focus on developing your analytical skills through the Socratic method, hornbooks actually tell you what the law is. However, hornbooks should not be used as primary texts for two reasons. First, hornbooks are too detailed for standard student reading. Even though hornbooks are less detailed than treatises, they are still relatively dense. Second, simply reading about applicable legal principles in the abstract does not develop a student's ability to understand how those principles are developed and applied in a novel fact pattern. This is precisely the reason why students should not rely on commercial outlines when trying to learn a new subject. Instead, hornbooks should be used to answer particular questions that a student cannot figure out on his or her own.

Hornbooks, like commercial outlines, cannot be used as primary study materials, though they are an excellent supplement.

D. Putting It All Together

Many student success guides suggest that you start outlining your course early, rather than waiting until just before your final exams. This is excellent advice, since the sheer scope of materials that you will be expected to know in law school far exceeds anything you saw during your years as an undergraduate. Furthermore, studies have shown that students understand and retain knowledge best when they spread their learning out over a period of time rather than trying to cram it all in at the last minute. The long-term approach is particularly effective when the material involves deep conceptual issues rather than simple facts.

The key to a good law school outline is not just the succinct repetition of relevant legal authorities, although a good outline certainly does that. Instead, a good law school outline focuses on the connections between different areas of law, thereby allowing you to undertake sophisticated analyses in your final exam essays.

NOTE

The best exam answers integrate legal principles from multiple parts of the syllabus. You need to identify these areas of overlap in advance if you are to do well on the exam.

In fact, the process of creating your own outline and identifying those connections for yourself is one of the most important ways to ensure that you will get a good grade on your final exam. Many students rely on outlines created by former students or their classmates. Some classes have a legendary outline, handed down through generations of law students who swear by its power. Don't be fooled. Having an outline—even a magic one—is no substitute for creating one.

Furthermore, empirical research proves that making an outline is more important than having an outline.[4] As a result, those who want to excel on their law school exams should put the time into creating their own study materials.

EXAM

Highlighting your textbook is not the same as outlining. You need to rewrite the casebook's language using your own words.

Some students hesitate to create their own outline because they feel that they don't have a firm enough grasp on the substantive law to be able to organize their notes in a useful or "correct" manner. However, these concerns can be allayed by the fact that it is not necessary to come up with your own individual organizational approach. Instead, the easiest and perhaps best way of organizing your outline is to rely on your syllabus or on the table of contents in your casebook. Usually, both of those sources will not only have a number of major headings but will also break down each heading into several sub-issues. Each of these sub-issues will then have a number of cases, statutes, and/or law review articles associated with that topic.

Usually the first case or statute listed under a particular subheading will be the most important and general one, although some professors or casebook authors arrange their materials in historical order. Once you have found the leading precedents, you will be able to identify

---

4   *See* Cooper, *supra* note 1.

the general legal rule. Subsequent cases usually flesh out particular aspects of the basic legal principle and describe how that rule is applied in particular circumstances.

Understanding the structure of your materials is critical to doing well on a law school exam, since those efforts help you identify which cases will be discussed in your essay. For example, you should always mention the case or statute that identifies the broad principle of law. However, you should only introduce subsequent cases to the extent that they are relevant to the question posed by the professor. You should not try to discuss each and every case that falls under a particular sub-heading, since that would demonstrate a lack of judgment in deciding what was relevant.

Your outline should pay particular attention to conflicts or shifts in the law, since these are fruitful areas for discussion and testing. Obviously those areas of law that have experienced reform or a radical change are very likely to form the basis of an examination question, so you should also make particularly detailed notes of those lines of cases. Be sure to know how and why the change has occurred.

TIP

If you are presented with the opportunity to distinguish conflicting cases, you should rejoice, rather than groan, since that offers you an excellent opportunity to show off your legal talents.

Many professors allow students to bring a single-page outline into the final exam room. This document should essentially be a table of contents to your outline. Even if you have an open-book exam, you should create this kind of abbreviated document, since it will help you spot relevant legal issues without having to search through 40 pages of notes. Other open-book exam techniques include "tabbing" your outline with multi-color sticky tabs to identify chapter breaks in your outline. This technique allows you to save precious time during the exam itself. Furthermore, you are embedding important information into your head every time you work on organizing your study materials, so the mere act of manipulating your outline can be useful.

The preceding information should be helpful to you as you work to obtain the building blocks of a good law school essay. Having set the stage, we can now move to the IRAC method itself. The first item to discuss is the issue.

CHAPTER 3

Step One in the IRAC Method: The Issue

Many undergraduate students worry about studying law because they think the subject is too hard. In fact, there is nothing conceptually difficult about law. The hardest thing about law school is learning how to read cases and statutes and finding a way to organize the materials into a workable format. The previous chapter discussed those points. The second hardest thing about studying law is learning how to present the material in exam answers. That concern is the focus of this and the following chapters.

WRIT-ING

Law school exams seldom generate a single answer that is objectively "right." You must analyze all sides of the argument to earn a top grade.

During the exam, most of your time will be spent on the second step of the IRAC method, which requires you to identify the applicable law (i.e., the "rules"). That step is discussed in the next chapter. However, before you can discuss the legal rules, you need to narrow the scope of your response to certain key points. To do so, you must identify what the IRAC method calls the "issue."

This chapter shows you how to identify what question your professors want you to answer and how to write a two to three sentence opening paragraph that will take approximately one minute to write. This first paragraph is supposed to be short because the majority of your time should be spent on the second portion of your essay: the rules.

First impressions matter. Use a short but strong introductory paragraph.

By presenting the issue quickly and succinctly, you set yourself up to write a concise and on-point essay. You also give the reader the impression that you are in full command of the subject matter and the shape of your answer. First impressions are very important if you wish to receive a top grade on your essay. However, if you do not identify the appropriate issue or issues, it becomes nearly impossible to introduce all the relevant rules. Do not shortchange the importance of the "I" step in your analysis.

27

In order to apply the IRAC system effectively, you need to understand its relationship to the practice of law. That subject is introduced in the first section of this chapter. Once you have grasped that point, you will learn:

(1)   what an "issue" is under the IRAC methodology;

(2)   why it is important to identify the issue explicitly in an exam answer; and

(3)   how to spot the various issues that arise out of a question.

You will also be provided with a hands-on example of issue spotting.

A.   Relationship of the IRAC Method to Legal Practice

Although IRAC is primarily known as an exam-writing method, the system has its roots in the style and form of argument used by attorneys, particularly litigators. When an attorney presents a case to the court, he or she must identify and discuss:

(1)   the cause of action that is being alleged (the "issue" in IRAC);

(2)   each of the elements that must be proven in order to prevail on the cause of action (the first, more general, aspect of the "rules" in IRAC);

(3)   any particularly contentious areas of law relating to the elements that must be proven as part of the plaintiff's *prima facie* case (the second, more specific, aspect of the "rules" in IRAC);

(4)   how the facts in his or her case fulfil the *prima facie* case (the "application" of IRAC); and

(5)   the suggested resolution of the case (the "conclusion" of IRAC).

This same model is used in academic programs because the study of law is meant to prepare graduates for legal practice. Just as chemistry students must learn and be tested on how to conduct practical experiments in a laboratory setting, law students must learn and be tested on the tools of their trade, namely the construction of a legal argument.

This is not to say that the IRAC method attempts to duplicate the precise form of legal arguments and documents. Instead, IRAC merely uses a practice-based approach to essays in response to practice-based questions.

B. Defining the Issue in a Law School Exam

When initiating a civil lawsuit, attorneys bring what is known as a cause of action, which identifies the wrongs that have been done and the remedies that should be granted. In many subject matter areas, the issue in IRAC can be equated with a cause of action.

For example, a tort issue would be the same as the various torts: negligence, battery, trespass to chattels, etc. Criminal law may refer to an indictment rather than a cause of action, but the methodology is still the same: prosecutors are claiming that a particular crime (burglary, manslaughter, conspiracy, etc.) has occurred and must prove all the constituent elements in order to make out a *prima facie* case. Contract law is slightly different, since no one sets out to "prove" a contract in the same way one attempts to prove a tort or crime, but the issues in contract cases can be framed in terms of various matters relating to the creation of a contract (such as the presence of adequate consideration) or the termination thereof (such as circumstances leading to anticipatory repudiation).

> **TIP** ✓
>
> Do not try to format your exam answers like a legal memo or client letter, even if the professor asks you to draft a memo or letter. The professor is testing your ability to analyze a legal problem, not remember formats taught in legal research and writing.

When you are trying to identify what the issue is in any particular exam scenario, you should think about what types of actions you might bring. It is important to frame the initial issue (when at all possible) in terms of legal actions for the following reasons:

(1)   framing the issue in terms of a cause of action gives the reader the proper context for the following discussion (this is particularly important when you have multiple issues or multiple parties);

(2)   framing the issue in terms of a cause of action leads you directly to the elements that must be proven as part of the plaintiff's or prosecutor's *prima facie* case and, by extension, into the elements that must be proven for a defendant's affirmative defenses; and

> **EXAM**
>
> Many students lose points by failing to bring up any applicable defenses.

(3) framing the issue in terms of a cause of action gives you a quick and effective introductory paragraph when it comes time to write your essay.

It will be helpful to address each of these points briefly.

1. Putting the Essay in Context

Identifying issues in terms of causes of action is the first and best way to put your essay into its proper context. At first, this may not seem important, since you probably expect the reader of your essays (i.e., your professor) to know more than you do about the subject matter. However, when a reader picks up your essay, he or she has no idea where your essay is going to go. Students can adopt a wide variety of approaches to the same question, and what appears to the professor to be a simple question about the availability of rescission of a contract following a misrepresentation, can be construed by students as a question about breach of contract, consideration, or even intent to create a contract.

TIP

Never write an exam as if the professor already knows the relevant issue or issues. Your job is to demonstrate your knowledge, not to test the knowledge of your reader.

To be fair, this sort of variation is not always due to students misreading the question; some questions are just badly written. However, an experienced professor is often a skeptical professor. Therefore, it is your responsibility, as the author, to put your answer into its proper context and tell your reader precisely what aspects of the question you are going to address.

a. Multiple Issues

NOTE

Give your reader a roadmap to your analysis.

Clear identification of the issues is even more important when you have multiple causes of action or multiple parties arising out of the same fact pattern. This type of scenario is perhaps easiest to see in criminal law, since we're all used to hearing reports of defendants who are charged with multiple crimes arising out of a single event. For example, someone might be charged with both kidnapping and rape or both burglary and manslaughter. However, civil cases can also involve multiple causes of actions and/or multiple theories of liability. For example, a plaintiff in a tort case might simultaneously seek damages for assault, battery, and negligence.[1]

---

[1] *See* Spivey v. Battaglia, 258 So.2d 815 (Fla. 1972) (involving a defendant who pulled the plaintiff toward him in a "friendly unsolicited hug," thereby causing the plaintiff partial facial paralysis).

The rules of civil procedure indicate that plaintiffs do not need to choose one type of action over another but can instead assert any claim that is legitimately supported by the facts. This ability to pursue various actions is important because different types of actions carry different types of remedies: for example, one type of tort may only offer compensatory damages while another type of tort provides for injunctive relief.

Defendants can also assert competing or complementary legal theories. For example, a defendant in a contract case could argue that no liability exists because the plaintiff repudiated the contract (anticipatory breach). That same defendant could simultaneously argue that no contract ever existed due to vagueness of terms or the absence of consideration. Because parties may proceed in the alternative, students can and should do the same in their essays. However, in order to avoid confusing yourself and the person reading your paper, you need to be clear about what precisely you are doing.

b.   Multiple Parties

You also should break apart the different issues that arise between different parties. In an exam, no two parties will be situated in precisely the same manner. Sometimes the parties will be asserting different claims and sometimes they will be asserting different defenses. Even in those situations where two parties are subject to the same cause of action, the sub-issues (as discussed below) will vary slightly. This sort of overlap is not unduly problematic, since you can incorporate prior points by reference, as explained further in chapter four. However, you do need to set forth the relevant issues and sub-issues for each of the different party pairings so that your reader knows what you are doing.

YOUR TURN

Why should you frame the initial issue in terms of legal actions?

---

2.   Running Through the Elements of the Cause of Action

The second benefit to framing your issues as a crime, civil cause of action, or defense is that this technique requires you to recall and list each of the elements that must be established as part of the *prima facie* case or defense.

For example, when you decide that a party can make a claim for negligence, you list the five elements of negligence (duty, breach of duty, legal causation, factual causation, and damages), first to yourself in your notes and then explicitly in your essay. When you do this, you are forced to consider each of the constituent elements and whether you can or should enter into a detailed discussion of any of them.

For example, you may read a question about children who are injured on city park equipment after park hours and who then vandalize that equipment. If you were not using the IRAC system, you might immediately think that you should talk whether and to what extent the city owes a duty to the children. You might start writing an essay about the existence and breach of duty without telling your reader that you were talking about negligence. Not only could this approach confuse your reader, it could also cause you to miss the fact that you could also talk about causation, another of the necessary elements for negligence. You might also miss possible discussions about other torts, such as the city's action against the children for conversion or trespass to land.

TIP

A confused reader cannot give you a good grade.

Students who don't take the time to consider all of their various options often miss potentially fruitful areas of discussion or spend too much time on relatively minor points. The first area of controversy that you identify may not be the best or only matter that you can and should raise. You want to find the most pressing legal issues so that you have sufficient scope to demonstrate your sophisticated reasoning skills. Slow down and consider all potential issues before starting to write your essay.

WRITING

Think before you speak (or write). Law students have to evaluate all options before answering.

3. Creating an Easy Introductory Paragraph

The third reason why you need to learn how to identify the issue is so that you can create a simple introductory paragraph for your essay. As will be discussed later in this chapter, you need to run through all four steps of IRAC before you put pen to paper (or fingers to keyboard), since that will help you formulate a strong writing plan and thus a concise and effective essay. However, many students find that once it comes time to start writing, they struggle to find a way to ease themselves into their argument.

Poor essays typically begin with one, two, or even three superfluous paragraphs that either reiterate the facts or slowly get around to identifying the points that the writer wishes to make. Some essays spend so much time setting the scene that they don't truly start until the second page. Valuable time is lost as a result, and the reader begins to wonder whether the writer really knows what he or she wants to say. Presentation is an important part of legal argument, and you need to learn how to make your points quickly, logically, and effectively. By forcing students to start their essays by identifying the issue, the IRAC method provides an easy route into the substantive discussion.

C. Identifying Sub-Issues

Equating the issue with a cause of action requires you to generate a list of elements that must be proven for the plaintiff to establish a *prima facie* case. For example, to establish the tort of negligence, you must prove existence of a legal duty, breach of that duty, legal causation, factual causation, and damages. However, you should not try to analyze each of these elements in detail. Not only would it be impossible to get through all five elements in a timed exam scenario, but giving equal weight to each of the five elements would also suggest that you do not know what is important and what is not. Law school exams require you to exercise your legal judgment, and what you leave out is as important as what you put in. While it is important to introduce each of the elements that must be proven and provide some general legal authority to support that assertion (a point that will be discussed in more detail in the next chapter, which deals with the "rules" portion of IRAC), you need to focus your analysis on those sub-issues—i.e., those legal elements—that are most difficult to establish as a matter of law.

Remember, you are working from a litigation model. Judges don't want to see a treatise on basic legal premises that are not in dispute, and neither does your professor. Focus on the points that are controversial, not on matters upon which there can be no real disagreement between the parties. Similarly, for reasons discussed more fully in the next chapter, you should not spend your time on questions of fact.

Treat your reader as you would treat a judge.

Identifying the sub-issues that are in contention is a learned skill. Sometimes you see the sub-issue first and sometimes you see the basic issue first. Either way, you need to spend some time thinking about the matter so that you can see the problem in its entirety.

For example, if you have a question in contract law that presents you with a sixteen-year-old who wants to buy a house, your first thought may be to discuss the issue of capacity to contract. However, rather than sticking with that particular thought, you need to work backwards to see that the real issue is whether a contract exists. Although capacity is a concern, no one walks into a court and says, "Your Honor, my client is alleging lack of capacity." That statement gives no context and identifies no possible remedy. Instead, a lawyer would say, "Your Honor, my client alleges that no liability exists in this instance because no contract was formed [i.e., the issue] because a sixteen year-old lacks the capacity to enter into a contract [i.e., the sub-issue]."

D. Spotting Issues

The best way to spot issues is to proceed through the fact pattern considering why the professor has included those particular facts. During this analysis, you are looking for both issues and sub-issues. Operate under the assumption that each sentence is providing you with something to discuss. This is not always the case, but most professors only include facts that are legally relevant. If you use that assumption as your baseline, you will be less likely to miss potentially fruitful topics.

> **EXAM**
>
> Underline facts that raise issues and sub-issues. This will force you to mention those facts later, when you are in the third step of the IRAC analysis.

This approach is particularly important when the fact pattern shows a person speaking. In torts or criminal law, these words are likely relevant to questions of intent or mens rea. In contracts, the words often can be used to determine whether a person is attempting to create a contract. Read these lines particularly carefully.

> **TIP**
>
> If you think you have found the answer based on one case, look again. Law exams are seldom that simple.

Because law professors typically grade on a curve, they must include some elements that will separate excellent answers from average answers. Often this technique involves a question that seems to point down an easy (but ultimately incorrect) analytical route. Some students will take the bait and give a simple answer, based often on one case that appears to control.

Top students see through the deception and use the opportunity to discuss why the simple analysis is inappropriate and why the issue is either (1) a non-starter or (2) better resolved in a more complex manner. As you conduct this analysis, remember always to explain your thinking, even if you are deciding to set aside a point.[2] This technique allows you to show the professor that you are not only intelligent enough to see the potential relevance of a particular argument, but you are so astute that you know enough to set it aside on further analysis.

---

2   You will, of course, need to exercise some judgment. Describing why you have disregarded a point that was obviously irrelevant doesn't make you look intelligent. On the other hand, describing why you have declined to pursue a potentially relevant line of argument can show excellent discretion. This approach is also useful in covering your bases in case the issue you are disregarding is, in fact, relevant. At least you have something down on paper for which your professor can give you points.

Thus, for example, if you are told on a torts exam that "Ann sneaked up behind Lance and hit him on the head with a chair," the core issue is of course battery. However, you should also briefly mention that there could not be an assault because Lance did not see Ann coming and therefore could have been in apprehension of an imminent attack.

Always say why you're doing what you're doing. You don't win points for knowing that some aspect of the question is legally (ir)relevant; you win points for saying that it is legally (ir)relevant, and why.

As you work through your fact pattern, you need to differentiate between questions of law and questions of fact. As discussed further in the next chapter, your job, as a law student, is to argue the law, not the facts. Arguing the facts is something that attorneys do and involves poking holes in the evidence, noting what could have happened and delving into motivation. This often leads to "he said, she said" arguments that are useful in court but

NOTE

Don't argue the facts— argue the law. The distinction is discussed more in chapter four.

unhelpful in a law school essay. When you are looking for possible issues and sub-issues, you should concern yourself solely with legal disputes because your job is to argue various points based on legal authority that you will introduce in the second step of the IRAC analysis. While you definitely need to evaluate the law in light of the facts—a process that will be discussed in detail in chapter five—that is a different thing than arguing the facts.

There are several ways to identify potential issues and sub-issues. One is to look for similarities to well-known cases. For example, if your civil procedure professor gives you a question in which a plaintiff is attempting to sue a non-resident defendant in a jurisdiction where the defendant may have done business, you will immediately think of *Burger King Corp. v. Rudzewicz*[3] and *Helicopteros Nacionales de Colombia, S.A. v. Hall.*[4] You should also think about any other civil procedure cases that involve personal jurisdiction and non-resident defendants because those cases may also be pertinent and may give you an idea about issues to discuss (see chapter four for further discussion of the relevance of factually similar cases).

Notably, although you may not refer to all of these cases and rules when it comes time to start writing, you should at least consider their potential applicability. Of course, you cannot consider their applicability in the second stage of IRAC if you have not spotted the potential issues in the first stage.

---

[3]　*See* Burger King Corp. v. Rudzewicz, 471 U.S. 462 (1985).

[4]　*See* Helicopteros Nacionales de Colombia, S.A. v. Hall, 466 U.S. 408 (1984).

When trying to identify issues and sub-issues, consider whether your fact pattern is similar to any well-known cases.

Another way of identifying potential issues and sub-issues is to consider all the different ways someone might sue on a particular set of facts. While it is possible that an exam question might present only one cause of action, it is at least equally likely that a question will give rise to multiple torts, crimes, or contract concerns.

When trying to identify issues and sub-issues, remember that every person in a particular fact pattern (even those who are not given names) is situated differently. Find what makes these people different from a legal perspective. Small variations often give rise to extremely fruitful discussions.

Sometimes students become so excited about all the potential issues and parties that they forget that the question focuses specifically on one aspect of the fact pattern. For example, a question may give rise to the following issues: A v. B, A v. C, B v. C, and B v. A. In an open-ended question (for example, one that just says "discuss"), you can and should discuss each of the four plaintiff-defendant pairings and each possible cause of action, or issue.

Other questions do not allow you to be so broad in your response. For example, a question might ask you to identify and discuss all the issues that A can assert. In that case, you would only discuss A v. B and A v. C. However, it might be that part of B's defense is that C is entirely or partly to blame for B's conduct. In that case, you could bring up those aspects of B v. C that relate to B's or C's defense (for example, contributory negligence or whether B's act constituted a sufficiently superseding act so as to foreclose any liability to A on behalf of C). You would not, however, discuss B v. C directly, nor would you bring up B v. D, since those points fall outside the question set by the professor. Rather, you would include your discussion of contributory negligence under the heading of A's negligence claim against B.

Notice that any discussion you might have of B v. C or B v. D might be entirely correct as a matter of law. However, those matters are simply irrelevant to the question asked. Think about it: an attorney hired to represent A in court wouldn't suddenly start discussing the liability of C or D to B. The attorney would only be concerned with arguments relating to B and C's liability to A. Other arguments would be left for another day and another trial. Therefore, do as practicing attorneys do and answer only the question asked.

Only answer the question asked. Don't add additional material just because you know the answer.

Having given the basic parameters of identifying issues and sub-issues, we can turn our attention to how to write the "I" portion of your essay.

E. Writing the "I" Portion of an IRAC Essay

Scribble down notes to yourself on your scratch paper as you write your essay. There is nothing more frustrating than re-membering an im-portant case and then forgetting it before you have finished the paragraph you are currently writing.

The IRAC approach provides you with a four-step analytical framework for your law school essays. The goal is to produce a simple (but not simplistic), well-focused essay that answers the question asked with brevity, precision, and power. Because each step builds upon another, you need to plan out all four elements before you start writing. While it is perfectly acceptable to go back and make insertions into earlier paragraphs by using arrows or asterisks, you can and should try to minimize such efforts through proper advanced planning. Also, it's easier to insert one or two additional cases than it is to completely revise your argument when you suddenly remember a key decision or statute. Therefore, take your time in the planning stages. IRAC allows you write your essay much more quickly than you normally would, since the information and analysis speak for themselves once they are compiled. As a result, you have more time to spend planning your essay.

1. Taking Notes

The first thing to do is write down some notes to yourself to start organizing your thoughts. This step does not involve a complicated or wordy outline that takes as much time to draft as the essay. All you need to do is walk through each of the four steps for each issue, think about what you will say in each step, and write down some notes so that you don't have to carry that information in your head as you write. The note-taking process is most important for the "I" and "R" portions of your essay because they are the ones that tax your memory and analytical skills the most. The "A" and "C" portions of the essay merely require logic, although that logic is built on the first two elements of the essay (the "I" and "R" steps).

Your notes can be in any form you wish—cryptic abbreviations of legal authority, lists of party pairings and potential issues, mnemonics that you have devised to help you remember the elements of each claim—whatever works best for you. The point is to be creative and broad in your initial thinking; you can narrow the field down later, after you've covered everything. Once you have made a note of

NOTE

Most errors are made during the "I" stage. If you miss an is-sue you cannot discuss it.

something potentially relevant, you can move past the fear that you will forget it and can focus on figuring out whether the point is important enough to be put into your essay or whether it is too tangential.

When you have finished that process, stop. Do not start writing. Instead, re-read the question. Make sure you are answering the question as asked. Look for more issues and contentious sub-issues. Think again about whether you can supplement your legal authority. Only when you are sure you have considered everything and have prioritized your points should you start writing. Because IRAC gives you a straightforward approach to structuring your essay and eliminates the need for flowery rhetoric, you will not spend as much time writing as you usually do. Spend that time in thought—it will be well worth it.

WRIT
ING

When you think
you're ready to
start writing,
stop and think
again. Have you
identified all
possible issues?

2. Starting to Write

Once you have completed all four steps of IRAC in the planning phase, you can finally put pen to paper. However, there is no need to introduce your essay with a complex or thought-provoking paragraph that takes you forever to write. Instead, simply state the issue and sub-issues in contention.

EXAMPLE

A. Negligence

"According to these facts, Alex (A) can sue Bob (B) for negligence. To establish negligence, A must prove [here you would set forth, in one sentence, the basic legal standard for establishing negligence, as discussed in chapter four]. Of these elements, the only issue that can seriously be disputed is [identify which aspect or aspects you wish to discuss]."

NOTE

It's fine to abbreviate the names of the par-ties, as long as you de-fine the terms you're going to use at the out-set.

WRIT
ING

There's no need
to "ease" your
way into your
argument. The
best essays open
with simple, di-
rect statement.

That's it—that's your entire "I" analysis. You are now ready to move on to your second paragraph, which sets forth the legal standard concerning the areas of dispute (i.e., the rules).

You now see how quickly you can identify the issue and sub-issues in your essay. Notably, there is no need to ease your way into your discussion with background material like the history of negligence (or whatever your issue may be) or an outline of the facts of the case. Again, think of your essay in terms of a litigation model. No attorney would walk up to a judge and start giving a mini-treatise on the evolution of the negligence—that lawyer would be immediately asked by the court to focus on the case at hand. While an attorney may sometimes begin with a summary of the facts for the court or the jury, there is no need to do that in an exam because the professor is familiar with the facts. You are under time pressure and operating in an academic environment, so not everything must conform to professional legal practice.

A professor cannot give you points for simply rewriting the facts. Points come from legal analysis.

You can, however, imagine an attorney standing up and saying, "Your Honor, this case involves the tort of negligence. To establish that tort, the plaintiff must prove X, Y and Z. I propose to focus on Z, since the parties agree that there is no dispute about the existence of points X and Y." The attorney then proceeds to argue about whether the elements of Z have been met. That is what you are doing in your essay: you are arguing about the contentious sub-issue(s) in a particular tort, crime, or other cause of action. You're not trying to tell the professor everything you know about a particular area of law without any reference to the legal problem posted by the fact pattern.

Those who are being very creative and open-minded about potential sub-issues may come up with as many as seven or eight possible discussion points. While this demonstrates an admirable level of ingenuity, you should try to limit your discussion of sub-issues to two or three major points. This doesn't necessarily mean that you should discard your other ideas. Instead, you should try to group your sub-issues together under a larger heading. For example, you may have a question in contract that involves sub-issues including sufficiency of consideration, promissory estoppel, and modification of a contract. You could group these all together as an issue involving consideration: sufficiency as a necessary element under formal rules regarding consideration, promissory estoppel as a stand-in for consideration (although promissory estoppel could also stand on its own as a non-contractual basis for a remedy), and the need for consideration when modifying a contract. By combining these points under a single heading, you are not eliminating any potential areas of discussion. Instead, you are presenting a more cohesive argument about how the sub-issues relate to one another. In an academic essay, you don't have a lot of time or space to make your points, and it is better to focus on a few very strong arguments rather than dispersing your time and energy among many weak ones.

Why should you aim for two or three major points? The study of communications suggests that people grasp information better when it is arranged in groups of three. While you need not adhere to this rule slavishly, a three-tiered argument gives the appearance of balance and strength.[5] In addition, it is unlikely that all seven or eight points can really be justified as independent issues; no fact pattern is that complex. It is much more likely that some of those points can be combined in some way and those that cannot are either shadow issues (i.e., part of another larger issue) or too minor to merit mention.

Don't worry if you don't come up with that many sub-issues. It may just be that you are thinking in larger conceptual terms than your colleagues. What they may consider a sub-issue you may think is a sub-sub-issue falling under a larger heading. Neither style of analysis is inherently better. For example, someone who only comes up with one or two sub-issues may be in danger of missing something important. If you are the type who only sees one or two points to discuss, take an extra moment to re-read the question and see if you've missed anything. Don't think of this extra step as "wasting" time—your colleagues will be spending that time compiling their many sub-issues into two or three key points, so you're not losing anything by taking a second look at the question.

Once you have decided which issue(s) and sub-issues you are going to discuss, you need to organize your points in a logical manner and inform your reader how you will proceed. In most cases, you should start with the sub-issue that either comes first as a threshold matter or that yields the longest and most complex legal analysis. How to identify and present the relevant law is discussed in the next chapter. However, this point helps you see why you must proceed mentally through the various stages of the IRAC analysis before you put begin writing. If you don't know which legal points are most important before you start writing, you run the risk of spending too much time on something that will not win you a lot of points.

TIP

Use your one-page outline (table of contents) to ensure that you have identified all possible issues.

Be sure to frame the issue in terms of legal actions or legal remedies. If you focus too much on factual issues, your essay will often end up arguing the facts instead of the law (this point will be discussed in greater detail in later chapters). Try to use legal terminology when you identify your issue(s), since that will force you into a legal, as opposed to factual, analysis.

---

[5] Some of you may have been taught to follow a five-paragraph essay structure in school. A five-paragraph essay consists of an introduction, a conclusion, and three main points in the body of the essay. While this approach is too simplistic to be used in response to a problem question in law, it demonstrates the symmetry of a well-balanced essay.

YOUR TURN

What steps should you follow before you start writing your essay?

_____

_____

_____

_____

_____

3. Timing Concerns

One point bears mentioning. Although this book encourages you to spend a significant amount of time planning your essays, you still need to be aware of the amount of time you are spending on any particular question. This concern is particularly acute with respect to the first question you answer. Lots of students fall into the trap of spending too much time on the first point in their essay or on the first essay of a multi-essay exam. Typically, professors provide you with some idea about how much time to spend on each question, usually by telling you how many points are allocated to each part of your exam. Always do the math to determine how many minutes you should spend on each question.[6] If the first question gives you

Follow the suggested time allotments given for each question. Nothing hurts you more than not fully answering a question because you ran out of time.

---

6   Assume you have three hours to complete an exam with four questions. One question is worth 50% of your grade, one question is worth 20% of your grade, and two questions are worth 15% of your grade. Three hours is the equivalent of 180 minutes. Therefore, you should spend no more than 90 minutes on the first question (180 x 50% = 90), 36 minutes on the second question (180 x 20% = 36), and 27 minutes on each of the last two questions (180 x 15% = 27). Check your math by adding the minutes together (90 + 36 + 27 + 27 = 180). Then, figure out when you need to change from one question to another. For example, if your exam starts at 9:00 and you start with the first question, you should change to the second question at 10:30. Write this number down in the margin so that you don't forget it or have to recalculate it. You should start the third question at 11:06 and the fourth question at 11:33. However, it is often wise to build some "wiggle" room into your calculations. Thus, for example, you would give yourself 80 minutes on the first question, 30 minutes on the second, and 25 minutes on the last two. You would then calculate the times for switching over based on these numbers. This approach gives you some breathing room to read instructions, check your work, submit your exam electronically, etc. If your professor sends you the instructions to the exam in advance so that you can read them through before the day itself, do these mathematical calculations before you arrive in the exam room. You don't

ninety minutes, you must stop writing your essay to that question after ninety minutes. While you may be earning extra points if you continue writing, those points will be relatively minor as compared to the large number of easy points that can be answered on later questions.

One of the main reasons students do poorly on exams is because they do not devote enough time to each question. Rather than falling into this trap, force yourself to move on. If you have time at the end, you can go back.

When planning and writing your "I" step, remember that the best essays:

- include a lead-in sentence that goes straight to the point;

- separate issues according to the pertinent plaintiff-defendant pairings;

- precisely identify the issue(s) relevant to the question;

- use legal terms and concepts when framing the issue; and

- feature bold and direct use of language.

YOUR TURN

How should you allocate your time in an exam and why?

_____

_____

_____

_____

_____

F.   Worked Example

Now that you have the core principles and rationales in mind, it is time to see how the first step of the IRAC method is put into practice. We will use the same sample question through each of the following three chapters so that you can see how to build an essay. Additional examples appear in chapter ten.

---

want to spend any precious exam time on administrative matters if you don't have to.

Assume this question appears on an exam in torts.

QUESTION

Jack, a Formula One race car driver, was driving his standard-issue SUV home from his daughter's school, where he had just dropped her off for the day. On the way, he was involved in a traffic accident. Had he used his expert skill in braking, he could have avoided the accident, although an ordinary driver could not have done so. Is Jack liable for the injuries to the other party?

---

1. Identifying the Issue and Sub-Issues

The first thing you have to do is identify the issue and the various sub-issues in contention. As discussed above, you should work through the question, sentence by sentence, trying to spot as many potential issues and sub-issues as possible. Later you can cull through your list and cut those issues that are of minor importance.

2. Breaking Down the Question

SENTENCE ONE: "Jack, a Formula One race car driver, was driving his standard-issue SUV home from his daughter's school, where he had just dropped her off for the day."

ANALYSIS:

(1)   Jack is an expert driver. In the law of negligence, questions involving the defendant's skill level relate to the standard of care owed from the defendant to the plaintiff. If we recall that the tort of negligence requires the plaintiff to establish the existence of a duty of care, breach of that duty, causation (both legal and factual) and damages, then this potential issue (standard of care) relates to whether a duty of care exists. Therefore, we have a potential issue relating to the tort of negligence and a potential sub-issue relating to the breach of a duty (with a sub-sub-issue specifically relating to the standard of care).

(2)   Jack was not driving a Formula One race car, but was instead at the wheel of an average SUV. Can he be held to a higher standard relating to his expert skill if he is in a vehicle that cannot (presumably) take advantage of those higher skills? The issue and sub-issue/sub-sub-issue are the same as in point one, although this fact gives us another potential area of discussion.

(3)   Jack was driving home from his daughter's school, which indicates that he was not employed as a race car driver at the time of the accident. This point can relate to issues discussed in point one, since it is questionable whether people can be held to a higher standard of care when they are not holding themselves out as having that expert skill.

(4)   However, once we start thinking about Jack's employment, we immediately think of the tort of vicarious liability. Sub-issues regarding employment include questions relating to (1) whether the defendant was an employee or an independent contractor and (2) whether the defendant was acting in the course of his or her employment at the time of the accident.

(5)   The fact pattern does not say whether the school was public or private, but when you see a school, you might want to consider whether the question gives rise to issues involving public liability. The rest of the question should give you more of an idea about the relevance of this particular concern, so you should move on to the next sentence.

SENTENCE TWO: "On the way, he was involved in a traffic accident."

ANALYSIS:

(6)   The term "accident" suggests lack of intent; therefore you can probably discount any of the intentional torts (assault, battery, etc.). However, this term does suggest the possibility of negligence. Whereas the previous sentence gave rise to concerns about the existence of a duty of care, this sentence suggests that there has been a breach of whatever duty exists. Nothing has been said yet to raise the level of culpability from negligence (if, indeed, that can even be proven) to recklessness, but you will keep the recklessness question in mind as you carry on through the problem.

SENTENCE THREE: "Had he used his expert skill in braking, he could have avoided the accident, although an ordinary driver could not have done so."

ANALYSIS:

(7)   Here we see that Jack's expert skills are very much at issue, even more so than the question about the ability of the car to perform at a higher standard, as raised as a potential issue in point (2) above. The negligence claim and related issues, as noted in point (3), remain relevant, since the question of whether expert skill exists outside the realm where the skill is normally exercised is quite interesting, from a legal point of view. However, the vicarious liability claim raised in point (4) appears to be irrelevant, since the question says nothing more about Jack's employer or employment. The same is true of the public body liability question considered in point (5); since nothing more is said about what type of school the daughter attended or about whether the school or its employers played a role in the accident, we will conclude that public body liability is not an issue in this question.

SENTENCE FOUR: "Is Jack liable for the injuries to the other party?"

ANALYSIS:

(8)   The question here focuses you on Jack's liability, rather than on the liability of any other parties. The fact that the other party to the accident is not named suggests that he or she is not contributorily negligent in any way, but just because a party is not named does not mean you should always ignore any potential claims or defenses. In this case, however, no facts are given as to the relative negligence between the parties, so you should not assume the other party's (or any third party's) negligence is at issue. Don't hypothesize about possibilities that did not arise under the facts.

3.   Discarding Extraneous Parties, Claims, and Issues

Based on the analysis in point (8), we will focus on one plaintiff-defendant pairing, namely unnamed plaintiff v. Jack. For the reasons discussed in point (7), we will discard issues of vicarious liability and liability for public bodies. We will therefore proceed with one issue for the tort of negligence, with sub-issues relating to the existence of a duty of care and the breach of the duty of care (and within the sub-issue of breach of duty, focusing on the standard of care for people with an expert skill).

4.   Writing Your Response

DRAFT ANSWER (first paragraph)

The question at issue is whether Jack is liable to the plaintiff for the tort of negligence.[7] To establish a claim in negligence, the plaintiff must prove the existence of a duty, breach of that duty, causation (including both legal foreseeability and "but for" causation) and damages (*Detraz v. Lee* (La. 2007)).[8] Of those four elements, the plaintiff here will have the most trouble establishing that there was a breach of the duty of care.[9] The key sub-issue involves the appropriate standard of care.[10]

In four simple—but not simplistic—sentences, we have set up the framework for the written response. The reader knows precisely which points will be made and why. We have not wasted time with unnecessary rhetorical flourishes or repeating the facts of the question. While the language may not seem as elegant as that of a literature or history essay, it is effective, powerful, and clear. Having introduced the discussion

---

[7]   This is the issue, identified in one simple sentence.

[8]   These are the general elements of negligence. For a further discussion of how and why to set forth the general legal standard for the issue, see chapter four.

[9]   This sentence introduces the contentious sub-issue, which arise out of the plaintiff's *prima facie* case.

[10]   This sentence narrows the intended scope of discussion even further for the reader.

succinctly and precisely, we are now ready to begin discussing the most important part of your essay: the rules.

You now have a basic understanding of how to approach the first step in the IRAC method. For a further discussion of how to handle this step in "discuss" type questions, see chapter seven. The issues in those kinds of questions cannot be equated with legal causes of action, since "discuss" questions are not analogous to litigation, but the analysis is similar in many ways. For more worked examples of various questions, see chapter ten. We will now move to the second step in the IRAC method, namely the analysis and presentation of the legal rules.

YOUR TURN

What are the hallmarks of a strong "I" section and why?

_____

_____

_____

_____

_____

CHAPTER 4

Step Two in the IRAC Method: The Rules

The preceding chapter discussed how to identify the issue in the IRAC method of essay writing. In many problem questions, the issue will be the same as the cause of action that would be brought in court if the situation came up in real life. "Discuss" type questions use a slightly different analysis, at least in the early stages, but follow the same general model.

Identifying the issue is not enough, of course. Certain sub-issues will be more difficult to establish than others as a matter of law, and these are the points that are important to you as a student. Practitioners need to concern themselves with issues that are difficult to establish as a matter of fact as well as those that are difficult to establish as a matter of law, but as students, you focus on questions of law, not questions of fact. The difference between the two will be discussed in this chapter and the next.

NOTE

Focus on questions of law, not questions of fact.

If you follow the suggestions outlined in chapter three, you will have a three- or four-sentence opening paragraph that will take approximately one minute to write. The first paragraph of your essay is supposed to be short because the majority of your time should be spent on the second step of the IRAC analysis: the rules. However, if you spend the proper amount of time in analysis and thought, you will find that the "R" section of your essay writes itself as easily as the "I" portion does.

To write a high-scoring essay in law, you must understand:

(1)   the purpose of supporting authority ("rules") in legal writing; and

(2)   what constitutes supporting authority in legal writing.

Once you have grasped those points, you must learn how to:

(3)   compile the relevant supporting authority; and

(4) communicate the relevant supporting authority in your essay.

Each of these points will be discussed in turn.

A. The Purpose of Supporting Authority in Legal Writing

Law is unlike other subjects you have studied at school because it has both practical and academic applications. Indeed, that's what many people find so interesting about law school. However, the practical aspect of law means that the purpose of supporting authority in legal writing differs from that used in any other subject you have ever studied. Still, some analogies can be drawn to other academic subjects to help you understand how to structure your legal writing and how you can adapt your existing skills for use in law school.

1. Supporting Authority in Other Fields

People who studied the humanities (literature, history, politics, and the like) as undergraduates have a leg up in law school because they are familiar with the need to use supporting texts to illustrate various theories created in response to an exam question. To do well in a humanities course, you need to find as much support as possible for the position stated. While some students have been known to introduce and rebut contrary arguments, the most popular exam model is to identify a position and provide as much logical support as possible without considering any evidence that would lessen the forcefulness of the argument.

Those of you who have studied the humanities know that sometimes it is easy to incorporate the primary texts into your essays. For example, the question "analyze the character of Mr. Rochester in *Jane Eyre*" requires you to refer to the plot and dialogue of the novel. You can refer to secondary texts (such as articles written by scholars in the field) to support your argument as and when you like.

WRITING

Refer to primary sources (statutes and cases) in the same way that you would refer to the novel or poem in question in a literature essay.

However, humanities questions don't always provide students with such an easy route into the primary texts. For example, a question about the causes of the Crusades allows you to refer to the commentary of expert historians but does not require you to do so. You will earn points by quoting other people, but you must also construct an independent theory out of facts that you have gleaned from various sources. While those sources can be named, they need not be, since the year that Constantinople fell exists objectively, regardless of who reports that fact. You can obtain a very good grade on your essay even though you refer to only one or two authoritative sources, since your ability to analyze the problem creatively is at least as important as your ability to reproduce facts and commentary.

Humanities students often do well in law school as a result of their ability to think creatively about various legal arguments. Students who studied the humanities in college are also well trained to argue by analogy, since they know how to draw fine points from seemingly disparate sources. This skill is central to the task of a common law lawyer, who must sift through numerous cases and statutes before identifying those that are most relevant to the problem at hand.

People who studied the sciences have a slightly different understanding of supporting authority, but one that is no less useful. Math and science majors are used to walking through their analysis so as to demonstrate how they reached their conclusions. Even if you didn't major in math in college, you probably remember having to "prove" an algebraic equation in high school by proceeding step by step through different mathematical principles in a logical manner.

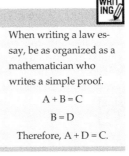

When writing a law essay, be as organized as a mathematician who writes a simple proof.

$$A + B = C$$

$$B = D$$

Therefore, $A + D = C$.

When conducting a mathematical or scientific analysis, the source of the information is of minimal importance. For example, in a physics question, it is more important to know that $E = mc^2$ than to report that Albert Einstein said it or that it appears in a particular textbook on physics. Of course, you must know and state the significance of the equation $E = mc^2$ in your answer. You must also make sure that the equation is relevant to the question asked. Producing that particular equation in response to a question about organic chemistry will not win you any points, even if the equation itself is correct, since the information you produce in your answer must pertain to the question asked. The same is true in law. You must produce correct and relevant statements of law to prove your point. You must also introduce those statements in a logical order if you are to persuade your reader that your conclusions are correct.

Including irrelevant legal principles in a law essay is as useful as saying that $E = mc^2$ in a chemistry exam. The proposition may be correct, but it won't win you any points.

2. Supporting Authority in Professional Practice

It is also helpful to consider how practicing lawyers think about supporting authority. Although not everyone who studies law goes on to become a lawyer, the study of law is influenced by the demands of legal practice. You see this influence clearly in the use and purpose of supporting authority in legal essays. If you understand how legal authority is used in the practice of law, you will better understand how to use supporting authority in your legal essays.

One of the most basic principles of law involves the ancient concept of *nulla poena sine lege*, which translates to "no punishment without a law." The idea underlying this principle is that the state cannot punish someone unless that person violated an established legal principle. The law in question had to (1) exist prior to the taking place of the act and (2) be well-known enough so that the defendant could be said to be on notice that a penalty would occur if he or she acted in that way. The justification for this principle is that it is unfair to punish someone for doing something that wasn't illegal at the time.

Although the concept of *nulla poena sine lege* developed in the context of criminal law, the principle applies in other subject matter fields as well. For example, contract law describes the circumstances in which people will be required to live up to their agreements. If an agreement doesn't fall into the recognized pattern, courts— i.e., the law—will not impose liability, since it's unfair to hold someone accountable for acts that were not legally required at the time.

NOTE

Your job is to show what the law was at the time the act took place. Liability will be then measured against that known standard, following the concept of *nulla poena sine lege*.

In deciding what is legally required in a particular situation, courts do not look to logic or common sense alone. Instead, judges must look to the established law at the time of the event in question. If common sense dictates one course of action, but the law was not clear on that point, the court cannot follow common sense. Courts must follow established legal precedent in the form of judicial decisions and statutory law. While a judge may suggest that a change in the law would be wise, he or she cannot change the law retroactively, since to do so would violate the concept of *nulla poena sine lege*.

3. Legal Authority in Law School Exams

When considering whether and to what extent legal authority is required in a law school exam, law students can draw certain lessons from each of these examples. For instance, the fact that law school is built on a litigation model means that law students must respect the concept of *nulla poena sine lege* when writing their law school exams. While there may be good reason to change the law—and, like the courts, you may wish to recommend legislative reform—your final conclusion must be based on pre-established legal principles, not on common sense or even on logic.

Law students can also benefit from techniques used in undergraduate courses. For example, law students should emulate analytical processes seen in the hard sciences and create essays that define various principles that have been proven and accepted by the relevant community as reflecting the true state of knowledge at the time the essay is written. Lawyers and scientists must cite these pre-existing principles (be they theorems, axioms, statutes, or judicial opinions) in an orderly fashion to demonstrate that their conclusions are correct. Both lawyers and scientists must also guard against the introduction of irrelevant information—such as $E = mc^2$ into an organic chemistry problem—since such information is extraneous to the problem at hand.

A great way to earn easy points is to define your terms.

Law seldom has one "right" answer, although a number of answers will likely be wrong.

Law is dissimilar to the hard sciences in that there is seldom (if ever) one correct answer or one correct statement of the law. As will be discussed in the next section, law is a matter of nuance and persuasion, and you must look at all the evidence—even conflicting evidence—before you can come to a reasoned conclusion.

Those who have studied the humanities will appreciate the way that the law exists in shades of gray, rather than in black and white. Historians, for example, will know that while one person may argue that the Crusades were caused by X, another person may argue equally persuasively that the Crusades were caused by Y. A first-class historian will explicitly consider all possible theories before discussing why one particular approach should prevail. A second-class historian will construct a plausible theory that contains sufficient supporting authority but that ignores any conflicting evidence.

The best essays discuss both sides of an argument. Average essays adopt only one perspective.

The same is true in the study of law. The best students explicitly consider all possible arguments before weighing them up. Average students focus on only one way of reading the supporting authorities.

You must explicitly cite legal authority in your essays if you want to earn a top grade.

The study of law differs from the study of history quite radically in one respect. As mentioned above, historians can refer quite easily to objective facts (such as dates) that do not require citation to underlying sources. As is discussed in the next section, lawyers do not have this luxury. They must indicate the source of the law they cite, since a principle alone does not constitute "law." The persuasiveness of a legal proposition depends on who said it. As a result, you must identify your source material if you want to do well on a law school exam.

B. What Constitutes Supporting Authority in Legal Writing

"R" in IRAC stands for "rules," meaning you have to discuss more than one authority and may need to pull elements from different sources to identify the legal standard governing your fact pattern.

Chapter two introduced the concept of supporting legal authority as part of the discussion of how to analyze case law, statutory law, and legal commentary. However, a few additional words may be helpful before we consider how to use this authority in legal writing. For ease of comprehension, we will break legal authority into two types: binding authority, meaning those sources that must be followed when they are found to be relevant, and persuasive authority, meaning those sources whose principles may guide courts but do not control the outcome of the dispute.

1. Binding Authority

Common law jurisdictions recognize two sources of binding legal authority:[1] statutory law (which for purposes of this discussion includes constitutional law and regulatory law) and case law. The essence of legal argument involves identifying which statutes and cases apply to the situation at hand and what those authorities require in your particular situation.

As your study of law progresses, it will quickly become apparent to you that the law is seldom clear. There are even situations where two sources of binding law appear to contradict each other. For example, you may have a case that says a person will be held liable for negligence if he or she does X, while another case says that a person will not be held liable for negligence if he or she does X.[2] These types of discrepancies appear

---

[1] This book considers all primary authority to be binding authority, since most law professors teach from national casebooks that include cases and statutes from many different jurisdictions. As a result, it is impossible for you to distinguish between primary persuasive authority (such as a Third Circuit opinion when you reside in the Ninth Circuit) and primary binding authority (such as a Ninth Circuit opinion when you reside in the Ninth Circuit) on an exam. Therefore, you should consider all primary authority to be binding authority on a final exam, unless your professor tells you otherwise. This rule would obviously differ when you take the bar exam, since those examiners are looking for you to know the law of that particular state.

[2] One of the most famous inconsistencies arises between *The Wagon Mound* (holding that negligence did not exist because the damage that occurred was held not to be reasonably foreseeable) and *The Wagon Mound (No. 2)* (holding that negligence did exist because the same damage was held to be reasonably foreseeable). *See* Overseas Tankship (UK) Ltd. v. Morts and Dock & Engineering

frequently on final exams, since professors know that only the best students will know enough to mention both cases and reconcile the apparent conflict.

EXAM

Professors often test in areas where there are direct conflicts in binding authority.

Although direct conflicts are often tested when they exist, such conflicts are relatively rare, given judicial respect for precedent. Instead, it is more likely that a broad, general principle (for example, the notion that people may not kill others) will be subject to various conditions and exceptions (such as the idea that people may not kill others unless in self-defense or unless the death was a pure and unforeseeable accident). Professors also like to test areas where there are exceptions to a general principle of law, so you need to be prepared.

EXAM

Professors often test areas of law where there are exceptions to a general rule.

Chapter two introduced the idea of distinguishing and harmonizing cases. As you recall, lawyers distinguish two cases that seem to require different outcomes by describing how the undesirable case is dissimilar from the fact pattern at issue, either as a matter of fact or of law. Lawyers who are trying to show how a line of cases works together are harmonizing those cases.

Learning how to distinguish and harmonize different cases is very important because practicing lawyers are not permitted to forget or ignore inconvenient law. Instead, practitioners are required by the rules of professional conduct to refer the court to relevant cases that go against their own arguments. Because practicing lawyers must know how to distinguish unhelpful case law, students must learn and display the same skill by discussing cases that are difficult to reconcile in the "R" section of their essays.

Because every judicial decision is tailored to a particular factual situation, it is very unlikely that your professor will give you a question that duplicates one case exactly. Instead, it is much more likely that your professor will give you a question that is similar to one line of cases in one respect and to a different case or line of cases in another respect. As you will see in this and the next chapter, you must not only introduce all of these arguably relevant cases but also discuss how they apply to your factual situation. What is "arguably relevant" is a matter of judgment, although you should rest assured that you should not be trying to list every case ever decided in that particular area of law. Instead, you must use your discretion to decide

EXAM

More than one case will be relevant to your essay question.

Co., *The Wagon Mound* [1961] A.C. 388; Overseas Tankship (UK) Ltd. v. Miller Steamship Co., *The Wagon Mound (No 2)* [1967] 1 A.C. 617.

which cases to discuss and which cases to discard. More will be said on this point below.

Just because a court has not specifically discussed your fact pattern does not mean that no law exists on the issues in question. Instead, your job in that situation is to argue by analogy, looking at principles enunciated in similar cases and describing why those rules apply to your case. You also need to look at any exceptions to the general rule and explain whether and to what extent those exceptions apply to your fact pattern. Remember, good legal argument involves showing how—*and why*—your situation resembles or doesn't resemble these pre-existing principles of law.

This principle is best illustrated through an example. For instance, early contract cases concerning the timing of an offer or acceptance often focused on when the offer or acceptance was put into the mail (i.e., the mailbox rule). As technology evolved, questions arose involving telexes, telephones, facsimiles, and electronic mail. However, courts did not create new rules of law to address these new innovations. Instead, judges simply looked at existing principles of law, evaluated those principles in light of new facts, and decided how new cases should be considered by using legal analogies. You can and should adopt the same approach when answering questions on an exam.

Students who want to earn high grades look beyond the facts of the cases they are citing and focus instead on the rationales supporting the judges' conclusions. Top students also make sure that they identify their sources. Remember, you may very properly say that it is illegal to kill someone, but that statement, on its own, carries little or no weight in a courtroom. The law according to Jane Smith is not the same as the law according to Judge Smith or the law according to Congress. Because your statements about the law do not come from a legally recognized authority, nor are they published in the same way that statements made by the legislature or the courts are, your statements about the law do not constitute binding legal authority. That is why you must identify the source of your legal statements, either by name or, if you can't remember the name, by description. For example, you can reference "the case where the defendant snatched the plate" for *Fisher v. Carrousel Motor Hotel, Inc.*[3]

WRITING

If a statement is not contained in a case or statute, it is not binding law.

CONCLUSION

In your writing, do as courts do and indicate three things:

(1)   what the legal principle is;

---

[3]   *See* Fisher v. Carrousel Motor Hotel, Inc., 424 S.W. 627 (Tex. 1967).

(2)   why it should apply in the current case; and

(3)   what the source of the legal principle is.

YOUR TURN

What do you do if your exam raises issues that courts have not specifically discussed?

_____

_____

_____

_____

_____

2.   Persuasive Authority

The term "persuasive authority" refers to those sources or principles that guide, but do not control, courts and lawmakers. Persuasive authority cannot be used to negate relevant binding authority but can be used to justify a particular course of action when there is no clear-cut answer contained in binding law.

There are at least four types of persuasive authority:

(1)   public policy;

(2)   legal commentary;

(3)   legislative history; and

(4)   case or statutory law from jurisdictions outside the United States.

a.   Public Policy

Public policy arguments arise out of logic and/or morality rather than a particular case or statute. These arguments typically involve the motivation for or consequences of a particular course of action, which can be very attractive to students who feel their knowledge of case and statutory law is sketchy. Humanities students who are used to offering their own opinions in essays have a particular tendency to over-rely on these types of arguments. Professors are well aware of students' propensity to rely on these kinds of "soft" legal arguments and typically do not award high marks for a legal discussion based entirely on public policy (unless, of course, the question specifically asks you to do so).

Students can become confused about the importance of public policy arguments because those types of discussions are frequently found in class discussions and in published judicial opinions. This phenomenon leads many students to give undue weight to public policy, even though public policy is not "law" in the same way that statutes and court decisions are. Public policy concerns give reasons why a judge or legislator should act in a certain way but do not dictate a specific outcome. As a result, public policy is persuasive rather than binding in nature.

When presenting a public policy argument, remember:

- public policy is persuasive, not binding, legal authority;

- there are two sides to every public policy argument; and

- you must define what you mean by "public policy."

If you decide to raise a public policy argument, you must do so in an even-handed manner. Every public policy can be met by a similarly persuasive policy that demands a different outcome. Any time you raise public policy, you must discuss both sides of the issue. Presenting one perspective alone does not make your discussion stronger and more cohesive; it is simply incomplete. The art of legal analysis lies in recognizing opposing arguments and stating why one position is more convincing than the other. This method of analysis holds true for both binding law (when you are noting which strand of cases and/or statutes is the most applicable to your fact situation) and for persuasive law (when you are noting which public policy rationale is the most convincing).

A third reason why public policy arguments fail to earn high marks is because many students allude to public policy generally, without stating precisely what they mean. The term "public policy" can refer to a variety of social interests, including those involving health, finances, and even morality. Students must be careful to define exactly what they mean by public policy in the context of the particular fact pattern before they use the term in an essay. The meaning cannot be simply gleaned from the context of the case, since, as stated above, public policy rationales exist on both sides of an argument.

For these reasons, public policy arguments can, and in appropriate cases should, be used to supplement your discussion of binding law, since policy analysis can help persuade the reader why your proposed course of action is wise. However, remember that you cannot replace a discussion of relevant statutory and case law with a policy analysis if you hope to earn one of the top grades in the class.

b.   Legal Commentary

The second type of persuasive legal authority involves legal commentary generated by academic lawyers. These types of works are found in hornbooks, treatises, and legal journals. Legal commentary describes existing law, offers critical analysis of current law and practice, and/or provides suggestions on legal reform. Because commentators have spent a significant amount of time researching and reflecting on the problems they discuss, their analyses are valued by courts and legislators who do not have the luxury of spending several months or years working on a particular issue. Referring to legal commentary broadens your analysis and can help persuade your reader of the wisdom of your recommendations and conclusions. However, like public policy, commentary does not constitute binding law and therefore cannot form the entirety of your essay.

Of the different types of commentary, articles and treatises are the most persuasive. Student hornbooks are helpful, but generally do not contain the type of detail and sophistication that is necessary to craft a first-class essay. Nevertheless, don't hesitate to refer to a helpful point just because it appears in a hornbook.

Whenever you refer to a commentator's ideas, you should provide his or her name. Not only does this technique avoid problems with plagiarism, it gives more persuasive weight to the statements themselves. As you are beginning to realize, the "R" portion of the IRAC method is all about law and legal authority. While it is important to give your opinion in your essay, that step does not come until later in the process. As intelligent or innovative as your ideas may be, they do not constitute legal authority. Therefore, focus at this point on the views and statements of others.

If you use the exact words of anyone else, be it court or commentator, use quotation marks and attribute the quotation. Failing to do so constitutes plagiarism and loses you points on your essay. Quotes are a good thing in law. Use them and acknowledge their presence fully.

c.   Legislative History

Although U.S. courts take differing views as to the importance of legislative history,[4] law students can introduce such materials in their essays if it helps answer the question asked. While legislative history is not binding on courts, it can be persuasive to the extent it suggests the purpose and/or scope of a particular statute. Courts often take this

---

[4]   *See* Abbe R. Gluck, *The States as Laboratories of Statutory Interpretation: Methodological Consensus and the New Modified Textualism,* 119 YALE L.J. 1750, 1834–46 (2010).

information into account when considering cases arising in front of them, and you can do the same in your essays.

d. Case or Statutory Law from Other Jurisdictions

Finally, U.S. courts occasionally consider case or statutory law from other jurisdictions.[5] Because these laws have been promulgated in other jurisdictions, they cannot be binding in the United States. However, U.S. courts respect the pronouncements of other lawmakers just as they respect the work of legal commentators and consider foreign law as suggestive of how the matter at bar should be decided. You, too, can bring up law from other jurisdictions as long as you recognize it to be persuasive, rather than binding.

CONCLUSION

You can find relevant legal authority in:

- statutory law;

- case law;

- public policy;

- legal commentary;

- legislative history; and

- case or statutory law from other jurisdictions.

Remember to consider each of these areas when planning your essay.

3. Legal Authority in "Discuss" Questions

In many ways, it is easier to identify what constitutes proper supporting authority in a fact pattern question because you can analogize the situation to litigation. "Discuss" questions are slightly more difficult and are handled specifically in chapter seven. However, at this point it is sufficient to say that "discuss" questions use the same types of authority that fact pattern questions do. You might need to rely on persuasive sources of law a bit more heavily in "discuss" questions, but you cannot

---

[5]   Examples have already been discussed in this chapter. *See* overseas Tankship (UK) Ltd. v. Morts and Dock & Engineering Co. (The Wagon Mound) [1961] A.C. 388, Overseas Tankship (UK) Ltd. v. Miller Steamship Co. (The Wagon Mound (No. 2)) [1967] 1 A.C. 617. Sometimes courts use comparative law to help fill a gap in U.S. law or to ascertain whether and to what extent the United States might be out of step with other countries. *See* S.I. Strong, *Religious Rights in Historical, Theoretical and International Context*: Hobby Lobby *as a Jurisprudential Anomaly?* 48 VAND. J. TRANSNAT'L L. 813 (2015).

and should not ignore binding sources of law when answering a "discuss" question.

C. Assembling Your Legal Authority and Planning Your Essay

Preparing the "R" section of an IRAC essay is a two-step process. First, you must consider the realm of potentially relevant law, both binding and persuasive. This process requires both creativity and knowledge of the law. Second, you must use your judgment to identify which legal authorities you will actually discuss and which you will discard. Most students fail to recognize that professors are more interested in testing your judgment than they are in testing your memory. Therefore, be sure to complete both steps of your legal analysis. Only after you have completed this two-step process should you begin to write the "R" section of your essay.

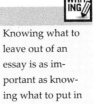

Knowing what to leave out of an essay is as important as knowing what to put in and requires ruthlessness and courage on your part.

1. Compiling Relevant Law

The IRAC system requires you to compile two sorts of relevant law: first, the law supporting the various elements of the issue, as that term is defined in the previous chapter, and second, the law relating to the various sub-issues that you have identified in the "I" section of your analysis.

a. Law Supporting the Elements of the Issue

As was discussed in the last chapter, the "I" in IRAC stands for "issue," which is analogous to a cause of action in a court case. The issue can be a tort, a crime, a dispute about the existence or terms of a contract, etc.

When it comes time to discuss the law relating to your issue, you must set out each of the elements that must be proven as part of a plaintiff's or prosecutor's *prima facie* case. For example, if you decide that your question involves the tort of negligence, you must state that negligence requires the plaintiff to prove the existence of a legal duty, breach of a legal duty, factual ("but for") causation, legal causation (foreseeability), and damages. If any one of those elements is missing, the plaintiff cannot prevail in a court case.

You should always try to support your statements, even statements as general as these, with binding legal authority. For example, one case that is discussed in a number of first year casebooks on torts, *Detraz v.*

Lee, contains a general reference to all five elements of negligence.[6] Cite *Detraz* (or a similar decision from your casebook) by name or by description to earn every possible point on your exam essay. Alternatively, you could cite to the *Restatement (Third) of Torts: Liability for Physical and Emotional Harm* to establish these basic elements, recognizing (both in your mind and explicitly in your essay) that the Restatement is only persuasive authority unless and until it is adopted in a particular jurisdiction.[7]

Negligence is a typically viewed as a common law cause of action, which means you must pull the elements of the tort from case law. However, some claims are based on statutory law. Thus, for example, a prosecutor who brings a case for robbery must prove that the defendant has

> use[d] or threaten[ed] the immediate use of physical force upon another person for the purpose of: (a) Preventing or overcoming resistance to the taking of the property or to the retention thereof immediately after the taking; or (b) Compelling the owner of such property or another person to deliver up the property or to engage in other conduct which aids in the commission of the theft.[8]

Committing this entire provision to memory may not be the best use of your study time. However, you should memorize the key components ("use[d] or threaten[ed] the immediate use of physical force upon another person" for certain purposes) and use those exact words, followed by a citation, in any essay you write concerning robbery.

NOTE

Specificity in your essays impresses readers and wins you points.

We will discuss how to go about writing your essay in greater detail below, including matters relating to quoting and citing legal authorities. However, this introduction gives you an idea of what you should hope to achieve.

You must complete this first step of setting forth the required elements because it requires you to slow down and think about all the different things you can discuss in your essay. As we mentioned in the last chapter, jumping straight to what you think is the most important sub-issue can lead you to miss other potential areas of discussion and lower your final grade. You may also find yourself in a situation where you have several potential issues. For example, a tort question might allow you to discuss both battery and assault. Although each of these

---

[6]   *See* Detraz v. Lee, 950 So.2d 557, 562 (La. 2007).

[7]   *See* Restatement (Third) of Torts: Liability for Physical and Emotional Harm § 6, cmt. b.

[8]   Mo. Rev. Stat. § 569.010(1).

torts has different elements that must be established before a plaintiff can prevail, there is considerable overlap. If you set down the basic elements as the first step in your discussion of each cause of action, you can insert internal cross-references into your essay that will save you time. As discussed in the previous chapter, professors often set questions with multiple issues and multiple parties; IRAC gives you the means to break down your responses in a straightforward and logical manner.

Setting forth the elements of the basic issue and the supporting authority is an important planning point but, as discussed below, should consist of one or two sentences at most. The majority of your time should be spent on identifying the rules relevant to the various sub-issues that you have identified in the "I" step as being in contention.

b.   Law Supporting the Contentious Sub-Issues

As we discussed in the last chapter, a contentious sub-issue is one that is difficult to prove as a matter of law. For example, there might be two lines of cases that point to different outcomes. Similarly, liability might hang on whether some act was "reasonable," in which case you must discuss previous cases or statutes that define when an act is reasonable.

Avoid pre-prepared treatises on the law. Tailor your response to the question asked.

As mentioned in the previous chapter, you have to undertake something of a mental juggling act when considering what is going to be contentious as a matter of law, since you have to think about the law while simultaneously remembering the facts of your problem. You won't discuss those facts until you get to the "A" element of IRAC, but there's no use raising some aspect of the law that isn't relevant to the question. Professors often complain that students provide pre-prepared treatises on the law that have little, if any, relevance to the question. Avoid that mistake.

The way to avoid bringing irrelevant bits of law into your essay is to make sure that you have enough relevant law from the very beginning. In this stage of your preparation, your task is to identify as many different sources of authority—both binding and persuasive—as you possibly can. You will discard some of these authorities later, but that's the second step. This first step is all about identifying as many potential discussion points as possible. In doing so, you should consider each of the types of legal authority introduced above:

Be as broad and as creative as possible at this stage of your analysis. You can discard material later.

i.   *Statutory Law*

Although most law students who are considering possible legal authority move straight to case law, statutory law is actually more important in the fields where it applies. You should therefore start your analysis by identifying any statutes or regulations that might apply to your fact pattern. While it is always important to discuss any constitutional issues that might arise, the U.S. Constitution is quite general. As a result, any citation to the Constitution or its amendments really needs to be supplemented by case law to be worthwhile.

ii.   Case Law

When considering which case law to include, think about the following categories of cases:

- cases that construe or supplement any statutes that you will be citing;

- cases that are factually similar to your problem;

  o   for example, if you have a question involving a driver, consider all the automobile cases you know;

- cases that are legally similar to your problem;

  o   for example, if you have decided that your question involves the standard of care in negligence of a person holding expert skill, consider all the expert skill cases you know, whether or not they are factually similar to your problem.

As you think about each category, write down any potentially applicable case in your notes. Later you will evaluate the relative importance of each item and delete those that are not relevant or useful.

iii.   Persuasive Authority (Public Policy, Legal Commentary, Legislative History, and/or Case or Statutory Law from Other Jurisdictions)

Some types of questions (such as "discuss" questions or invitations to reform the law) will require more discussion of persuasive authority than pure fact pattern questions. However, one hallmark of a top fact pattern essay is the ability to incorporate persuasive authority in a logical and relevant manner. Therefore, don't ignore these types of materials, even if you have lots of binding authority to discuss.

Discuss both sides of the dispute.

At this point, you should not try to create an argument for one side or another, no matter what the question asks you to do. Instead, look for cases or statutes supporting both sides of the dispute. Look also for any possible defenses, remembering that some defenses stand by themselves (for example, contributory negligence or self-defense), whereas other defenses can be seen as a negation of one of the *prima facie* elements of the plaintiff's case (for example, voluntary assumption of the risk can be seen either as a defense or as a negation of the existence of a duty).

This may sound like a lot to do under time pressure, but in fact you probably know quite a lot of law already. The important thing to do is to start organizing your ideas so that you can see how different aspects of the law interact.

You also must learn how to think creatively, as suggested in chapter two. Although most people easily see the relationship between cases that are factually similar, fewer people recognize cases that are legally similar, even if the underlying facts are somewhat diverse. Chapter two has given you some tips in how you can develop this skill, which is critical to the practice of law. You must learn to argue by analogy; if you can make a good, logical argument why a case relates to your problem, the professor will have to respect it. This is not to say that every case can be made relevant to every problem, only that arguing effectively by analogy shows the kind of legal sophistication that wins top grades. Don't be too hard on yourself if you find this process difficult at first. This technique is a learned skill, so it will take time to develop.

Cross-referencing your notes and outlines in advance is critical to carrying out a comprehensive "R" analysis in the exam room.

One of the realities of both legal practice and legal education is that the more law you know, the more creative and sophisticated you can be in your legal arguments. This makes the process much more enjoyable.

2. Discarding Irrelevant Law

At this point in the process, you have compiled a large amount of potentially relevant law to discuss in your essay. You should have more material than you will ever have time to cover properly in a timed exam. Now you must start to make decisions about what lines of argument you should discard.

It may seem odd to require you to identify more material than you will actually be able to use, but there is a method behind the apparent madness. First, forcing you to be creative and come up with all possible arguments stops you from starting to write the minute that you find a halfway decent case or theory. Often the best arguments or authorities are not the ones that you think of first.

NOTE

Your first thought is not always your best thought.

Second, you need to give yourself time to think not only of arguments in favor of one position, but also of arguments against that position. Sometimes one line of analysis will seem so overwhelmingly right that it will take a moment to figure out how it can be attacked. Taking the time to identify and make a good opposing argument can be the difference between a top grade and an average grade.

Third, having a large amount of law to discuss means that you will spend more time discussing the legal authorities and less time arguing the facts. Arguing the facts is something that practitioners do and involves poking holes in the evidence, noting what could have happened, and delving into motivation. This technique is irrelevant to your study of the law. Argue your points based on legal authority. Arguing the facts is like arguing public policy. Both are based on common sense, and both are given relatively few points in an exam scenario. While you will need to evaluate the law in light of the facts, that is a different thing from arguing the facts. We will return to this subject in the next chapter.

Argue the law, not the facts. You're in law school, not "fact school."

Finally, forcing you to create a large stockpile of material means that you will not be (as) tempted to include legal authorities or arguments that are not really relevant to the problem at hand. Students often worry that they will not know enough law to get a good grade. In fact, most students know more than enough law. They just don't present it well.

Most average students start writing about the first thing that comes to mind, even though that first thing may not be the most important. If you have identified a large amount of material, you will feel confident discarding some of it. You will also be past that first flush of enthusiasm that leads you to spend too much time on one case or statute. Because you know you have a lot to write about, you will prioritize your arguments and which aspects of the law you will discuss. Remember, you want to show the professor how discerning your judgment is.

Final exams test legal judgment as well as your understanding of the legal rules.

Eager students often believe that an effective method of studying involves preparing and memorizing large blocks of ready-to-use law that can be dropped into an essay. In fact, this approach is not helpful at all. Pre-prepared blocks of information demonstrate memory, not critical judgment. While you must know and remember the law before you can produce it in an examination scenario, simply regurgitating information will not win you high grades. You must use your judgment to tailor your response to the question asked. Obviously judgment is a more difficult skill to attain than simple memorization, which is why it is a hallmark of a top essay. Because you cannot demonstrate your judgment without having the information on hand, learning the law is the first necessary step. However, to get high grades, you must learn how to use your knowledge effectively.

How do you know which law should be discarded and which should be retained? That is something that is difficult to describe in the abstract, since it all comes down to judgment. However, one key element to remember is that you will only introduce those legal rules that support your overall arguments and that have some relationship to the facts that you will discuss in the "A" section of your essay. As a result, you have to plan all four steps of your IRAC essay before you start writing. Only after you know how the "R" and the "A" steps relate to one another should you put pen to paper.

YOUR TURN

When considering which case law to include, what categories of cases should you think about?

_____

_____

_____

_____

_____

D. Writing the "R" Portion of an IRAC Essay

As was discussed in chapter three, you must plan out the "I," "R" and "A" portions of your essay, at least roughly, before you start writing. While it is perfectly all right to go back and make insertions into earlier paragraphs if you remember a rule or an argument later, your essay will be much more persuasive if you limit the number of amendments and addendums. Therefore, take your time in the planning stages. With IRAC, the writing stage takes far less time than you are used to, since the information and analysis speak for themselves once they are compiled.

The "R" portion of your essay has two elements. The first involves explicit legal support for the various elements that a plaintiff or prosecutor has to prove as part of his or her *prima facie* case. This discussion is quite brief and requires one or two sentences at most.

The second part of the "R" analysis involves explicit and detailed support for each of the contentious sub-issues you have identified in the "I" portion of your essay. This discussion constitutes the majority of your essay.

Because this second aspect of the "R" step is relatively lengthy, you need to impose some kind of organizational structure on the analysis. For

Start with the most general rule, then give any supporting rules and exceptions.

example, it is often wise to cover each contentious sub-issue separately, beginning with the general rule (for example, it is unlawful to kill or injure others) before moving on to the exceptions and conditions to that rule (for example, it is not unlawful to kill or injure others if you are acting in self-defense). Each statement of law should come from a specific source, such as a statute or judicial decision, and be followed by a citation. You must include rules that support your anticipated conclusion as well as rules that suggest a different outcome.

Don't forget persuasive authority, particularly if the law is not clear or if the outcome required under the law seems unjust. While you cannot overcome bad precedent with persuasive authority, you can look to public policy, legislative history, and scholarly commentary to help fill gaps in the law or to suggest how a court should resolve a novel situation.

As you begin to write your "R" analysis, remember the following points. First, students who rely only on general statements of law will likely pass an exam, but they will not get top grades. You must demonstrate detailed knowledge of the law and provide an in-depth analysis to do well.

Second, use precise language—for example, the exact formula for *res ipsa loquitur*—and legal terms of art. Your essays will be tighter and more sophisticated if you can use phrases such as subrogation, servitude, or trespass *ab initio* correctly. Many students find it useful to start a vocabulary list for each of their subjects, both to help them understand the cases that they read and to help them as they study.

Third, cite to your sources. While the failure to provide attribution for specific statements of law will not cause you to fail (unless, of course, you are plagiarizing sources, which is an honor code violation), neglecting to include citations suggests that you have forgotten the first principle of legal analysis, namely that legal controversies are decided on the basis of existing law (the *nulla poena sine lege* idea). A rule or principle is not "law" unless someone in authority—a court or a legislature—

"The law according to Pat" is not law. It's opinion. The time for your opinion is in the "C" section of your essay, not the "R" section.

has said it is. If you are going to take the trouble to learn the rules, identify the source and get full credit for it.

Fourth, be sure to include enough information to demonstrate, even in the "R" section, why you are citing a case. A list of cases, statutes, or commentary, without more, is not legal argument. Some sources may be useful for several different propositions, and you need to indicate why you are including the reference. It's also true that some cases are important for their outcome whereas others are important for their analysis (i.e., why they come out the way they do). You do not always need to include a recitation of the facts of the cases you are citing—indeed, you should not do so—but you need to convey the reason why the case is important to your discussion.

You must indicate why you are citing a particular authority. Remember, you're trying to persuade your reader. Lists are not persuasive. Parentheticals are better.

CONCLUSION

Top-scoring essays show the following:

- detailed knowledge of the law;

   o you should be able to identify specific sections of statutory law as well as highly relevant cases (not just the big leading cases);

- precise use of terms;

   o you must use specific language from cases and statutes where necessary;

- creative and sophisticated analysis;

   o you must be able to craft arguments for and against your final position, using your knowledge of binding legal authority and, if possible and appropriate, persuasive legal authority;

- judgment;

   o you must know which arguments and legal principles to include in your essay and which to discard.

E. Worked Example

Now that you have the principles and rationales in mind, it is time to see how the second step of the IRAC method is put into practice. We will use the same sample question that appeared in chapter three, since you now know the issues and sub-issues in contention.

QUESTION

Jack, a Formula One race car driver, was driving his standard-issue SUV home from his daughter's school, where he had just dropped her off for the day. On the way, he was involved in a traffic accident. Had he used his expert skill in braking, he could have avoided the accident, although an ordinary driver could not have done so. Is Jack liable for the injuries to the other party?

1.   Identifying the Issue and Sub-Issues

We are building on the example begun in chapter three.

The first thing you have to do is identify the issue and the various sub-issues in contention. That process has been discussed in chapter three, where we concluded that the issue involved the tort of negligence. The sub-issues involve the existence and breach of the duty of care as well as the standard of care for people with expert skill.

2.   Compiling Relevant Law

The second thing you have to do is identify a list of potentially relevant legal authorities. Since legislative enactments take priority over judicial decisions, you should start by thinking about whether there are any statutes relevant to this fact pattern. While there may be some statutes that discuss automobile accidents of this nature, those statutes are not usually included in the first-year tort curriculum. Therefore, we will conclude there are no relevant statutes on automobiles.

Our analysis does not stop there, however. Whenever you are faced with a negligence question, you should consider the potential relevance of statutes concerning contributory or comparative negligence. Every state will have enacted something on this subject, although not every statute will apply to all fact patterns.

You also need to identify any relevant cases. Here, you should consider factually relevant cases and legally relevant cases for both the issue and the sub-issues. You also need to be sure to look for cases that favor liability and those that oppose liability.

To establish liability in negligence, a plaintiff must prove the existence of a duty of care, the breach of that duty, factual causation, legal causation, and damages. These elements are found in virtually every case and treatise on negligence, so you can provide support for this proposition by citing to the *Restatement (Third) of Torts: Liability for Physical and Emotional Harm*[9] or to cases that either include all five

---

[9]   *See* Restatement (Third) of Torts: Liability for Physical and Emotional Harm § 6, cmt. b.

elements (such as *Detraz v. Lee*[10]) or that stand as the seminal decision on a particular aspect of negligence (for example, *Palsgraf v. Long Island Railroad Co.*[11] for legal causation).

The notes you make regarding the cases you will initially consider will be quite brief. No one will see them but you, so use your own shorthand. Factually relevant cases include any automobile case that you know, while legally relevant cases will include (1) cases establishing the general standard for duty of care (the reasonable person), (2) cases involving special skill, and (3) cases involving professional negligence. You can find source material in your casebook (which would include cases appearing in footnotes, in notes following excerpted decisions, and cases cited within excerpted decisions) as well as in any study guides that you have used. While many commercial outlines are too general to provide you with much assistance, hornbooks can be quite useful in identifying relevant sources.

It is impossible to identify in the abstract how many legal authorities you should identify during this step. However, it would not be inappropriate to have ten or more cases, statutes, or other authorities listed in your notes at this point. You want to have a lot of material from which to choose so that you can pick your best alternatives in the next step of the process.

Be expansive during the brainstorming portion of your "R" analysis. You can cut down your list of authorities later.

3.   Discarding Irrelevant Law

The third step in the core "R" analysis involves culling out extraneous cases. When undertaking this step, it is critical that you keep the facts of your problem question in mind. When discarding authorities, what you want to do is identify and cite the "best" cases, which can be defined as either:

Prioritizing your legal authorities and eliminating those that are unnecessary is a high-level legal skill that is deeply satisfying.

- the leading cases (first precedents or highest courts);

- the most specific cases (meaning they have the most precise and complete legal language); or

- factually similar cases that are also legally relevant.

---

10   *See* Detraz v. Lee, 950 So.2d 557, 562 (La. 2007).

11   *See* Palsgraf v. Long Island R.R. Co., 162 N.E. 99 (N.Y. 1928).

Ask your professors whether they prefer you to focus your discussion narrowly on a few cases or more expansively, with more issues in play.

As you will see in the worked example, some authorities are discussed in detail while others are noted only in passing. While it is impossible to say in advance how many legal authorities you should discuss with respect to any particular issue or sub-issue, that number will always be more than one. Quite often, a top essay will refer to somewhere in the range of four to six authorities, which would include both case law and persuasive authority such as the Restatement. However, not all of these sources can be considered "standalone" references; instead, several will likely appear in different parts of the syllabus, thereby making them easier to remember, since they will be reinforced by constant cross-referencing.

It is important to remember that there is no standard number of authorities that you should discuss in the "R" step. Some professors prefer to see more authorities and some prefer less. This discrepancy arises because some professors value issue spotting while other professors prefer to see in-depth analysis. However, four to six authorities would appear to be a good starting point in either type of situation.

You will need to cite multiple cases in your essay.

4. Writing Your Response

DRAFT ANSWER ("I" section, with general "R" reference)

The question at issue is whether Jack is liable to the plaintiff for the tort of negligence.[12] To establish a claim in negligence, the plaintiff must prove the existence of a duty, breach of that duty, causation (including both legal foreseeability and "but for" causation) and damages (*Detraz v. Lee* (La. 2007)).[13] Of those four elements, the plaintiff here will have the most trouble establishing that there was a breach of the duty of care. The key sub-issue involves the appropriate standard of care.[14]

We have now set up the framework of our response quickly and concisely. We have wasted no time and no words on rhetorical flourishes or repetition of the facts. While the language may not seem particularly elegant, it is effective, powerful, and clear. More importantly, the opening paragraph is exactly what your professors—who are all trained in law and who are used to that kind of precision and brevity—want to see. After three sentences and two minutes of writing, you are now ready to

---

[12] This is the "issue," as defined in chapter three.

[13] These are the general elements of negligence.

[14] This sentence introduces the contentious sub-issues, which arise out of the plaintiff's *prima facie* case.

begin discussing the most important part of your essay: the legal rules concerning the contentious sub-issues.

DRAFT ANSWER ("R" section)

The legal standard relating to duty of care[15] is that of the reasonable man (now person),[16] taking into account the circumstances of the case. *See* Oliver Wendell Holmes, Jr., *The Common Law*. This standard is less rigorously applied in emergency situations. *See Cordas v. Peerless Transportation Co.* (involving a taxi driver whose cab hit a family following a car-jacking);[17] Restatement (Third) of Torts.

What constitutes a "reasonable person" depends on whether the defendant has any expert skill and whether that person holds him or herself out as having that expert skill. Restatement (Third), s 12. Thus, *Clark v. University Hospital* held that two medical residents should be held to the standard of a practicing physician rather than a resident, since they held themselves out as being practicing doctors.

Drivers are held to the same "reasonable person" standard as workers and professionals. *Daniels v. Evans* involved a 19-year-old driver who was still held[18] to the standard of a reasonably competent driver, despite the fact that the driver was only a minor. *Breunig v. American Family Insurance Co.* involved a defendant who had a mental lapse (the notion that her car could fly like Batman's) while driving. She was held to be negligent.

These cases involved defendants who asked to be held to a standard lower than that of a reasonable person.[19] The question of whether a person with expert skills should be held to a higher standard is somewhat open. Section 12 of the Restatement (Third) suggests that persons with superior abilities could be held to the standard of a reasonable person with those superior abilities. However, comment a to Section 12 recognizes that this approach could be unwise from a policy perspective, since people might be discouraged from acquiring superior skills if they are held to a higher standard. Therefore, *Fredericks v. Castora* (Pa. Super.

---

[15]   Note that you have already introduced the general elements of negligence, so you can start with the sub-issues.

[16]   Use gender-neutral language when possible.

[17]   This parenthetical helps contextualize the case reference and show its relevance to the discussion.

[18]   When writing your "R" analysis, you should focus on the legal holding of the cited case, with only enough factual information to place the holding in context.

[19]   This sentence shows good legal judgment in the way it distinguishes cases cited up until this point.

1976) rejected the notion that truck drivers, as professionals, should be held to a higher standard of care in traffic accidents.

Depending on how fast you write, you may decide to stop here. You have included legal support for your major points and could go on to evaluate the law (the "A" in IRAC) in light of the facts of your case if you wanted. The next chapter will discuss how to apply the law to the facts of your question. As you will see, certain rule-related statements can be made in that section as well.

However, some people write very quickly. If you fall into that category of students, you could go on to introduce a few less-important cases.

DRAFT ANSWER ("R" section — optional additional section)

Several defenses can be raised in negligence actions. Contributory negligence is the most common. *See Gyerman v. United States Lines Co.* (involving a longshoreman who was injured after failing to report a dangerous work condition). However, contributory negligence must contribute to the actual injury incurred. *See Gyerman.* Some states use comparative negligence instead of contributory negligence, either by statute or as a matter of the common law.

Older cases discuss the last clear chance rule, which indicates that the last person who was able to avoid the accident has the burden of doing so. *See Fuller v. Illinois Central R.R.* (involving a collision between a train and a wagon). The relevant standard might differ, according to the Restatement, depending on whether the plaintiff was helpless or merely inattentive.[20]

Both of the "R" responses feature a number of elements that bear mention. First, both discussions incorporate citations that briefly refer to the facts of the case cited as well as citations that refer only to the legal rationale. Both approaches are appropriate, depending on what you hope to accomplish with the citation. For example, you may need to include a slightly higher number of facts in situations where you are distinguishing between two lines of conflicting cases. Fewer facts are warranted when there is little or no dispute about the applicability or boundaries of the law (for example, the general applicability of the reasonable person standard).

Second, both discussions also rely heavily on succinct statements of the law and do not make judgments about the state of the law or discuss

---

[20] The author knows that the facts will not support a detailed discussion of comparative or contributory negligence or the last clear chance rule and therefore only mentions these concepts in passing.

the facts of the question. Those elements are more appropriate in the third step of the IRAC method, which will be discussed in the next chapter.

The organizational style of the "R" step is simple. Begin with the general rule associated with the issue, then move to the general rule associated with each of the sub-issues. Here we had only one real sub-issue, but if you look at the worked examples in chapter ten, you will see how to handle multiple sub-issues.

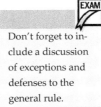

Next, identify any exceptions to the rule and introduce any cases you need to distinguish. You can categorize your case law by facts or by areas of law, as was the case in the preceding response. Possible defenses usually come at the end of your discussion. If you are discussing a line of cases, try to relate your later, more specific cases to your more general standard. That makes your discussion look more cohesive and less like a list of cases and holdings. Again, you will see examples of this approach in the worked essays in chapter ten.

Don't forget to include a discussion of exceptions and defenses to the general rule.

You now have a basic understanding of how to approach the "R" step in the IRAC method. For a further discussion of how to handle this step in "discuss" type questions, see chapter seven. In those situations, you may rely more heavily on persuasive sources of law, since you may be discussing the theoretical propriety of a certain reform movement or contextualizing a certain public policy position. However, you will still need to refer to binding sources of law and prioritize your arguments, as we have here. For more worked examples, see chapter ten. We will now move to the third step in the IRAC method, namely the application of law in light of the facts.

YOUR TURN

When should you give the facts of the case cited and when should you simply describe the legal rationale?

CHAPTER 5

Step Three in the IRAC Method: The Application

The preceding chapter discussed how to identify the rule in the IRAC method of legal essay writing and how to present legal analysis in a concise and logical manner. Up until this point, you have not explicitly referred to the facts of the case but have instead focused on identifying the issue and relevant sub-issues and setting forth the applicable legal authorities. Now, in the third part of your essay, you can begin to bring the specific facts of your question into your essay. This is also the section where you can demonstrate some originality in your thinking and writing style, since this is where you attempt to persuade the reader of your argument. Although the "R" portion of the essay is, in many ways, the most important, since it demonstrates your knowledge of the materials presented during your course, the "A" portion comes a close second, since a properly written evaluation of the facts in light of the law demonstrates your legal judgment.

When undertaking your "A" step analysis, you need to remember that you are being asked to think about the fact pattern as if you were a practicing lawyer, and a lawyer would not be giving proper legal advice if he or she merely identified the leading cases and statutes for a client and left it at that. The client would not know how to interpret that information and how to apply it to his or her case. A lawyer's job is not only to find the relevant information but also to explain how it relates to the problem affecting the client. Explaining the relevance and role of each of the legal authorities is particularly important because many of the same materials will be used by the lawyer's opponent to argue precisely the opposite outcome.

When answering a fact pattern question, think of yourself as providing legal advice to a client who needs things explained at a relatively basic level. Connect the dots explicitly, as if your reader knows nothing about the law.

To excel on a law exam or essay one must show both knowledge (i.e., recollection of the law) and judgment (i.e., the ability to apply and analyze the law.)

Therefore, practicing lawyers must evaluate the facts in light of the relevant law if they are to serve their clients properly. The same is true in an academic course. To carry out your "duty" to your reader, you need to indicate both what law applies to the question and how it applies to the facts reflected in that question. Both elements—law and application—are necessary if you wish to earn a top grade.

To implement the third step of IRAC properly, you must understand:

(1) what "application" means under the IRAC system;

(2) the need for the application step in legal writing;

(3) how to distinguish "application" from "rules" in the IRAC system; and

(4) various stylistic and practical issues concerning the application of the facts in light of the law.

Each of these points will be discussed in turn.

A. What Constitutes "Application" in the IRAC Method

The third step of your IRAC analysis requires you to apply the law to the facts of your case, although you could think of it, conversely, as applying the facts to the law. Either way, you must demonstrate the connection between the rules you have presented in the second step of the essay and the facts in the question. In the "R" step of the IRAC analysis, you set forth the general legal standard that exists independent of any particular fact scenario. Although you were not writing a mini-treatise on the law, in the sense that you were not merely listing the legal principles that exist in a certain area without any regard to how those principles would eventually apply to your case, you were providing an objective analysis of the standards that apply to all persons and situations. However, you were careful to tailor your analysis to your particular fact scenario by only introducing those cases, statutes, and commentators that were relevant to the question you were answering. Essentially, the "R" step provides the foundation for the "A" step of your essay.

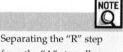

Separating the "R" step from the "A" step allows you to weigh up competing legal authorities in the "R" step and come to an objective conclusion about the relevant legal standard. If you try to apply the law to the facts too quickly, you might forget to do the legal analysis.

As you progressed through your discussion, you weighed up any competing authorities and came to some sort of conclusion about how a court would decide any particular issue, as a matter of law. Of course, you could not come to any final conclusions about the outcome of your particular problem, since you had not yet introduced any facts particular to your question. However, because you went through all four steps of the IRAC analysis in the planning stages, you knew, in your mind, why you were introducing each case and statute.

The "A" step of your essay is where you explicitly discuss the relevance of your legal sources to your fact pattern. Remember, you cannot win points unless you put your thoughts down on paper; professors are not mind readers.

Many students are convinced, at the time of writing that their arguments are clear and easy to follow. Very often, they are not. Walk your reader through each step of your analysis. You may feel as if you are being incredibly obvious, but it is virtually impossible to be too clear.

You cannot be too clear in your writing.

What connections must you draw between the facts and the law in your application analysis? Essentially, you must explain how your facts do or do not live up to the objective standard identified in the "R" step. The application stage is where you use logic and common sense to argue your position. As you recall, arguing on the basis of logic and common sense was discouraged in chapter four, primarily because logic and common sense do not constitute binding principles of law. Legal precedent, in either case law or statutory form, is what is important when you are defining the rules governing your dispute. Once you have an objective basis upon which to build your arguments regarding how these particular parties are situated under the law, you can then look to logic and common sense.

For example, in the "R" stage of an essay on defamation, you would have stated that publication of the allegedly defamatory material must be proven as part of the plaintiff's *prima facie* case. You would have gone on to define, with appropriate references to relevant legal materials, what constitutes publication under the law. You then would have moved on to introduce the next issue or sub-issue. Now, in the "A" stage of the essay, you are in a position to state how and why the defendant's actions constitute publication.

In some cases, the analysis is simple: for example, if the defendant, Jim, wrote "Felix embezzles the company's money" on a piece of paper and stood on the street, handing photocopies of the message to passersby, you would have few problems proving publication. When it comes time to do the application step for this particular aspect of the defamation claim, you would simply need to note how the act falls under the definition of "publication" and move on.

Sometimes the facts are slightly more problematic. Suppose, for example, that Jim is in the middle of photocopying the defamatory statement when a fire alarm goes off. What if he runs out of the building, leaving a copy in the machine? You would have noted in the "R" portion of your essay that publication exists if it ought to have been foreseen. Is publication here foreseeable? Possibly. You can argue it either way. What if Jim had an inordinate, unusual, and unreasonable fear of fires that caused him not only to run out of the building in a panic as soon as he heard the alarm but also to refuse to reenter the premises, even after the firefighters gave the all clear? Would publication exist if the photocopy was found a day later, after everyone else had returned to the building? What if the paper jammed in the machine just as the fire alarm went off, and a colleague pulled Jim out of the building as he tried to clear the jam? As this example shows, the legal standard relating to negligent publication remains the same even though the facts change.

You may or may not have cases that help describe what constitutes negligent publication, but you can identify a reasonable standard by pulling together cases dealing with defamation and cases dealing with negligence. Although this fact scenario may look bizarre, professors do their best to come up something unusual so that you can discuss how and why Jim's acts do or do not constitute publication. Notably, professors are not only testing your ability to identify the relevant legal standard when they give you a question, they are also testing your ability to judge whether the facts fall within that standard. Professors see these as two separate skills, which provides yet another reason why your essay should differentiate between issues relating to the law and the evaluation of the facts in light of the law. This phenomenon also explains why you must be explicit about when you are applying the facts to the law (or the law to the facts): it is the only way you can demonstrate the kind of legal judgment that your professors want to see.

> **EXAM**
> A lot of professors look to real life for inspiration. Keep up to date with current events if you want to do well on a final.

When conducting your analysis, you should be aware that your final conclusion about the outcome of the case is usually nowhere near as important as how you arrived at that answer.[1] If the study of law simply involved the determination of a single, objectively correct answer, then there would be no need for essays: a single sentence ("Jim is liable") would be sufficient. However, you know that if you submitted a single sentence like that in an exam scenario, not only would you fail to earn a high grade, you would most likely fail to pass the exam, even if the

---

[1] There are, of course, exceptions to this general rule. For example, if your question includes a person who drove a car on a dark and stormy night, knowing that the brake lights didn't work, it would be difficult to argue successfully that the person was not at least partially responsible when an accident arising out of the faulty brake lights occurred.

professor agreed with your conclusion. Therefore, you must admit that how you arrive at your final answer is as — if not more — important than the final answer itself.

There is typically no simple, single "right" answer in law. Why you conclude as you do is more important than what you conclude. The "A" step shows your "why" analysis.

Sometimes the application step involves the straightforward determination of whether a particular act falls within the legal standard established in the second section of the essay, as described in the preceding paragraph. Other times, you may have two conflicting cases which you had to harmonize or distinguish in the "R" section of your essay. You will have drafted that portion of your discussion with an eye to your facts, anticipating how you were going to handle a fact pattern that either puts you halfway between the two cases or squarely under the less attractive outcome.

Professors often play on your sympathy. You need to be ruthless and analyze the law and facts objectively.

Sometimes you can weigh up the competing authorities in the "R" section and indicate which way the court will rule, as a matter of law. Your application analysis will be much easier if you can come to this sort of legal conclusion. However, there may be times where it is impossible to come to a definite conclusion about the state of the law (for example, if the cases are utterly irreconcilable, a situation that occurs far less often in practice than students think). If that happens, you may want to wait to resolve the conflict until the application section of your essay. Once you start discussing the facts, you can show how your problem resembles one of the two lines of cases more than the other.

If your facts fall halfway between two lines of conflicting cases, you must state why your facts are more similar to one of the two lines of precedent. Hopefully, you have also been able to argue in the "R" section of the essay that the same line of cases is better or more likely to control as a matter of law and/or policy. However, you must always acknowledge the extent to which your facts resemble the troubling cases or the extent to which your facts fall outside the general standard.

Arguing persuasively is not the same as ignoring difficult precedent. In fact, a really good legal argument anticipates rebuttal and proposes a solution that is in keeping with your preferred outcome. If you fail to discuss opposing arguments, you are throwing away an opportunity to demonstrate your legal acumen.

You can't ignore troubling precedent. You must address it head-on.

When your facts place you squarely under a rule that you don't like or don't intuitively feel is correct, you can try to argue for another outcome, based on persuasive authority. For example, you might cite to a case that has been overruled on other grounds (taking care, of course, to note that the case is no longer binding authority but is persuasive on the point in question) or refer to a judicial decision from another jurisdiction. However, adopting this approach requires you to state explicitly that you are arguing for an extension and/or change in the law. While this technique may be appropriate at times (without extensions or alterations, the common law would stagnate), it is not the same thing as arguing that a certain set of facts falls squarely under an established legal standard.

If you argue for a change in the law, you should show, in the "R" section of your essay, that such a move would be possible as a matter of law (for example, to fill a gap in existing law) and then argue in the "A" section that your current fact pattern gives good reason for that extension. When demonstrating the wisdom of your suggested path, you need to show why public policy supports your proposal (and, as stated in chapter four, you need to enunciate precisely which public policy is at issue and discuss any opposing policies). Public policy argument can become very abstract, so use care and tie your statements to established legal principles as often and as closely as possible.

Never assume that your reader's sense of fairness corresponds with your own. Show why your course of action is best.

Even if you adopt all of these techniques, there will be times when your analysis leads you to conclusions that you believe are unjust. In those cases you should double-check your work to make sure that you have identified all the possible legal authorities and made the proper evaluations. Because the law is based on a shared sense of morality, cases often turn out the way we would expect or want them to. However, justice is determined at a relatively high level of generality, and sometimes a very sympathetic party will not prevail in a particular case. Stick to your legal analysis. The law does not remedy all ills, and you cannot distort the evaluative process just so that you arrive at a conclusion that satisfies you emotionally. Use your intuition to double-check your response, but don't try to follow your instincts in every situation. Professors commonly set questions that intentionally tug at your heartstrings. Don't let yourself fall into this particular trap.

Listen to your gut instinct, but don't let it control your legal judgment.

Chapter four admonished you not to argue the facts but instead to argue the law. Hopefully, you are now beginning to see the difference between the two techniques. When you argue the law and then apply the facts to the law, you are building your argument on an objective foundation. Although you use logic and common sense to ascertain whether the facts fall under the relevant legal standards, you are not basing your entire argument on factual concerns: every argument you make has its roots in the rules that you described in the second step of your essay. You sometimes have to argue by analogy, particularly when your fact pattern falls into a gap between two conflicting lines of cases, but you are still basing your position on the legal authority that you have previously identified.

YOUR TURN

How should you conduct your application analysis if the law has two competing lines of cases, each dictating a different outcome?

_____

_____

_____

_____

_____

The situation is very different when someone argues the facts per se. In those cases, the author skips the discussion of legal principles and goes straight to the facts of the case, often arguing that reasons of justice, fairness, morality, or public policy require a certain outcome. Sometimes the author is quite clear in his or her mind about what the law is, which is why the analysis begins with the factual discussion. While the intent is laudable to the extent that the author wants to show the reader how particular facts should be analyzed, people who move straight into a factual analysis do not give themselves the opportunity to (1) show that they know the law or (2) demonstrate legal judgment by comparing, contrasting, and manipulating legal authorities.

It may be that your unspoken presumptions are absolutely correct. However, your professor can't read your mind and can't know the assumptions on which you are operating. More importantly, the professor can't award points for something that is not written on the paper.

> **TIP** ✓
>
> The most important word in a law school exam is "because."

When you jump ahead of yourself and start discussing the facts before discussing the law, you also run the risk that your unspoken understanding of the law is only partially correct, in which case your analysis will be faulty or one-sided. Something about writing down the law, by itself, without any explicit consideration of the facts (though they are always in the back of your mind, since you know better than to introduce cases or statutes that have no bearing on your particular question) gives structure to your thoughts. Jumping straight into the facts often leads to emotive or muddy thinking. The first idea that comes to you might not reflect the best approach to the question.

For all these reasons, the IRAC method suggests that you discuss the facts only after you have presented the law. Many students who use this technique find that many questions can be answered satisfactorily without recourse to inherently ambiguous concepts such as morality or public policy. Since legal arguments are always stronger than arguments based on general principles of fairness, justice or logic, frame your response in terms of the law.

Your analysis must be based on law, not opinion.

B. The Need for Application of the Facts to the Law in Legal Writing

Once students become accustomed to the IRAC system, they sometimes become enamored by the "R" step and begin to short-change the "A" step. The underlying philosophy seems to be that the reader knows that the law would not be presented if it did not apply to the question and that, therefore, to analyze the facts in light of the law is simply belaboring the point.

While this approach shows an admirable respect for legal authority, objective presentations of the law, without more, are nothing but narrowly focused mini-treatises. While your discussion of the law should make sense on its own and should be placed in the kind of context that suggests how the materials will be used in the application section, a well-written "R" section does not eliminate the need for a well-written "A" section. Remember the example of the practicing lawyer from the beginning of this chapter: a practitioner cannot just present his or her client with a list of legal authorities and consider that list to constitute adequate legal advice. The lawyer must explain how and why those authorities are relevant to the question at hand. You must do the same thing in your final exams. No matter how clear and obvious the link between the law and the facts is in your mind, you must connect the dots for the professor, for several reasons.

Avoid "submarine" arguments that invoke the law implicitly rather than explicitly. These arguments exist just underneath the surface of the essay, like a submarine. Professors cannot give points for implied analyses.

First, you need to include an adequate "A" analysis because your "R" section may not be as clear as you think it is. Often a professor can see that a student is trying to make a point, but that point is submerged beneath the surface of the essay—a kind of "submarine" argument. Be explicit. Spell things out. No essay has ever been marked down for being too clear.

Second, you need to apply the facts to the rules that you identified as relevant earlier in the essay because law does not operate in a vacuum. Although legal principles can be studied and learned in the abstract, they cannot be divorced from real life. Indeed, problem questions mimic the kind of questions practitioners face on a daily basis. Law becomes relevant only when it is placed in a particular factual context. Therefore, you must individualize every legal analysis by relating the rules to the question asked.

Finally, almost any fact pattern can be read in several different lights. What appears obvious to you as requiring one type of outcome may not seem so clear to someone else. As strange and as wrongheaded as it may seem, people really do take very different views of the same set of facts. Therefore, when answering a question, you cannot assume that others will follow your unspoken train of thought, nor can you assume that others will be persuaded by the same things which persuade you. One of the great misconceptions in life is that everyone thinks as we do. Rather than hope that your reader is one of the few people who shares your beliefs and values, you need to rely on influential legal authority and detailed, logical arguments to persuade your reader of the wisdom of your perspective.

Although the "A" step is somewhat subjective to the extent that you are identifying how you weigh up various facts in light of the law, the analysis includes an objective element to it, since you need to discuss how certain aspects of the problem relate to the rules outlined in the preceding section of your essay. Your goal in the "A" step is to demonstrate either that (1) each element of the plaintiff's *prima facie* case can be sustained by reference to the fact pattern or (2) some element of the *prima facie* case can be defeated, because it either (a) fails to rise to the legal standard set forth in the "R" section of the essay or (b) falls victim to a defense asserted by the defendant.

The above analysis needs to be conducted regardless of whether the question directs you to take the perspective of one of the parties (e.g., "Advise Company A regarding its liability") or instructs you to simply discuss the dispute more generally. In either case, you must consider both the viability of the claims asserted as well as any defenses that can be brought to bear.

The application step also includes a certain amount of advocacy. Although you should not identify so closely with your so-called client's case that you ignore arguments and facts that support your opponent's point of view, you should frame the argument in a way that shows your perspective in the best light. Notably, good advocacy does not include ignoring facts or legal authorities that go against you. Instead, good advocacy is demonstrated in the way that

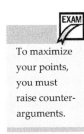

To maximize your points, you must raise counter-arguments.

you minimize the importance of such elements and demonstrate how and why those facts or rules are not determinative in your case.

C. Distinguishing the Application Step from the Rules in the IRAC Method

Some people naturally see the difference between rule and application. Other people have difficulty either distinguishing between the two or trusting that an entire section of an essay can be written without reference to the facts. If you remember that the "R" step of your essay relates to the rules applicable in the matter at hand and then organize the rules in a logical manner, beginning with more general statements and then narrowing your focus with greater precision to address the specific area that will be important in your case, then you will have fewer difficulties in leaving consideration of the facts until after you have completed the discussion of the law.

Be rigorous about separating the law and the facts, especially at first. What may initially seem odd quickly becomes second nature.

The "A" step of an IRAC essay requires you to demonstrate very different skills than the "R" step. In the application analysis, you are building on the rules identified in the second part of the essay and explaining how those cases and statutes affect the situation in question. However, this technique does take practice. For example, although you must refer to the materials cited, you need to do so without repeating everything that you have said before. Similarly, you must to refer to the facts in the question, but without repeating everything verbatim. Your goal is to tie the rules together with the relevant facts so that you can justify the conclusion proposed in the final step of the IRAC analysis.

Some people have difficulty trusting in the IRAC process and think that it would be better to introduce the facts at the same time you introduce the law, since that would appear to be more concise and logical. Certainly it is true that separating the "R" step from the "A" step can sometimes lead to unnecessary repetition. In the beginning, however, you should try to keep your legal analysis separate from your factual analysis, because it is extremely likely that you will shortchange your discussion of the rules if you don't separate your legal analysis from your factual analysis. It is very easy to fall into the trap of arguing the facts, rather than the law, especially in the early stages of your studies, when you are still learning how to read and analyze the materials.

Once you get used to presenting the rules on their own, the "R" analysis will look less sterile, particularly as you learn how to shape your discussion of the legal principles to foreshadow your discussion of the facts. In time, you may even start to think that any combination of law and facts in the "R" section of an essay looks sloppy and unprofessional.

The key benefit to separating out the facts from the law is that it allows you to parse out the finer nuances of your legal argument. If you mix your discussion of the rules with your analysis of the facts, you can forget to point out why one line of cases should control as a matter of law in your enthusiasm to show why the facts fall under another series of decisions. You could also fail to see a gap in the existing law and, as a result, miss an opportunity to discuss various policy considerations. As a result, the IRAC method separates out the two analyses.

Some students try to hedge their bets by conducting the application immediately after introducing the legal rule, leading to an organizational structure resembling the mnemonic IRARARAC. If well done, that approach can be as effective as a straight IRAC analysis. However, students who use IRARARAC are much more likely to miss some of the more sophisticated legal arguments, since the analytical structure suggests there is only one case or authority relating to each fact, when there might be several authorities that need to be considered. Students who use an IRARARAC approach also run the risk of arguing the facts, rather than the law, particularly if they evaluate each case as soon as it is mentioned. Remember, you want to introduce lines of cases rather than individual cases so that you can demonstrate your skills of legal analysis. IRARARAC can also become repetitive if you're not careful. Try different techniques to find out what works best for you, but do so only after you have given the regular IRAC method a proper chance.

If you are going to discuss several plaintiff-defendant pairings and/or several different issues (meaning causes of action rather than sub-issues), you should separate out the rule for each party pairing or issue and follow it with its own application. Remember, as stated in chapter four, you can incorporate previous discussions by reference, thus avoiding the need to repeat points of law or relevant facts. The emphasis here is on incorporation by reference—you must refer to the previous discussion explicitly rather than just assuming your reader will know that you mean to apply the same principles in your current discussion. You can provide a single joint

Separate your "R" and "A" steps for each party pairing and each claim. Incorporate prior discussions by reference.

conclusion at the end of the essay or indicate the outcome after each cause of action, whichever suits you best.

YOUR TURN

What are your options if you believe the outcome of your essay is unjust?

D. Writing the "A" Portion of an IRAC Essay

As mentioned above, you can adapt the IRAC system in several different ways, such as by separating out each individual sub-issue and following it with its own application in a type of IRARARAC approach. However, your biggest stylistic concern will likely relate to how strictly you adhere to the separation of rules and application. As you will find, there are times when an overly rigid application of this technique can lead to confusion. For example, you might undertake a rigorous analysis of two conflicting cases and feel that to add a short reference to a minor case that is only tangentially related to your facts would detract from the power or logic of your discussion of the law. In that case, it's perfectly acceptable to pop the reference to the case into the "A" section of the essay. This is particularly true if the point you are making regarding the additional legal rule is very brief and would have to be repeated nearly verbatim in your application section.

Similarly, there may be times when a very abstract discussion of the law could give the impression that the writer does not have the relevant facts in mind. While you should learn the art of structuring your legal analysis so that the links to your problem are apparent—for example, by highlighting the facts or legal issues in your cited authority that apply most directly to the question you are answering—sometimes a quick reference to the facts can be helpful in the "R" section.

Applying the facts to the law requires you to refer to the relevant cases and/or legal standards as you go. The link to your earlier discussion may be clear to you, but it may not be clear to your reader.

However, if you have identified the issues and sub-issues properly, you should be able to wait until the "A" section of your essay to discuss the facts. However, you still need to be strategic when it comes time to begin writing that section. For example, don't start with a general recitation of the facts. Instead, start evaluating the rules that you have already introduced in the preceding section in relation to the facts, beginning with the general principles that must be established to satisfy the plaintiff's *prima facie* case.

As you will see in the worked example below, you can run through the relevant facts and relate them to the legal standard outlined in the "R" section in a very short amount of time. Notably, when you are applying the facts, you are not repeating the discussion found in the "R" section, though you can and should refer to cases or statutes as appropriate to contextualize your analysis. Furthermore, you are not simply repeating the facts that were outlined in your question. Instead, your task is to identify which aspects of the facts bear a similarity or dissimilarity to the legal standards introduced in the "R" section.

As you can see, the application step of an IRAC essay cannot be conducted unless and until the "R" step has been completed. If there is no discussion of the relevant legal standards, any factual analysis simply looks like opinion and guesswork. You may very well know the law inside and outside, but if you don't put your knowledge on the paper, you can't win points for it. While it will take some time to master the technique, just as with any new skill, with practice you can learn how to manage your time and the amount of detail you introduce into your essays.

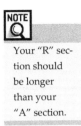

NOTE

Your "R" section should be longer than your "A" section.

During the "A" portion of your essay, you are, in a sense, justifying the inclusion of every legal reference you have made in the "R" portion of your essay. If you can't draw a direct link from a fact to any of the cases and statutes you have mentioned, then reconsider whether you should include that fact in your essay. This is what is meant by having the facts in the back of your head as you plan and write the "R" section of your paper. Of course, the reverse is true as well: do not introduce a case or statute unless it relates to a fact you intend to discuss in the "A" section of your essay. While this may seem difficult, all it requires is advance planning. If you take the time to think about the process of applying the facts to the law before you begin writing your essay, then you know that you are introducing each of your cases and statutes in the "R" section for a reason. The "A" step is when you explain that reason. That's why you outline your IRAC analysis before you start writing: to figure out what rules you need to adduce in the "R" step so that you can apply them in the "A" step.

TIP

Never simply repeat the facts in your essay—you win zero points for reiterating what the professor already knows. Applying the facts to the law is different than repeating facts.

Once it comes time to discuss the sub-issues that are most in contention, you should focus on explaining how the facts apply to the more specific cases that flesh out the general precepts of law. Because you have explained in the "R" section that these cases are merely more specific manifestations of the general standard, you can often get by without applying the facts to the general cases. Alternatively, you might find that you can demonstrate how your facts fall under the general rule, but not the more nuanced cases. If this result arises, then you need to conclude that the plaintiff has failed to meet the required standard for the *prima facie* case.

Use your judgment as you balance what needs to be said versus what can be implied. As stated above, it is dangerous to rely implicitly on a reader's understanding of your mental processes, but there are times when you do not need to spell out everything.

E. Worked Example

> **NOTE**
>
> We are building on the same worked example that was discussed in chapters three and four.

Having discussed the application step in the abstract, it is time to put that discussion in context by working through the example we have used in previous chapters.

QUESTION

Jack, a Formula One race car driver, was driving his standard-issue SUV home from his daughter's school, where he had just dropped her off for the day. On the way, he was involved in a traffic accident. Had he used his expert skill in braking, he could have avoided the accident, although an ordinary driver could not have done so. Is Jack liable for the injuries to the other party?

As you recall, the issue in the above example involves the tort of negligence, while the sub-issues involve breach of the duty of care and the standard of care for people with expert skill. The relevant legal standard has been set forth in detail in chapter four. Now you need to apply the facts in light of the law you have introduced.

1. Considering Your Facts

Chapter three suggested that you proceed through the question, line by line, to identify potential issues and sub-issues. While you could use the same procedure to identify those facts that you wish to bring to the

> **EXAM**
>
> The general organization of the "R" and "A" portions of your essay should mirror each other. Thus, they should follow the same general structure and both discuss and apply the law in the same order.

professor's attention, you should have already figured out those facts in your analysis of the issue and sub-issues (see the line-by-line worked example in chapter three). What is most useful during the "A" analysis is to track your legal analysis, as described in the "R" section of your essay, and demonstrate how the facts apply to each of those legal standards. This approach of course assumes that you have presented your legal materials in a logical fashion and have anticipated which concerns are most relevant to your question. If you have not planned out your essay ahead of time, you will find it difficult to correlate your application analysis to the rules found in the second part of your essay. If, however, you have taken the time to consider what legal points you wish to make and how those points fit in with the fact pattern before you start writing, you will find that the "A" portion of your essay writes itself.

To walk through the application analysis, we need to recall the rules, as they have been presented in the sample essay. Of course, as noted in chapter four, before you decided which law to present, you took the facts into account.

DRAFT ANSWER ("I" section, with general "R" reference)

The question at issue is whether Jack is liable to the plaintiff for the tort of negligence. To establish a claim in negligence, the plaintiff must prove the existence of a duty, breach of that duty, causation (including both legal foreseeability and "but for" causation) and damages (*Detraz v. Lee* (La. 2007)). Of those four elements, the plaintiff here will have the most trouble establishing that there was a breach of the duty of care. The key sub-issue involves the appropriate standard of care.

DRAFT ANSWER ("R" section)

The legal standard relating to duty of care is that of the reasonable man (now person), taking into account the circumstances of the case. *See* Oliver Wendell Holmes, Jr., *The Common Law*. This standard is less rigorously applied in emergency situations. *See Cordas v. Peerless Transportation Co.* (involving a taxi driver whose cab hit a family following a car-jacking); Restatement (Third) of Torts.

What constitutes a "reasonable person" depends on whether the defendant has any expert skill and whether that person holds him or herself out as having that expert skill. Restatement (Third), s 12. Thus, *Clark v. University Hospital* held that two medical residents should be held to the standard of a practicing physician rather than a resident, since they held themselves out as being practicing doctors.

Drivers are held to the same "reasonable person" standard as workers and professionals. *Daniels v. Evans* involved a 19-year-old driver who was still held to the standard of a reasonably competent driver, despite the fact that the driver was only a minor. *Breunig v. American Family Insurance Co.* involved a defendant who had a mental lapse (the notion that her car could fly like Batman's) while driving. She was held to be negligent.

These cases involved defendants who asked to be held to a standard lower than that of a reasonable person. The question of whether a person with expert skills should be held to a higher standard is somewhat open.

Section 12 of the Restatement (Third) suggests that persons with superior abilities could be held to the standard of a reasonable person with those superior abilities. However, comment a to Section 12 recognizes that this approach could be unwise from a policy perspective, since people might be discouraged from acquiring superior skills if they are held to a higher standard. Therefore, *Fredericks v. Castora* (Pa. Super. 1976) rejected the notion that truck drivers, as professionals, should be held to a higher standard of care in traffic accidents.

As you recall from chapter four, you could stop at this point if you run out of time. However, because the IRAC method streamlines your analytical and writing process, you may be able to carry on with the following section.

DRAFT ANSWER ("R" section—optional additional analysis)

Several defenses can be raised in negligence actions. Contributory negligence is the most common. *See Gyerman v. United States Lines Co.* (involving a longshoreman who was injured after failing to report a dangerous work condition). However, contributory negligence must contribute to the actual injury incurred. *See Gyerman.* Some states use comparative negligence instead of contributory negligence, either by statute or as a matter of the common law.

Older cases discuss the last clear chance rule, which indicates that the last person who was able to avoid the accident has the burden of doing so. *See Fuller v. Illinois Central R.R.* (involving collision between a train and a wagon). The relevant standard might differ, according to the Restatement, depending on whether the plaintiff was helpless or merely inattentive.

2. Writing Your Response

Following on from the draft response begun above:

DRAFT ANSWER ("A" section)

Next, we will apply the facts of the current case to the law discussed above.[2] Drivers have a general duty not to hit pedestrians, and causation (both legal and factual) exists here, as do damages.[3] However, the question is the scope of the duty of care and whether Jack breached that duty.

Jack will be held to the standard of a reasonable person in an emergency situation. Although Jack is an expert driver, he was not "holding himself out" as having that higher degree of skill in this

---

[2]   Use a brief introductory sentence to take the reader into the next section. Your reader may not be familiar with IRAC, so you have to explain your essay structure.

[3]   Run through the facts relating to the general (non-contentious) elements quickly.

situation. Because an ordinary driver would not have been able to avoid the accident, Jack should not be held liable for having failed to do so. Notably, some jurisdictions might apply the Restatement (Third) strictly and hold Jack to the higher standard of a professional driver, but that is the rule in a minority of states.

If for some reason Jack were to be held liable, he might be able to minimize or avoid liability by asserting an affirmative defense like contributory negligence, comparative negligence, or the last clear chance rule. However, there are insufficient facts in the question to allow a full analysis of any potential defenses.[4]

Again, the author avoids hypothesizing about contributory or comparative negligence, since the facts here do not support a discussion of such issues. Many exam questions will allow or even require a detailed analysis of defenses. However, it is appropriate to mention possible defenses briefly, even if they don't apply, so long as they are not entirely outside the facts. Thus, a brief mention of contributory negligence, comparative negligence, and the last clear chance rule is appropriate in the context of a car accident, but raising the possibility of self-defense (i.e., that Jack was fending off some intentional act by the other driver) would not.

You now have a basic understanding of how to approach the "A" step in the IRAC method. For a further discussion of how to handle this step in "discuss" type questions, see chapter seven. "Discuss" questions do not have the same sort of facts as a problem question, but they still require you to pay attention to the particular context of the question and answer it as asked. For more worked examples, see chapter ten. We will now move to the fourth and final step in the IRAC method, namely the conclusion.

YOUR TURN

Why is it generally wiser to use IRAC rather than IRARARAC?

_____

_____

_____

_____

_____

---

[4]   This identifies a factual question that could be determinative. However, the author rightly refuses to hypothesize about the matter.

CHAPTER 6

Step Four in the IRAC Method: The Conclusion

The first three steps of the IRAC system are, in many ways, the most important. If you do not properly identify the issue, you cannot present the relevant rules, nor can you construct a persuasive argument once it comes time to apply the facts to the rules. The fourth step, which relates to your conclusion, is the least important element of the essay.

NOTE

How you ultimately decide the legal issues in your exam or essay is far less important than how you arrived at your decision.

Nevertheless, an essay that fails to provide a conclusion about the arguments made by the parties is incomplete and cannot be given the highest grade. Again, drawing on the litigation analogy, a lawyer who discusses the applicable legal authorities and states how those authorities apply to a client's situation but fails to tell the client how the case is likely to be resolved cannot be said to have given proper legal advice. Just as a judge or practicing lawyer must come to some sort of conclusion about the outcome of the dispute, so too must you.

To implement the fourth step of IRAC properly, you must understand:

(1)   what a conclusion is under the IRAC system; and

(2)   the need for a conclusion in legal writing.

Both of these points will be discussed in turn.

A.   What Constitutes a "Conclusion" in the IRAC Method

In the conclusion, you indicate how you believe a court would decide the issues posed by the exam question. All legal advice—whether it is given in the context of litigation or a transaction—revolves around how a court would resolve various contentious issues. Therefore, when you are faced with a fact pattern question, you must anticipate how a court will act in response to that particular problem. Part of the question may ask you

NOTE

You must decide the issue presented, one way or another. Waffling is not "being lawyerly."

how you might reform the law, in which case you can consider the issue from the point of view of the legislature. For the most part, however, you should look at the outcome as if you were a judge.

What constitutes a conclusion in an IRAC essay depends to some extent on what you have said in your earlier discussion. Parts one, two, and three of your essay required you to consider all of the relevant law and facts. Because you have already explicitly discussed both the facts and the law, you do not need to summarize either in the "C" step of your essay. What you do need to do is tie up loose ends and come to a final determination about which part of the preceding argument controls the disposition of the case, to the extent you have not already done so. For example, during the "R" and "A" portions of your discussion, you indicated how much weight you would give to each aspect of your argument and whether the individual facts fulfilled the requirements needed to establish the plaintiff's *prima facie* case. In that sense, you have already indicated what your conclusion is. Further discussion is unnecessary except to make the final determination absolutely clear.

Therefore, the "C" step in an IRAC essay is very different than a conclusion in an undergraduate essay. When you were in college, you used the concluding paragraph to tie the threads of your argument together and put the argument into context, perhaps by repeating your main themes or indicating why one particular piece of information should be determinative. An IRAC conclusion, on the other hand, simply clarifies which party has ultimately prevailed. That result should be apparent from your earlier discussions, if your essay is as tightly constructed as has been suggested here. However, it is good practice for you to get into the habit of concluding your essay with a single sentence stating the resolution of the dispute, for two reasons.

First, professors want to see a clear conclusion at the end of an essay. The outcome may be implicit in your earlier discussion, but it does not hurt to add the words, "On these facts, the plaintiff will prevail and will receive damages in X amount" at the end of your essay.

Second, your "R" and "A" discussions may not make the outcome as clear as you think it is. In the heat of the moment, it is very easy to think that you have said something explicitly when in fact you have only thought of saying it. Take the time to make your essay complete by indicating who will win.

Your conclusion can and should be quite brief. As will be discussed in chapter nine, which deals with legal writing in professional practice, practicing lawyers typically set forth their legal arguments in great detail and then conclude their court submissions with the simple phrase, "For the aforementioned reasons, [my client] should prevail." That is the type of brevity to which you should aspire. As demonstrated in the worked example below, you

An IRAC conclusion is much shorter than a conclusion in an undergraduate essay.

can, in many cases, conclude your IRAC essay with a one-sentence paragraph stating which party prevails. Why that party prevails has already been demonstrated in the "R" and, to an even greater extent, the "A" portions of your discussion. Therefore, you need not repeat those reasons in the "C" step.

The one exception to the rule of brevity is if your "R" and "A" steps contain a lot of sophisticated and complex arguments that make it difficult for you to weigh up the opposing positions in those portions of the essay as either a matter of substance or style. In that case, the essay might be better served by recapping the weight of the various points in the final paragraph. For example, if you have a checklist of six attributes that define whether a particular act is "fair and reasonable," and your evaluation of the facts demonstrates that two attributes exist and four do not, you may want to note in your final paragraph that because Judge So-

Most conclusions need only a single sentence. Only a few essays require more.

and-So required all six elements to exist prior to a determination that the defendant was liable, and only two elements (i.e., X and Y) could be proven, the defendant could not therefore be held liable for the damages claimed. If Judge So-and-So did not require all six elements to exist, but merely stated that a court should consider those elements in considering whether a defendant could be found liable, then you could spend slightly more time and indicate why X and Y either should or should not outweigh the four elements that were not proven. In both cases, the closing paragraph would be more than one sentence in length, although it would still not attempt to summarize or recap the preceding paragraphs. Notably, this type of situation arises very infrequently and you should try to keep your conclusions quite brief, since the bulk of your analysis will already exist in the "R" and "A" sections of your essay.

Another example of when you might need to write a longer concluding paragraph is when your "A" step suggests that there is not enough factual information to come to a reasoned conclusion or when your "R" step suggests that the state of the law is too unsettled to provide a firm answer. Both circumstances are extremely—repeat, extremely—rare. In the first place, professors seldom create fact patterns that do not contain all the information necessary to dispose of the dispute. An incomplete question yields problematic answers, and professors want to give students every opportunity to show off their learning. In the second place, professors seldom create fact patterns that cannot be resolved as a matter of law, first because it is impossible to create a problem that is so evenly balanced that no conclusion is possible and second because every legal dispute must be decided one way or another, no matter how close the balance of equities or law may lie. Litigation is a zero-sum game: it does not allow for ties. A court must come to some conclusion about a pending case, and so too must you.

If you decide that you do not have sufficient facts or the law is too evenly balanced to suggest a firm conclusion, check your analysis again. You may be missing something or you may not be weighing up the evidence or the legal authorities as well as you thought. Nevertheless, if you do conclude that a straightforward outcome is impossible, say that the case cannot be decided without additional facts (which you should identify generally, without hypothesizing about what would happen if the question were written in the way you propose) or that the legal position is too complex or too much in a state of flux for you to suggest an outcome. Do not hesitate to make a decision just because you think it is not what the professor had in mind. Your professor wants you to make some sort of decision, even if it is different from the decision that he or she would make. Being a lawyer is all about using your best professional judgment. Even experienced lawyers can end up being "wrong" (in the sense that the court may ultimately disagree with their analyses), but clients still need to know what their lawyers think the outcome will be. Trial judges can

NOTE

Do not hypothesize about the question you wish had been asked.

also be "wrong" (in that a trial judgment may ultimately be overturned on appeal), but judges can't just say "it's a tie" when they see a close case. The judge still must come to a reasoned decision. You are in the same position. Make the best judgment you can, given the realities of your situation.

EXAM

Don't try to second-guess your professor. Provide a conclusion that is consistent with the law and facts as you have analyzed them in the "R" and "A" steps.

As has been mentioned before, the final determination about the outcome of your dispute is not as important as how you get there. As you recall from your high school and undergraduate days, mathematicians still get credit for how they work out a problem, even if the final number at the end of the equation is wrong as a result of an arithmetical error. How the mathematician evaluates the question is ultimately more important than the final answer.

The same is true for law students; you still get credit for how you analyze a problem, even if you reach a different conclusion than the professor would. Of course, there are exceptions to this general rule. For example, you will get very little credit if you attempt to rewrite the law with no legitimate basis for doing so, such as by claiming that a trial court need not adhere to principles set down by the Supreme Court based on your belief that the concept of *stare decisis* is nonsensical and outmoded. However, you will not be making these sorts of outrageous claims. Therefore, your conclusion will focus on indicating what the outcome of the dispute will be.

Some of you may be nervous about coming to a conclusion in case you have missed or misread a key case or statute. Of course you will lose points if you miss a big, important case, but you won't avoid that penalty by failing to come to a conclusion. Instead, you will simply compound the error by failing to come a conclusion based on the information you have presented in your essay. At the end of the day, you simply need to do the best you can with what you have. A well-written and well-reasoned essay can still earn a very good grade, even if you have had a lapse of memory or understanding.

TIP

Students often worry about missing the key case and coming to the wrong conclusion. In fact, the common law provides multiple routes to the same result. For example, you can get from L.A. to D.C. via I-40 or I-80. I-40 is faster and a bit more direct, but both routes work. The analogy holds true in law.

YOUR TURN

Under what circumstances will you need a conclusion that is more than one sentence long?

_____

_____

_____

_____

_____

B.   The Need for an Outcome in Legal Writing

As suggested in the preceding section, practicing lawyers must come to a conclusion when dispensing legal advice to a client or arguing a case in court. Sometimes the conclusion is not the one a client wants to hear. As a matter of good professional ethics, you cannot say that a case can be won just because that is what your client wants to hear. You must identify the likely outcome based on the law and the facts in front of you. It is better for a client to know bad news early on, when settlement is possible and less expensive, than to go to court not knowing that failure is likely.

Although law students are obviously under no professional or ethical obligations to speak the truth, you still need to give your honest opinion about the dispute rather than trying to force the decision one way or another. Just because the question directs you to advise one party does not mean that you should try to persuade the reader that that party should or will prevail. Instead, as the preceding chapters have indicated, you should present a balanced analysis of the dispute. If your designated client is likely to lose, say so. You may be able to identify and exploit certain weaknesses in the other side's case, but don't overestimate your client's chances of success. Many practitioners purposefully take a conservative approach to legal advice so that their clients do not get their hopes up too high. While you need not adopt a particularly conservative approach to your academic essays and examinations, you do need to be realistic.

The exception to this rule is when the question directs you to make the best possible case for a particular party. However, professors seldom ask students to adopt this approach.

One of the reasons why a conclusion is so important in an IRAC essay is because it allows your professor to evaluate how you exercise your judgment. Part of the task you have been given in a legal examination involves the question of judgment and discretion: how do you weigh up the conflicting legal authorities and how do you prioritize

Law exams test your judgment and discretion as well as your knowledge of the law.

the facts outlined in the question? If you don't offer a conclusion, your professor cannot evaluate your judgment. You may be absolutely correct about how you think the case will play out, but the professor can't get inside your head to access that information. It has to come out on the page. You may think that the outcome is obvious from your discussion of the law and your evaluation of the facts, but don't take the risk of offering an incomplete analysis. Take the time to write one sentence stating your conclusion.

Some students fear putting down a conclusion because they think they will lose points if they "get it wrong." However, if you don't put down an explicit conclusion, you have already demonstrated that you lack the kind of forthright, decision-making ability that is necessary in a legal career. The conclusion is the last thing your professor will read: make sure it counts in your favor.

If legal disputes had a single "right" answer, no one would go to litigation. The "right" answer is identified through persuasion.

Therefore, there is no downside to making an educated guess and stating your conclusion. Conversely, failing to provide an outcome will lose you points. Therefore, be bold and don't worry about finding the single "correct" answer that probably doesn't exist anyway. Remember, law is more about persuasion and argument than it is about finding an objectively identifiable, universally accepted "right" answer.

C. Writing the "C" Portion of Your Essay

As you recall, IRAC involves two stages: the planning stage, in which you work your way through the potential issues, rules, and factual analysis, and the writing stage, in which you present your best arguments after discarding the more tangential or minor points. In your planning stage, you come to a preliminary decision about who will win the case. You then shape your legal and factual discussions with this outcome in mind so that you can have as brief a concluding paragraph as possible (optimally one line long).

However, it is altogether possible that you will think of additional arguments as you write your essay. Alternatively, you may become convinced that what seemed to be a straightforward win for one side is actually closer than you thought. By the time you're done with your essay, you could have an entirely different opinion as to the outcome of the case.

If this happens, don't worry. While your goal is to be as organized as you can be before you start writing, the process of writing often clarifies your points for you in an entirely new way. Your shift in perspective will probably be visible in your writing, which is objective (i.e., non-biased) but which still takes a view as to the weight of the opposing arguments. However, because you have begun your essay with a discussion of the basic principles of law that are applicable to the situation (the "R" step), you should be able to make a mid-course correction in the "A" step without too many problems. In any event, there is no shame in changing your mind. If you suddenly recall a new case or realize that you misread the question, it is better to say so than to hold firm to an indefensible point out of a misplaced sense of pride or the fear that any sort of waffling will undermine your argument.

EXAM

Professors know you're under time pressure and evaluate your submission accordingly. Just do the best you can.

This concept is particularly true in timed essays. Professors know that you're under time pressure and don't have time to go back and refine your arguments. When you realize you want to change directions, you have two choices: either go back and amend your preceding language through inserts or scratch-outs or explicitly state that you are changing your analysis going forward, based on your reconsideration of X case or Y fact. Professors are used to seeing both techniques, so do whichever makes the most sense and is the most time-efficient in the circumstances. While changing your mind midway through your essay is not recommended (and you can generally avoid it

TIP

Don't create your own time pressures by waiting until the last minute to draft a take-home examination. The best writers draft early, let the piece sit for a time, then revisit their submission later with a fresh and critical eye. Good writers are really good re-writers.

in a non-timed essay), it does happen and you should do whatever it takes to make your point in an exam scenario.

Once you get to the writing stage, you should aim to use one sentence to describe the legal outcome of the dispute. For example, in a tort case, you might write, "For the reasons mentioned above, Joe will fail in his claim of negligence but will prevail on his claim of nuisance, and will receive compensatory damages equal to the cost of his damaged rhododendrons." One sentence should be enough.

In the beginning, it may feel somewhat abrupt to end with just one sentence. You may have felt the same about starting an essay with a single sentence identifying the key issue(s) (cause(s) of action). However, the following discussion demonstrates the wisdom of ending an essay on a concise note.

One exception to the rule of brevity occurs when you want to include a short discussion about potential reform or the direction in which the law is moving. This technique is used when you want to exceed the expectations of the professor and go beyond the question to demonstrate your understanding of legal theory or policy. As you recall from chapter one, one of the things that distinguishes a top essay from an average essay is a strong understanding of the policy and context of the area of law under discussion. Because you have so much information to cover in a response to a problem

EXAM

If you have time, exceed the professor's expectations by discussing some aspect of public policy.

question, it can be hard to find the opportunity to include some comments on policy. Such information can also seem out of place in what is primarily a pragmatic response to a real-life legal dispute.

Nevertheless, if you want to earn good grades, you should try to find a way to contextualize your discussion into the larger debate in that field of law. Sometimes your comments can be incorporated into the "R" or "A" steps, but you might want to be cautious about spending too much time on "extra credit" material in the early stages of your essay, in case you run out of time. A discussion about reform measures may also seem out of place in the body of a tightly written IRAC essay. As a result, it may be useful to save your more philosophical points until the end of your essay and place them in a short paragraph following your stated outcome. Remember, the important part of writing an answer to a problem question is to answer the problem. Including policy discussions shows good versatility and a wide understanding of the subject, but is like icing on a cake: nice, but not necessary.

D. Worked Example

Having discussed the conclusion in the abstract, we can now put that discussion into context by working through the example we have used in previous chapters.

Here we are returning to the same essay that has been developed in chapters three, four and five.

QUESTION

Jack, a Formula One race car driver, was driving his standard-issue SUV home from his daughter's school, where he had just dropped her off for the day. On the way, he was involved in a traffic accident. Had he used his expert skill in braking, he could have avoided the accident, although an ordinary driver could not have done so. Is Jack liable for the injuries to the other party?

As you recall, the issue in the above example involves the tort of negligence, while the sub-issues involve breach of the duty of care and the standard of care for people with expert skill. The relevant legal standard has been set forth in detail in chapter four and the relevant facts have been evaluated in chapter five. The last thing to do is to identify the outcome of the dispute.

1. Writing Your Response

First, we identified the claim, adding in the general legal standard as part of the introductory paragraph.

DRAFT ANSWER ("I" section with general "R" reference)

The question at issue is whether Jack is liable to the plaintiff for the tort of negligence. To establish a claim in negligence, the plaintiff must prove the existence of a duty, breach of that duty, causation (including both legal foreseeability and "but for" causation) and damages (*Detraz v. Lee* (La. 2007)). Of those four elements, the plaintiff here will have the most trouble establishing that there was a breach of the duty of care. The key sub-issue involves the appropriate standard of care.

Next, we introduced the most important legal authorities.

DRAFT ANSWER ("R" section)

The legal standard relating to duty of care is that of the reasonable man (now person), taking into account the circumstances of the case. *See* Oliver Wendell Holmes, Jr., *The Common Law*. This standard is less rigorously applied in emergency situations. *See Cordas v. Peerless Transportation Co.* (involving a taxi driver whose cab hit a family following a car-jacking); Restatement (Third) of Torts.

What constitutes a "reasonable person" depends on whether the defendant has any expert skill and whether that person holds him or herself out as having that expert skill. Restatement (Third), s 12. Thus, *Clark v. University Hospital* held that two medical residents should be held to the standard of a practicing physician rather than a resident, since they held themselves out as being practicing doctors.

Drivers are held to the same "reasonable person" standard as workers and professionals. *Daniels v. Evans* involved a 19-year-old driver who was still held to the standard of a reasonably competent driver, despite the fact that the driver was only a minor. *Breunig v. American Family Insurance Co.* involved a defendant who had a mental lapse (the notion that her car could fly like Batman's) while driving. She was held to be negligent.

These cases involved defendants who asked to be held to a standard lower than that of a reasonable person. The question of whether a person with expert skills should be held to a higher standard is somewhat open.

Section 12 of the Restatement (Third) suggests that persons with superior abilities could be held to the standard of a reasonable person with those superior abilities. However, comment a to Section 12 recognizes that this approach could be unwise from a policy perspective, since people might be discouraged from acquiring superior skills if they are held to a higher standard. Therefore, *Fredericks v. Castora* (Pa. Super. 1976) rejected the notion that truck drivers, as professionals, should be held to a higher standard of care in traffic accidents.

Because we had sufficient time left over, we introduced those legal principles that were of secondary importance.

DRAFT ANSWER ("R" section—optional additional analysis)

Several defenses can be raised in negligence actions. Contributory negligence is the most common. *See Gyerman v. United States Lines Co.* (involving a longshoreman who was injured after failing to report a dangerous work condition). However, contributory negligence must contribute to the actual injury incurred. *See Gyerman.* Some states use comparative negligence instead of contributory negligence, either by statute or as a matter of the common law.

Older cases discuss the last clear chance rule, which indicates that the last person who was able to avoid the accident has the burden of doing so. *See Fuller v. Illinois Central R.R.* (involving collision between a train and a wagon). The relevant standard might differ, according to the

Restatement, depending on whether the plaintiff was helpless or merely inattentive.

The third step required us to evaluate the facts in light of the law. That step tracked the legal principles that had already been introduced in the essay. See how you have already begun to suggest to your reader what the outcome will be.

DRAFT ANSWER ("A" section)

Next, we will evaluate the facts of the current case in light of the law discussed above. Drivers have a general duty not to hit pedestrians, and causation (both legal and factual) exists here, as do damages. However, the question is the scope of the duty of care and whether Jack breached that duty.

Jack will be held to the standard of a reasonable person in an emergency situation. Although Jack is an expert driver, he was not "holding himself out" as having that higher degree of skill in this situation. Because an ordinary driver would not have been able to avoid the accident, Jack should not be held liable for having failed to do so.[1] Notably, some jurisdictions might apply the Restatement (Third) strictly and hold Jack to the higher standard of a professional driver, but that is the rule in a minority of states.

If for some reason Jack were to be held liable, he might be able to minimize or avoid liability by asserting an affirmative defense like contributory negligence, comparative negligence or the last clear chance rule. However, there are insufficient facts in the question to allow a full analysis of any potential defenses.

Now we must explicitly state the conclusion, even though it is implicit in the draft text. Because we have weighed up the legal authorities as we progressed through the application analysis, the final, concluding paragraph is quite simple, along the lines of a practitioner's "for the abovementioned reasons, my client should prevail."

DRAFT ANSWER ("C" section)

Based on the above, Jack will likely not be liable for the injuries to the other party.[2] Although there is some uncertainty about whether all jurisdictions would adopt this approach, the absence of liability promotes

---

[1] These lines suggest that you will conclude Jack will not be liable.

[2] Be sure you answer the question asked: here, whether Jack is liable to the other party.

good public policy by allowing expert drivers to get behind the wheel without fear of opening themselves up to a higher duty of care.[3]

You now have a basic understanding of how to handle each of the four steps in the IRAC method of essay writing. For a further discussion of how to handle "discuss" type questions, see chapter seven. As you will see, a conclusion is just as important in those essays, though it may not be as brief as an outcome in a fact pattern question. For more worked examples, see chapter ten.

Using the IRAC method helps you write powerful essays, but there is more you need to do to get high grades. As important as structure and content are, style also plays a role in a persuasive legal argument.

In law school, good spelling and grammar are critical.

Although they may seem trivial, spelling or grammatical errors can detract from an otherwise persuasive essay and pull you down from a high grade to an average grade. By the time you move into the working world, you are expected to have mastered the art of writing. Although you can always ask the advice of your supervisors, your peers, and your assistants, you cannot expect them to proofread every piece of writing you produce. You are responsible for your work and must know the basic rules of grammar, punctuation, and spelling. While there are entire books devoted to this subject, chapter eight will give you some tips in these areas. Before moving to that discussion, however, we will address the second type of law essay: the response to the "discuss" question.

---

[3] This is how you incorporate a public policy reference in your "C" step.

CHAPTER 7

Adapting IRAC to "Discuss" Questions

Although the IRAC system of exam writing is particularly helpful in answering problem questions (also known as fact pattern questions), it can easily be adapted for use with so-called "discuss" questions, meaning questions that focus on matters of legal policy, legal reform, or legal history rather than on litigation-type scenarios. The preceding chapters have already provided you with some tips on how to use IRAC to answer discuss questions.

NOTE
"Discuss" questions require you to analyze ideas rather than litigation scenarios.

This chapter will address a number of additional items in more detail, including:

(1) what a discuss question is asking you to do;

(2) how to structure your discuss essay; and

(3) how to adapt each of the four IRAC steps to discuss questions.

A. What a Discuss Question Is Asking You to Do

NOTE
A discuss question is not asking for an opinion only. You must offer legal authority to support your analysis, just as you do in problem questions.

Problem questions are designed to probe your ability to identify the relevant legal issues in a particular fact pattern, discuss the pertinent legal rules, apply the facts in light of the law, and come to a reasoned conclusion about the outcome of the dispute. Discuss questions have similar aims but place a slightly different emphasis on each of the elements. You still need to identify the relevant legal issues, but they will not be as numerous or as diverse. Most issues will appear on the face of the question, which means that you do not have to worry about red herrings. In fact, many students run into trouble by trying to get too tricky with a discuss question.

When answering a discuss question, you need to introduce relevant legal rules, just as you do in fact questions. However, the type of rules that you use may be slightly different. To do well, you may also need to discuss the relationship between ideas from different parts of the syllabus, which will require a different approach to the "A" step than that used in problem questions. Finally, you need to come to a conclusion about your analysis, although the outcome will probably not be a yes/no or win/lose scenario, as is the case with problem questions.

Discuss questions are designed to give you an opportunity to discuss legal policy, legal reform, or legal history. You must cite cases and statutes in your response, but you will be using the materials to support theoretical, rather than practical, arguments. In some ways, discuss questions generate essays that are somewhat similar to the types of papers that you wrote during your undergraduate career.

As mentioned above, discuss questions tend to focus on three basic areas of inquiry: legal theory, legal reform, and legal history. The following discussion details the basic skills that professors are hoping you will demonstrate on each type of discuss question.

1. Legal Policy

Legal policy evaluates why the law is the way that it is. You can often spot a legal policy question by the way it asks you whether a certain course of action is wise, just, or fair. Alternatively, the question may ask you to identify what rights or interests are at stake and to weigh them accordingly. The key is that the question will, most likely, be asking you to evaluate some statement, event, or course of action. To answer the question, you must ascertain what was done, why it was done, and whether the result is worthwhile.

Source material for these sorts of discuss questions can be found in judicial opinions and legislative history and in academic books and articles. Legal academics and judges will argue about competing policy interests (for example, how to allocate the risk of loss or the need to encourage potential tortfeasors or victims to take out insurance) or attack the empirical assumptions underlying the policy arguments. When you answer a discuss question, you should follow the same approach, since legal policy questions are all about weighing competing interests.

Never discuss one side of a policy argument without also discussing the other side.

Chapter four noted that you should never introduce a policy argument without identifying the opposing policy on that grounds that any issue that is so clear-cut as to have no competing policy arguments will never be in dispute. Discuss questions operate on the same assumption; never will one theory be so persuasive as to eradicate the need to introduce counter-arguments. You—and the experts you cite—may have very good reasons to believe that your approach is best, but you need to explain why you have arrived at your particular conclusion. Other people will not necessarily agree with your analysis and your value system; that is why you must persuade the reader to adopt your way of thinking. Discuss questions are just as much about developing an argument as problem questions are, which means that you have to walk your reader through your analysis in order to persuade him or her that your conclusions are correct.

When discussing your opponent's position you need to be objective, but that does not mean you need to avoid coming to any conclusions. Take a position and defend it against all reasonable arguments; that is how to do well on these sorts of discuss questions.

While discuss questions are similar to undergraduate essays in some ways, you still need to introduce legal authorities into your arguments. Not many undergraduate majors use authorities in the same way that law does, although political science comes close. Political science students must use political theory to support their arguments, citing eminent thinkers to explain how certain political structures and movements came about. However, political science students also point to certain historical events to illustrate their own ideas about why a certain political structure or concept is a good or poor idea. As a law student, you need to distinguish these types of "social" examples from "legal" examples and focus primarily on examples drawn from the law (i.e., cases, statutes, etc.) rather than on current or historical events.

Discuss questions still need legal authority.

The one exception to this rule is constitutional law. Although students often over-cite social examples in constitutional law essays, there are times when you must refer to real-life events to illustrate the development of certain constitutional principles (e.g., economic theory during the *Lochner* era).

When writing essays regarding legal policy, it is better to rely on principles espoused by eminent judges and academics than to simply cite common sense. You shouldn't discard common sense altogether, nor should you avoid bringing in your own original ideas, but you should be aware of how and when to use the different types of argument.

Law schools vary greatly in the amount of emphasis they put on legal theory in course work. Some law schools are known for focusing on the "black-letter law" rather than on law's theoretical and philosophical underpinnings. Other law schools take the reverse approach. Although you need to be aware of how your particular school approaches the issue, don't be fooled into thinking that a "practical" stance is either superior or inferior to a more theoretical approach. Once you move into professional practice, you will need to be familiar with both methods of analysis.

YOUR TURN

Why should you give counter-policy arguments?

_____

_____

_____

_____

_____

2. Legal Reform

Discuss questions may also ask you to comment on legal reform. You can identify these questions relatively easily, since they will often include the word "reform" or "change" or they will refer to a recent or prospective legislative shift. There may be some reference in the question to the interests or rationales supporting (or opposing) the change, which will suggest the need to discuss legal policy, but the focus will primarily be on the state of the law before and after the reform efforts.

Questions involving legal reform often include elements of legal policy.

Reform questions do not exist in a vacuum. To answer such questions well, you must have some knowledge of legal policy, since the issue of reform presupposes the question "why the need to change?" However, a legal reform question is slightly different from a question relating strictly to legal policy, in that legal reform questions typically allow (or require) you to focus more on the black-letter law. For example, if you are answering a question about a recent amendment to the law, you need to know what the law was (and why) as well as how it has changed (and why). You then need to weigh the facts and policy interests to see whether the change was successful. Remember, you are not just recounting what has happened; you need to have an opinion about the events you are recounting. In so doing, you also need to be guided by the question itself.

When discussing whether legal reform was successful, be sure you identify what you mean by "success."

Previously you were discouraged from providing stock answers to problem questions, and the same is true here. You must adapt your response to suit the question asked. Questions about past reform can be the most problematic to students, since they may have read numerous articles or heard several lectures about what changes were made and why. Unwary students will eagerly recite this information, thinking that the professors want to see their own ideas presented back to them. Don't fall into this trap. Law is about analysis, not about memory recall—or, better said, not only about memory recall, since you do need to remember the law to do well on law school exams. Think back to the standards given in chapter one describing a top essay. According to those guidelines, you must demonstrate some independent thought if you want to do well in an essay or examination. Use the information you have learned as the building blocks for your own unique analysis.

Don't just regurgitate information gleaned from books and professors. Manipulate your knowledge to suit the question rather than trying to do the reverse.

If the question refers to the possibility of future reform, you need to discuss more than the theoretical or policy reasons why change should occur; you also need to discuss any cases or statutes that are currently causing problems. This element demonstrates why you cannot answer a legal reform question only from a policy perspective. You must know the black-letter law as well.

Legal reform questions require you to use the same kinds of materials as legal policy questions. You can find useful information about the need for and success of legal reform in judicial opinions, legislative history, and academic works. You can and should cite any and all of these materials to support your arguments. Of course, you will need to take a position about the merits of the different viewpoints and identify the strengths and weaknesses of others' analyses before forming your own conclusions.

While it is possible to answer a question on legal reform without having read any articles specifically discussing the subject, you will obviously do better if you are familiar with others' thinking. Academics' thinking is bound to be more sophisticated than yours, if only because they have spent weeks or months considering the subject while you have less than an hour. However, even if you came up with the same conclusions as an academic lawyer, there is still good reason to read and cite these sources. As noted in earlier chapters, law is not merely about logic. Law is about precedent. Common sense rationales gain additional weight when they come from recognizable legal rules, be they binding or persuasive. If you are able to base your discussion on these outside sources, you will be arguing like a lawyer (i.e., not just from logic, but from rules) and will therefore receive a better grade.

3.   Legal History

Legal reform questions generally relate to a sudden change in the direction of the law, typically as a result of legislative action. Legal shifts can also come about through judicial action, but that doesn't happen too often. Judicial change is more likely to arise slowly and gradually. These are the types of issues that are usually the focus of a legal history question.

Legal history questions typically ask you to discuss how a certain area of law has changed over time. You might also be asked to consider whether a certain case is still good law in light of recent developments or whether two strands of law are growing closer together or farther apart. Notably, all these examples focus on a line of cases rather than a single event, as is the case with reform questions.

Top essays identify themselves by the number and quality of authorities they discuss. Law is more than just case law.

Questions about legal history require a high degree of familiarity with both case and statutory law. Although you can answer a legal history question adequately if you know the authorities well, you may want to have recourse to the work of legal commentators. Remember, citing additional sources doesn't just improve the quality of your analysis, it also demonstrates that you know that good legal arguments are based on precedent.

Often the most difficult aspect of answering a legal history question is identifying the proper point at which to start the analysis. Scholarly articles provide misleading models, since they sometimes go all the way back to the founding of the nation. It is rarely necessary to reach that far back in a law school exam essay, although there may be exceptions.

When trying to identify an appropriate starting point, you should be guided less by what you know and more by what is relevant to the question. If your main focus is on presenting the complete width and breadth of your knowledge on a particular subject, you run the risk of including lots of factually correct but irrelevant information. Remember the tips from previous chapters: you will know more law and policy than you are able to present. You must pick the best information to include in your essay. What constitutes "the best information" depends, as always, on the question. While leading cases and statutes will be relevant to any discussion of the subject, other materials may be used or discarded at your discretion.

YOUR TURN

What are the main differences between the three types of "discuss" questions?

_____

_____

_____

B.   Structuring Your Discuss Essay

Over the course of your education, you have gained numerous essay-writing skills. These skills have obviously contributed to your academic success, and you should continue to use them. This is particularly true in your responses to discuss questions, since the discuss format is most similar to the type of essays you wrote in your undergraduate career. You may, however, find a few additional tips helpful.

As discussed in earlier chapters, people seem to understand information better when it is grouped in threes. Therefore, a common way of organizing an essay is to rely on a five-paragraph structure with an introduction, three substantive paragraphs, and a conclusion. This basic format can be translated to IRAC terminology: the introductory paragraph can be equated to the issue, the three substantive paragraphs can be equated to the rule and application, and the final paragraph is the conclusion. Notably, you should not try to reverse the process and use a standard five-paragraph model in a response to a problem question, since fact pattern essays are more naturally organized by issues, sub-issues and plaintiff-defendant pairings.

If you have problems structuring discuss essays, try using a standard five-paragraph model.

Journalists use the "inverted triangle" approach to writing. They lead with their broadest, most important point and progress downwards to their least important point (the thin tip of the upside-down triangle). Try doing the same in your essays.

Organizing your thoughts into a five-paragraph format in a discuss question gives you a strong, logical structure, even if you actually end up with six or seven paragraphs. There is no magic in five paragraphs *per se*, and you should feel free to start a new paragraph to create additional white space[1] or to begin a new thought.

When writing a five-paragraph essay, you want to group your thoughts into three major points, preferably of equal weight. Usually you lead with your strongest argument and progress to your weakest argument, although there may be times when you alter that strategy. For example, you may need to establish one element

---

1   The term "white space" refers to indentations and breaks in paragraphs. Readers become daunted by a solid page of prose and are much more likely to pay attention to a text that has lots of breaks in it. Paragraph breaks also demonstrate the author's organizational plan and thus guide the reader.

as a threshold matter before you can proceed to the other parts of your discussion. Remember that each of your three points must be supported by case law, statutory law, or scholarly commentary.

Usually the three middle paragraphs are the easiest to write, since they contain the information you have learned in class. The first and last paragraphs tend to be more challenging, which is why the IRAC system is so helpful in problem questions (there the form of your introduction and conclusion comes automatically).

If you're having difficulties, focus on the purpose of each paragraph. An introductory paragraph is simply meant to introduce your discussion. Therefore, the easiest way to proceed is to state what you intend to argue (i.e., the issue) and how you plan to organize your essay. You should not spend a lot of time setting the stage for your argument or giving background information. All of that information should be contained in your substantive paragraphs. If the information is not critical to your argument and doesn't fall into one of your substantive paragraphs, then consider omitting it as irrelevant to this particular essay. Remember, what you leave out is as important as what you put in.

The best style is one that is clear, brief, and logical.

One of most common errors that students make in discuss essays is trying to cram too much into the introduction or spending a lot of time in the introduction setting the stage for arguments that are to come. Students fall into these traps because they worry that they don't have enough to say in their essay or because they don't want to "waste" any of their hard-earned information.

Remember the advice from earlier chapters: if you plan your essays before you start writing, you will find that you have plenty to write and you will not be tempted to waste your time on tangential matters. You may not be able to present all of the information that you know, but if your aim is to achieve high grades, you need to resist the temptation to throw everything into one essay and instead focus on writing a strong and relevant response to the question asked. This is particularly hard to do when you get excited about a certain question. The best thing you can do then is to slow down and make sure that the point you are most enthusiastic about is actually relevant to the question asked. Too many students have started writing in the first blush of excitement, only to find halfway through their essay that they're off track. Remember, your first idea is not always your best idea.

NOTE

What you leave out of a discuss question essay is as important as what you put in, just like in fact pattern responses.

The conclusion is the second most difficult paragraph to write. If you have just drafted a relatively complicated argument, then you can use the concluding paragraph as the means of pulling all the various strings together. Many essays, however, will not be that complex.

The burden of relevance falls on you, the writer. Don't make the reader do the work of figuring out why something relates to the question asked.

Some students are taught that it's a good idea to include some new point in their conclusion so that it is more than a mere summary of what has already been discussed. Be careful. If your new point is highly substantive or involves a reference to a case or statute not discussed in the body of the essay, then it may not be appropriate to mention it only in passing. Consider giving the point its own paragraph. If it doesn't deserve its own paragraph, consider again why you want to include it. Don't just add extra information as a tactical move. Such tricks seldom work.

Nevertheless, there may be times when it is appropriate to introduce new points into a final paragraph. For example, you might make some suggestions for reform (if the question itself was not about reform measures) or provide practical arguments about the likely success of the suggested action (for instance, the likelihood that political pressure would lead to a certain outcome). This approach would be similar to adding a policy point to the final paragraph of a fact pattern essay. In both cases, you are showing your knowledge of the related issues, though you are wise enough to remain focused on the main points. It is a fine distinction, but one that you can learn to recognize with practice.

C. Issues in Discuss Questions

The first step in an IRAC essay involves the identification of the issue. In a problem question, the issue is analogous to the crime charged or a civil cause of action. Discuss questions frame the issue slightly differently. In this context, the issue can be characterized as your overarching theme or the point of your essay.

When identifying your issue, you need to remember that every law essay, whether it is in response to a problem question or a discuss question, has to build an argument and take a perspective on the issues discussed. A good exam essay cannot be absolutely indifferent to the merits of the different viewpoints, although you must be objective in your analysis of the opposing arguments.

Base your conclusion on logic and facts rather than on emotion or unsupported beliefs.

If your question constitutes a controversial statement, followed by the single word "discuss," use your issue statement to identify the position you intend to take regarding the statement. Some students think that they can write a stronger and more memorable essay if they attack or disagree with the statement. Be careful. This technique can backfire unless you believe that the statement is indeed wrong and you can support your position with binding or persuasive legal authority. It is always better, in an academic essay, to base your arguments on the facts and the law rather than try to be overly tactical. There may come a time in professional practice when you have to find some sort of plausible argument even though you believe your opponents have the better case, but you do not need to take this approach during law school.

If your issue is your basic, overarching response to the question, then your sub-issues are the three main points made in support of your main issue. You need to think of these sub-issues as support rather than merely as points to be stated, since your goal is to build an argument rather than just present objective information in written form. Those of you who have studied literature can analogize the construction of a legal argument to the typical plotline of a novel. You open the novel by introducing the characters and the scene, build the tension to a climax, resolve the ultimate conflict, and end the book.

A legal argument opens with some sort of stage-setting device (an issue), builds the tension through point and counter-point argument (the "R" and "A" steps in an IRAC essay, whether that essay is in response to a problem question or a discuss question), then reaches its climax and denouement (the outcome plus any additional points to be made in the conclusion). Too many students fail to see the need to build an argument to an inescapable (or hopefully inescapable) conclusion. The plotlines of their essays are virtually flat. While there is a place for strictly expository writing, it is not in a law essay.

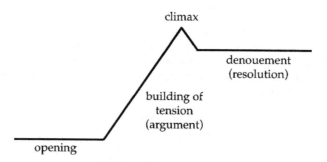

Remember, the study of law is not just about the acquisition of legal facts; it is about applying the facts you have learned to practical problems and using rules and judgment to come to a conclusion. This purpose does not change simply because you are answering a question that focuses on legal policy, legal reform, or legal history.

The organization of your essay may depend on the information you need to impart—for example, you may have sub-sub-issues to be raised within each of your sub-issues, just as you did with problem questions—but you must structure your essay to build to a logical determination about the outcome of the dispute. The disputes in discuss questions may seem slightly more academic than the kind of practical disputes you address in problem questions, but there is still a dispute at issue.

To identify your issue and the relevant sub-issues, you must read the question carefully, just as you did with problem questions. Use the same techniques you mastered with other types of IRAC analyses: proceed through the question slowly, line by line, picking out relevant words and correlating them to areas of law that you know to be contentious. While you can and should frame your response in a way that shows your knowledge to its best advantage, you should not change the question to suit your pre-conceived notions about how to discuss a particular point.

Don't try to change the question to suit your knowledge. Answer the question as asked.

When you identify your issue and begin your essay, don't be afraid to use the precise words of the question. In fact, you should purposefully do so, even if it feels somewhat mechanical or trite. For example, if a question asks whether it is "just and equitable" to undertake a certain reform, use the words "just" and "equitable" in your response. You should also be sure to define those terms. That way, both you and your reader will be sure that you are answering the question as asked. A lot of points can be gained by defining terms.

Be sure to define your terms, even if the terms originate in the question.

Once you've identified the key language in the question, figure out which cases, statutes, and law review articles relate to those terms and issues. Then delve into your memory bank and, without reference to the question, make a note of those issues that are listed on your outline as potential discussion points in this area of law. Cross out those ideas and source materials that do not correlate specifically to the question as asked and then organize whatever remains into a five-paragraph essay. Again, you must be ruthless, just as you were on problem questions. If there's a small point that doesn't seem to fit with the rest of the essay, consider whether you really need to include that element. A strong essay is not littered with minor points of tangential relevance.

Don't try to put everything you know into an essay. Instead, rely on your best arguments and authorities.

D. Rules in Discuss Questions

There is just as much need to include legal authority (i.e., rules) in discuss questions as in problem questions, although the type of authority that you use may vary slightly according to the type of question you're answering. Problem questions focus primarily on the types of disputes that arise in practice; therefore, the type of source material you use will resemble that used in practice. You can include some academic material (treatises and scholarly articles) in your essay, but only to supplement binding legal authority and fill gaps in the existing law.

NOTE

Discuss questions tackle the kind of issues and policies that legislators consider.

Discuss questions, on the other hand, are more wide-ranging in scope. They deal with critical questions of policy, theory, and equity. Therefore, your source material should resemble the materials used by academics and policymakers in their work: scholarly commentary, legislative history, and, of course, cases and statutes.

The breadth of your supporting materials should match the breadth of your analysis. Therefore, the "rule" portion of your discuss question essay should include both primary and secondary authority. For example, a legal history question may ask you to discuss the evolution of a particular line of cases or statutes. Obviously you need to know what the law is to discuss it intelligently, but you should also be able raise points made by esteemed commentators. Alternatively, a legal policy question may ask you to compare and contrast two competing strands of legal thought. In that situation, you need to use particular cases and statutes to illustrate your hypothesis, which will be supported by the views of scholars, judges, and legislators.

When deciding which authorities to introduce, be creative. Remember, your job as a law student is not just to repeat the thinking of others without any additional analysis of your own. You still need to weigh the competing arguments yourself and come to some conclusion about their relative merits (more on this step below). Legal authorities are building blocks; they are not the building itself. Use the building blocks to create a structure—i.e., an argument—rather than just tossing the blocks into a cordoned-off area and hoping that the structure will make itself known without any effort on your part.

Problem questions and discuss questions both require you to think independently about the issue at stake. Obviously this is difficult to do in a timed situation, particularly if you have never considered the issue before. If all you do is repeat back the information you have learned over the course of the semester, you will pass your examination, but you will not do well. To do well, you need to indicate a deep understanding of the issues raised (which is different than simply reciting legal authority) and an ability to think critically about those issues.

There is no way that you can anticipate what questions will show up on the exam. However, as mentioned in chapter two, you can develop your critical thinking skills by considering these deeper issues throughout the term and during your exam preparation. That way, when you are presented with a novel question in an exam, you will know how to go about analyzing the question.

Discuss questions are designed to test your ability to think independently about the law. Professors want to see what type of analogies you draw to different areas of law, what materials you present to support your thinking, and how you apply those materials. This concept of application is the third step of the IRAC process and is discussed in the next subsection.

YOUR TURN

How will the authorities cited in the "R" section of a discuss question differ from those used in a problem question?

E.   Application in Discuss Questions

The application step in problem questions involves applying of the facts of the question to the rules introduced in the second stage of the essay. The application process is not as clear-cut in discuss questions because the question does not provide a series of facts that need to be considered in light of the legal rules you have adduced.

Instead of separating out the two analytical steps and presenting a separate section containing the rules and a separate section containing the application, you may want to combine the two steps in a discuss question. Be careful, though: rather than making things easier, the combination of these two analytical steps may make things more difficult for you because you won't be able to rely on IRAC's easy structural framework quite as much as you do in problem questions. To offset this concern, you may need to spend more time in the preparation stage, making sure that you know what legal rules you will present and how you will critically analyze (i.e., apply) them in light of the question asked.

The main reason why you might want to combine the two steps is to avoid repetition. As you know from earlier chapters, you have to use a fair amount of discretion when writing IRAC essays, since a too-rigid application of the steps can lead you to repeat some of the "R" material in the "A" section. If you combine the two steps, you can avoid the risk of duplication. However, you also run the risks identified in earlier chapters, such as failing to identify the full scope of the relevant legal rules and arguing the facts (or, in a discuss question, your beliefs and impressions) rather than the law. Therefore, you should use caution if you decide to apply your legal rules as you present them.

As mentioned above, it is a good idea to use the precise words of the question as you evaluate the legal authority you have presented. If the question asks you whether a certain course of action is "fair" or "efficient," use the words "fair" and "efficient" in your response as your guiding standard. You may even want to highlight those words by using them in the opening sentence of a paragraph so that your reader knows that you are addressing that portion of the question.

Using the precise words of the question will also help ensure that you answer the question as asked. Discuss questions are notoriously confusing, and it can be difficult to know exactly what you are being asked to do. The encouraging thing about discuss questions is that there is usually a wide variety of good responses; if you can argue your point persuasively and retain some connection to the question, you can do well.

Using the same words in your response that were used in the question may seem somewhat mechanistic at times, but it is an effective way to check yourself and keep your focus. It is also a way to make sure that you and your reader are talking about the same thing. For example, you may see no harm in substituting the word "equitable" for "fair" in your essay, since you believe the two words are synonymous. Some readers might disagree, however, due to the special legal connotation given to the word "equitable." What you believe is a matter of style can become a matter of substance. Avoid those problems by using the words that appear in the question and by defining all necessary terms early in your essay. Often the most important evaluative step you can take is in how you define terms. Don't assume that definitions are clear or that defining terms is a rudimentary task.

F. Conclusions in Discuss Questions

Discuss questions need to have an explicit conclusion, just as problem questions do. However, discuss questions do not allow you to give a simple and succinct opinion on which party will win the dispute at hand. Instead, you need to use your conclusion to tie together the various strands of your argument to give a final answer to the question.

If you have used a five-paragraph essay structure, you will have three substantive paragraphs, each with its own main point and supporting ideas. Use the final paragraph to weigh the relative merits of the three substantive discussion points and indicate how the question

WRIT‑ING

Remember, there is nothing magical about five paragraphs *per se*—you can break one of your substantive paragraphs into two or three parts if it is getting too long.

should be resolved. Remember to walk the reader through your analysis step by step; do not merely state your conclusion.

Discuss questions are unlike problem questions in that the essay does not focus on yes or no issues. In a problem question, your analysis proceeds until you hit a yes/no issue: does action X constitute a breach of duty in tort, does action Y constitute an anticipatory repudiation of contract, etc. That is why your final paragraph can be so short in a problem question: you have already either proved or disproved the critical elements of the claim in the body of the essay.

Discuss questions, on the other hand, do not contain any intermediate yes/no questions. It all comes down to persuasion, and to persuade, you must illustrate your thinking to your reader. Therefore, discuss question essays have longer conclusions than problem question essays, since you must persuade your reader that your thinking is correct.

Always remember to show your analysis step by step. Don't just tell the reader your conclusion.

Some students have been told that a good conclusion should contain at least one new point not previously discussed in the essay. This technique can be risky, as mentioned above. If the new point is relatively minor, then one wonders whether it should be included at all. If the new point is relatively important, then one wonders whether it should have been given its own substantive paragraph. Usually the better route is to avoid introducing new material in the conclusion.

You now understand how you can adapt the IRAC method for use in discuss questions. Although this should give you some idea of how a discuss question in law school differs from a discuss question in other academic subjects, you should not forget the substantive and stylistic techniques that you learned in your undergraduate career. Rather than discarding all that you have learned up until this point, focus on adding to the skills that you can bring to your essay writing. As you have learned, presentation and persuasion lie at the center of good legal writing. No matter how good your ideas, you cannot receive good grades if you do not communicate well. Therefore, the next chapter will discuss the various elements of good writing.

CHAPTER 8

General Tips on Legal Writing

As the previous chapters have discussed, a good law school essay presents clearly identified legal rules through sophisticated and well-organized legal arguments. Although the IRAC method of essay writing does not offer instruction on the content of the law, it provides you with an effective means of conveying your knowledge of the substance of the law. The IRAC model therefore constitutes a substantive, rather than merely stylistic, approach to writing law school essays.

However, as mentioned before, law is as much about style as it is about substance. How you write affects how the reader perceives your argument. People make judgments about the quality and merit of your legal thinking based on elements that have nothing to do with the content of your writing. If you doubt this to be true, think about your most recent trip to a bookstore or library. When you're browsing for something to read, do you pick up the book that looks crisp and pristine, with clean pages and impeccable type, or do you naturally gravitate towards the one with a bent corner, faded printing, and crooked lines?

When you scan a newspaper rack and look at the headlines, do you trust the publication that states, "Prez Sez, 'We Want More!' " or do you think the one that states, "Union Leader Seeks Wage Increase" is more credible? Chances are, you perceive the latter as more persuasive and informative, though perhaps less colorful. You know that the first paper is misspelling the words "President" and "says" on purpose, but there likely have been other occasions when you have found errors in newspapers, magazine articles, books, or advertisements. In all honesty, haven't you felt just the slightest bit smug when you discovered another person's mistake? A bit superior perhaps? Maybe a bit disdainful that the other person either didn't know better or didn't care enough to check his or her work?

NOTE

Poor writing detracts from the substance of an essay. The best lawyers and law students are not only good substantive analysts, they are good writers.

If there is one thing you do not want to do as a lawyer, it is to make your reader feel either superior to or disdainful of you. You want to appear intelligent, diligent, and infallible, and certainly not the kind of person who is likely to make a mistake on any level. Someone who is too harried or careless to check his or her spelling and grammar may very well be the kind of person who is too harried or careless to check that a case or statute is still good law. If your reader doesn't trust you, he or she may be more inclined to double-check or argue with points that might otherwise have been simply accepted on face value. To avoid giving the impression of someone who is prone to errors, you need to make sure that your writing style is crisp and professional and that your use of language is correct at all times.

NOTE

Details matter. In law, issues of form or style can quickly turn into issues of substance.

Unfortunately, many people—students, professors, lawyers, and other well-educated professionals—cannot consciously describe what constitutes good writing or good grammar, although virtually everyone can distinguish between good and bad writing. To some extent, this lack of knowledge can be attributed to the widespread belief that good writing "just comes naturally" to some people and cannot be taught. In fact, nothing could be further from the truth. While not everyone can become a Nobel Prize-winning author, almost everyone can improve his or her writing style by learning a few simple techniques. Therefore, this chapter discusses the following points:

(1) why it is important to have a good writing style;

(2) why you need to learn the rules of good writing yourself;

(3) why you should work to develop that style now; and

(4) what constitutes good legal writing.

The chapter concludes with a series of self-tests and exercises to help you overcome any problem areas.

A. The Importance of Good Writing

There are two very good reasons for writing correctly. First, by so doing, you will advance your own career. Think about it. Your written work is aimed toward a very small, very discriminating audience. Almost every time you set pen to paper (or fingers to keyboard), your professional reputation is on the line. For example:

- If you are a student, your work is going directly to professors who will (1) write your job references and (2) award you the grades that will affect your job prospects.

- If you are an attorney, your work is going directly to a partner, a peer, a client, the court, or opposing counsel.

- If you are in business or working in a corporate legal department, your work is going to your superiors, your peers, other departments, outside attorneys you have hired, potential adversaries, and possibly even the press.

In none of these cases do you want to look careless. Signing off on a piece of work that contains spelling or grammatical errors makes you look ill-informed at best, sloppy or incompetent at worst. Don't do it.

Good writing often goes unnoticed. It is a quality that is most appreciated in its absence. Seldom does someone say, "Well done, nothing misspelled in that memorandum" or "fabulous use of commas!" However, fill that same piece of writing with typographical errors, misplaced modifiers, and passive voice, and just watch your reputation plummet.

It may be that none of your teachers has ever corrected your grammar, so you may be operating under the assumption that you are a fantastic writer. However, many teachers do not focus on grammar because they either feel their job is to focus on the substance of your argument or because they are themselves uncomfortable about issues relating to incorrect antecedents, sequential commas, and dependent and independent clauses. The problem is further exacerbated by virtue of the fact that grammar is no longer taught in schools and universities. As a result, few people graduate from college knowing what constitutes good writing or what the key rules of grammar are.

Now that you are studying for a law degree, things have changed. Presentation is as important as substance. Your professors, employers, opponents, and clients may not know why your writing is awkward or confusing, but they will subconsciously consider you to be a less competent lawyer then someone who has a strong writing style and who avoids errors. Since people who are considered better lawyers get better jobs and better work, you want to avoid anything that would make other people think less of you.

The second reason why it is important for you to learn how to write well is to improve your actual job performance. Poor writing is not just bad for you personally; it can also lead to bad results for your client and your employer. Think of the contract cases you have read. How many of them have turned on the placement of a comma or the existence of a misspelled or misplaced word? You may have thought at the time that the judges were being rather nit-picky, but contract construction requires precisely that type of objective, analytical, linguistic analysis.

Poor writing can have legal consequences.

Errors end up in court, and you don't want to be the one explaining such mistakes to your client or your supervisor.

You are responsible for your work and for overseeing the product of those whose work you direct. You may also be responsible for making sure that your client doesn't write anything that is legally problematic. Furthermore, you may need to correct your supervisor's language from time to time. In short, you must know what constitutes good writing if you are to carry out your job properly.

B. The Need to Learn the Rules of Grammar

Lawyers, particularly those in large firms, are spoiled. Not only do they have lots of staff at their disposal—secretaries, associates, and interns—they have the most modern computer equipment at their fingertips, complete with spellcheck and grammar check. However, there are still a number of reasons why you must learn the rules of grammar for yourself.

First, if you as a senior lawyer don't know what constitutes good writing, why would you suppose a junior associate would know any better? Furthermore, is there any way to be sure that your associates and interns will feel inclined to tell you about your errors? They might think it is easier or more polite to let the errors pass. After all, it's not their job to correct your writing. On the other hand, you may need to learn the rules of grammar because you will be starting your career at the bottom of the ladder and either need to check your own work or check the work of those who are more senior to you and who allegedly don't have the time to write properly. Whether you're at the top or the bottom of the ladder, you need to know the difference between good and bad writing.

Second, good writing is not something that can be programmed into computer software. For example, a good spell-checking program can correct your spelling of "there," "they're," and "their," but it can't tell

you whether you've used the right one in the right place. Grammar-checking programs are now standard, but not every highlighted phrase is incorrect. As a result, you cannot rely on a computer to pick up your errors, assuming that you have even remembered to run the spell and grammar check before printing out the final draft of your document.

NOTE

Computer programs cannot replace human proofreaders.

Another problem with relying on others or on computers to check your work is that you often run out of time to do justice to any suggested revisions. Because most people know that an error can creep into their work at any point during the rewriting process, they often don't run checking programs until the very last minute. Unfortunately, if lots of errors are found, you may not have time to correct them all. If you make fewer errors during the writing process, there will be fewer to correct at the last minute, thus improving the quality of your final product.

Therefore, it is up to you to learn how to write well. You cannot rely on others, nor can you rely on computers to check your work for you. By all means, you should seek feedback from other people and run a spell and grammar check on your computer, but you shouldn't expect others to do the hard work for you. The hard work is yours alone.

C. The Need to Develop a Good Writing Style Now

You may admit that there are good reasons for developing a good writing style once you enter the professional world, but why work on acquiring it now? Don't you have enough to do learning the substantive law? Quite simply, there's no time like the present to learn new skills. In fact, now is the best time to work on your writing style, since you are not under the same kind of pressure that exists in professional practice. Internships and associate positions are notoriously demanding, and you will be constantly scrambling to learn new skills and satisfy the requests of your supervisors.

Feedback on your work is even rarer in practice than it is in law school, and time is at even more of a premium. Because it takes time and practice to acquire a good written style, you should start ingraining these habits into your routine now. Students are expected to make errors, since there is no other way to learn; professionals, however, are expected to have already mastered these skills and can damage their careers if they make too many basic mistakes.

However, there's another, more immediate reason why you should work on your writing style now. Quite simply, people who write well get better grades than people who don't write well. Students with good grades get better jobs than students with low grades.

Law is about persuasion as much as it is about content. The art of persuasion involves getting the reader on your side and demonstrating the ease and logic of your position. If you confuse the reader in any way or make it difficult for the reader to follow your thoughts, either through the introduction of difficult concepts, illogical structure, or awkward language, you cannot communicate, let alone persuade.

D. The Elements of a Good Legal Writing Style

Good writing consists of two basic elements. First are the mandatory elements of style: grammar, punctuation, and spelling. You cannot consistently break mandatory rules and hope to be considered a good writer. Second are the discretionary elements of style: organization, word choice, pacing, etc. While people can follow their individual taste with respect to these discretionary elements, deviating too far from the norm can be distracting and therefore undesirable. This is particularly true in legal writing, which is highly conventional. We will begin with a discussion of the mandatory elements of style before turning to the discretionary ones.

1. Mandatory Elements of Style

Good grammar is the key to good communication. While not everyone can enunciate the rules of grammar, people become confused when the rules are not followed. Grammar is often absorbed subliminally rather than taught formally, at least in the United States. However, the U.S. educational system's failure to focus on grammar does not mean that those rules don't exist or that they do not facilitate understanding.

Consider the following text, for example.

EXAMPLE

Ethan borrowed Andrew's coat and scarf one winter day, but didn't return it. He became quite angry when the holidays were coming and everyone left college to go home. He called Ethan, but he had already gone, along with his things.

This example does not illustrate all possible grammatical errors, but it demonstrates how improper use of language both grates on one's nerves and leads to confusion. In the first sentence, you immediately see that "it" is incorrect. If the writer means *both* the coat and scarf, the word "them" should be used. If the writer means *either* the coat or the scarf, then the item should be clearly identified by using the noun.

The second sentence contains a lack of clarity regarding who is meant by "he." Because Ethan was the subject in the first sentence, one might think that "he" means Ethan. However, "he" might also refer to Andrew, who is the last person mentioned in the preceding sentence. From the context of the second and third sentences, it becomes apparent that "he" is Andrew. The use of "his" in the third sentence is equally confusing; "his" could mean that Ethan has left with Andrew's things (meaning the coat and scarf, presumably) or that Ethan has left with Ethan's things.

NOTE

Errors concerning antecedents are extremely common and extremely problematic in legal writing.

This example demonstrates the various problems that can arise when a pronoun ("he," "she," "it," "that," or something similar) refers to the wrong antecedent. To be correct, the pronoun should refer only to the immediately preceding noun or clause. To fix the problem, you need either to repeat the relevant noun or change the sentence structure altogether.

As this example shows, major misunderstandings can arise as a result of minor errors. Although most law students have a relatively strong intuitive grasp of the rules of grammar, many people can use a few tips regarding common problem areas. Therefore, this chapter clarifies a number of basic areas of concern.

The following discussion is by no means comprehensive. If you want more detailed instruction in grammar, you can refer to one of the many books dedicated to the subject. Time spent studying the art of writing is never wasted.

We will now consider several basic problem areas concerning the following:

- parts of a sentence;

- constructing a sentence;

- subject-verb agreement;

- verbs and verb phrases; and

- punctuation.

a. The Building Blocks: Parts of a Sentence

To discuss the rules of grammar, we need a common vocabulary. Here are a few terms that you may know, as well as a few that you may not.

Noun A person, place, or thing

Proper Noun The actual name of the person, place, or thing

Pronoun A reference to a proper or common noun (e.g., "he," "she," or "it")

Adjective A word modifying (describing) a noun

Verb A word showing action

Adverb A word modifying (describing) a verb (an adverb usually ends in "-ly," e.g., "slowly" or "coldly")

Gerund A verb form ending in "-ing" that stands in for a noun (e.g., "my understanding of the situation" contains a gerund)

Preposition A word that shows a relationship between a verb and a noun (e.g., you walk *through* a door or *by* a door but generally not *under* or *into* a door)

Conjunction A word that connects words or clauses (e.g., "and," "or," "but," and "since")

Clause A group of words acting together[1]

Independent clause A group of words that can stand alone as a sentence

Dependent clause A group of words that cannot stand alone as a sentence

These phrases will be supplemented and described in more detail as we progress through this chapter.

b. Constructing a Sentence

Simple sentences require a noun, acting as a subject, and a verb.

John ran.

(noun as subject) (verb)

Many sentences have a subject, a verb, and an object, which is the noun the subject is acting upon.

John threw the ball.

(noun as subject) (verb) (noun as object)

As you may have noticed, the sentences used in these two examples are quite simple. As a lawyer, you will sometimes use simple sentences. They are good for effect. However, you will often use more complex sentences. For example, you might write a sentence that has a dependent clause describing the way something is done (an adverbial clause) or describing one of the nouns in the sentence (an adjectival clause).

Good writers vary the length and complexity of their sentences for effect.

Flicking his hair out of his eyes, John threw the ball.

(adjectival clause describing subject), (subject) (verb) (object)

John threw the ball, which was coming apart at the seams.

(subject) (verb) (object), (adjectival clause describing object)

Notice how these adjectival clauses appear next to the nouns that they describe. The clauses are also offset by commas. As a general rule, a descriptive, dependent word or phrase should be placed as close as possible to the word it modifies. Placing the word or phrase that is being

---

[1] Some grammar experts distinguish between phrases and clauses, but there is no need to do so for our purposes.

described farther away from the descriptive clause often confuses the reader. For example:

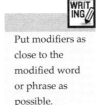

Put modifiers as close to the modified word or phrase as possible.

Hungry and tired, Darius gave the baby a bottle.

In this example it is unclear who is hungry and tired. While the author likely means the baby, the sentence seems to say that Darius was hungry and tired.

The rule about commas offsetting clauses is slightly more confusing and will be discussed in more detail below. Generally, however, you use commas when the clause is describing an aspect of the noun rather than when the clause is helping to identify the noun. For example, when you write, "John threw the ball, which was coming apart at the seams," you are describing the ball's qualities. There is no question about which ball you are discussing, and you could delete the clause without confusing the reader about which ball John threw. This is known as a "nonrestrictive clause."

If, however, you write, "John threw the ball that was coming apart at the seams," you are not just describing the ball's qualities. Instead, you are identifying the ball that John threw as compared to other possible balls (for example, if he had a selection of three and he threw the one coming apart at the seams, as opposed to the two new ones). Therefore, this clause could not be deleted. It is a "restrictive clause."

Sometimes you can have two verbs both relating to the same subject. For example:

John threw the ball and dodged the tackle.

(subject) (verb) (object) (conjunction) (verb) (object)

Notice how this sentence is different from the following, which has two verbs and two subjects.

John threw the ball, and Waseem dodged the tackle.

(subject) (verb) (object), (conjunction)[2] (subject) (verb) (object)

There is a comma between the two clauses in the second example because each clause can stand alone as its own sentence (two independent clauses). The first example contained no comma because

---

[2] Some students use commas correctly with the word "and" but not with the word "but." The rules are the same for both words. If you want the subject to apply to both verbs (the one preceding and the one following the conjunction), then do not use a comma. If you do not want or need the subject to apply to both verbs (i.e. when both clauses can stand independently as sentences), you can split the sentence with a comma.

that would improperly separate the subject of the sentence (John) from the second of the two verbs (dodged). In that sentence, the phrase "dodged the tackle" cannot stand on its own apart from the subject (John).[3]

People often make mistakes when they realize that two clauses are independent and therefore can stand alone. Thinking they don't need a conjunction, they simply slip in a comma:

> *John threw the ball, Waseem dodged the tackle.*

This technique[4] leads to a *run-on* sentence, which is a phrase used to describe a sentence that continues on after its logical end. It would be better to either use the "and" that was used in the first example or use a period and start a new sentence.

Run-on sentences continue on after their logical conclusion.

> *John threw the ball. Waseem dodged the tackle.*

While the meaning in this example is relatively clear either way due to the extreme simplicity of the sentence, think about a more complex example using legal terms:

> *The contract between the parties does not provide for a modification in terms except by written agreement between the parties, no such written agreement exists here.*

Everything is correct except for the misuse of the comma. Replace it with a period and all will be fine.

Sometimes you experience the reverse problem by creating a sentence that is incomplete. Such partial sentences are called *sentence fragments* and lack a necessary element such as a subject, a verb, or an object. For example, the following phrase lacks a subject:

> *Threw the ball.*

> (verb) (object)

---

3   There is one exception to the general rule that you should not separate a verb from its subject. If a comma is necessary to make the meaning clear, then you can insert one. For example, the comma in the sentence, "The contract allowed the defendant to deliver apples or oranges, and therefore was not breached upon delivery of oranges," is technically incorrect. However, because the comma groups the term "apples or oranges" visually, it helps the reader understand the meaning of the sentence and is therefore an exception to the general rule. Usually the "extra" comma occurs (properly) in sentences that have multiple conjunctions and need clarification.

4   You could classify this example as either a run-on sentence or a comma splice.

While some types of sentences can have an implied subject (for example, the imperative tense, which commands an implied subject to do something: "Throw the ball!"), most sentences require a subject.

Sentence fragments stop before their logical conclusion.

Other errors occur when you use a verb that requires an object to make sense. For example, the following sentence is incomplete:

Susan met.

(subject) (verb)

The verb "to meet" requires an object to make sense—you must meet someone. Technically, this is the difference between a transitive verb (a verb that transfers its action to an object) and an intransitive verb (which can stand on its own). Some verbs can be both transitive and intransitive, depending on the circumstances. Check a dictionary if you're unsure whether the verb you're using requires an object or not.

Sentence fragments can be quite long and can thus look like well-drafted sentences. However, a fragment is often introduced by a word, such as "which" or "that," which is normally used to introduce a descriptive clause. For example, the second sentence in the following excerpt is a fragment:

Numerous errors exist in this contract. Because the defendant misunderstood UCC 2–207.

Here, it looks as if all the elements of a sentence exist—subject (defendant), verb (misunderstood), object (UCC 2–207). However, the clause is dependent and cannot stand alone. In this case, the word "because" explicitly links the defendant's misunderstanding to the errors in the contract. To correct the error, the author either needs to combine the two sentences by taking out the first period and putting the word "because" in lower case or by taking out the word "because" and capitalizing "the." As it stands, however, the phrase is improper.

Many sentence fragments start with the word "that." For example, the second sentence here is a fragment:

Jameela signed the contract. That had errors in it.

In this case, the second sentence is actually a fragment that needs to be joined with the first sentence. Of course, there are times where you can begin a sentence with "that"—for example, when "that" refers to a noun or concept described in the previous sentence.

NOTE

This example could be improved if the author replaced "That" with "That principle."

Capital punishment is morally wrong. That has been accepted by jurists in many nations.

"That" may also describe a subject.

That party was boring.

You may also begin a sentence with "that," "which," or a similar word if you then follow that dependent clause with the noun that it modifies or if the clause itself stands as a noun. For example:

That reform is necessary is an idea whose time has come.

Notice, however, that such phrases are awkward and wordy. You can write much more clearly and powerfully if you cut straight to the important point: "reform is necessary" or "reform is an idea whose time has come."

YOUR TURN

What is the difference between restrictive and nonrestrictive clauses?

_____

_____

_____

_____

_____

c. Subject-Verb Agreement

Everyone knows how to conjugate a verb. For example, the verb "to be" is conjugated "I am," "you are," "he is," "we are," and "they are." In the abstract, you would never try to say "I are" or "we am." You know that when you have two subjects you use a plural verb: for example, "Nick and Rachel *are* outside." However, when writing, you can sometimes become confused about how many subjects relate to the verb.

Often, the problem occurs when you have a descriptive phrase that ends in a noun with a different number than the noun relating to the verb. Because the last noun is closest to the verb, you think that you should conjugate the verb according to the last noun. For example, an author might write:

A group of birds fly over the lake.

Here the author is incorrectly conjugating "fly" to correspond to the plural "birds." In fact, the author should write:

A group of birds flies over the lake.

The noun "group" is the sentence's subject. The author could take "of birds" out of the sentence and write, "A group flies over the lake." The author cannot write, "A group fly over the lake." "Group" is a singular noun; "fly" is a plural form of a verb. Of course, the author could avoid the potential for confusion by writing, "Birds fly over the lake." What the author cannot do is use the first example, since it violates the rule that the verb should match the subject in number.

Often the easiest and best solution to a grammatical problem is simply to change the sentence structure.

The proper pronoun for a court is "it," not "they."

Confusion often exists in cases involving collective nouns. For example, the words "audience," "team," "staff," and "council" describe groups but are themselves singular. You therefore need to use a singular verb, no matter how many objects exist in any descriptive phrase that follows.

Another area of confusion involves sentences that use "either/or" constructions or pronouns that appear to be of one number, but are classified as another. Just remember:

Either X or Y[5]   Requires a singular verb

Neither A nor B[6]   Requires a singular verb

Everyone   Requires a singular verb

Anyone   Requires a singular verb

No one (or none)   Requires a singular verb

The rise in the use of gender-neutral language can also lead to problems relating to subject-verb agreements. As you likely know, the standard convention in legal writing is to use gender-neutral language. This means avoiding "he"[7] as a generic pronoun and using a substitute such as "he or she," "s/he," or "one." Another alternative is to change the

---

[5]   This rule applies when X and Y are both singular nouns. If one noun is singular and one is plural, conjugate the verb to correspond with the noun that appears closest to the verb.

[6]   Again, this rule applies when A and B are both singular nouns. If one noun is singular and one is plural, conjugate the verb to correspond with the noun that appears closest to the verb.

[7]   Also avoid "man" as a so-called genderless noun.

Gender-neutral language is here to stay. Get used to using it correctly.

sentence so that you can use a plural pronoun ("they"). Problems can arise, however, if you try to use "they" without making the rest of the sentence plural. For example, at one time, you would have written:

A defendant is innocent until he is proven guilty.

Modern versions might include "A defendant is innocent until he or she is proven guilty," "A defendant is innocent until s/he is proven guilty," or, avoiding the pronoun altogether, "A defendant is innocent until proven guilty." You could also change the first noun to a plural form, thus requiring a change in the verb but also allowing the neutral "they" to be used: "Defendants are innocent until they are proven guilty." Up until recently, the phrase "A defendant is innocent until they are proven guilty" would be grammatically incorrect. However, some individuals who are non-binary with respect to gender prefer the pronoun "they." This is an area where language is evolving, and you should be sensitive to the requests of your clients and others. Since it is easy to avoid gendered language, that is probably the best course of action to adopt.

d. Verbs and Verb Phrases

Most people have no problems conjugating verbs once they get past a few minor subject-verb agreement problems. Sometimes verbs are in the past tense, sometimes they are in the present tense, and sometimes they are in the future tense. What is confusing is when they are in the subjunctive. Most problems with the subjunctive arise in an if-then scenario. Normally, you use the subjunctive when you have a situation involving an imaginary, doubtful, or wished-for outcome. For example, the following phrase is correct:

If I had more money, I would travel the world.

Normally you would conjugate the verb "to have" as "have" with the pronoun "I." However, because the speaker here is not rich and is speaking about a hypothetical situation, the subjunctive is used. Compare this sort of situation with the following:

If I have enough money, I will visit you next week.

In this case, there is no doubt, or at least not the same kind of doubt. The visit will take place if and when the money is found. While you can have the subjunctive in sentences that do not use if-then phrases—for example, "Julio wished he were dead" or "I wish I were rich," which both use the subjective "were" rather than the indicative "was" to indicate that Julio is not, in fact, dead and I am not, in fact, rich—if-then sentences are usually the ones that cause the most trouble. These sentences, however, are the easiest to resolve once you know the rule.

Another issue with verb phrases involves gerunds, which are words ending in "-ing." Although these words may appear to be verbs, gerunds act as nouns. Therefore, you can use gerunds as subjects or objects of sentences. For example:

Running is beneficial to your health.

Melody loves reading.

The thing you need to remember with gerunds is that they need a possessive when preceded by nouns or pronouns.[8] Therefore, you should write:

Dad told me that Corey's driving skills were not very good.

Junko's dancing is only getting better.

Finally, you may have heard the phrase "dangling participle" at some point during your education. The term "participle" refers to the two verb forms known as the present participle (words ending in "-ing," referred to in the discussion on gerunds) and the past participle (words ending in "-ed" or the equivalent irregular form). Sometimes phrases beginning with a participle can be used to modify another word in the sentence. For example:

Enjoying their hay, my sons watched the horses.

Rotten to the core, Alex smelled the fragrant apples.

In these two examples, the dependent clauses that begin the sentences are misplaced and are called dangling participles. As you recall from the discussion above, you should always put dependent, modifying clauses as close to the words they modify as possible. The two sample sentences put the phrases containing the participles in the wrong place, thereby changing the meaning of the sentences. If we put the participles in their proper place, then the true meaning of the sentences becomes clear.

WRIT ING

Place modifiers close to the words they modify.

My sons watched the horses enjoying their hay.

Alex smelled the fragrant apples, rotten to the core.

---

[8] Gerunds act as a singular noun, not a plural noun. Conjugate your verbs accordingly. For example, "Driving in cities is frustrating."

Sometimes you need to correct a misplaced modifying clause by including additional words or altering the sentence somewhat, but if you remember to put modifiers as close as possible to the word that they modify, you will avoid most problems.

e. Punctuation

A number of common errors fall under the heading of punctuation. While some of these errors may be more confusing to the reader than others, all violate the technical rules of grammar.

i.   *Capitalization*

Only capitalize words that appear at the beginning of sentences and proper nouns, i.e., formal names of people and places. For example, capitalize "Paris" and "New York" but not "my city." Similarly, capitalize "Uncle Joe" or "Mom," but not "my uncle" or "my mom." A good rule of thumb is that if you have to put a possessive word (my, her, their) in front of a noun, it's not a proper noun.[9]

Titles are another kind of word students often capitalize incorrectly. If a title is used as a common noun describing the position, rather than describing the person, then don't capitalize it. For example:

I interviewed the president of the company.

I interviewed President Clark of Acme Plumbing Company.

Students commonly make similar errors with words like "court" and "judge." If you are identifying a particular court or judge by name, capitalize both words. If you are not naming something or someone in particular, don't capitalize the term. For example:

Guadalupe Martinez is a judge on the Ninth Circuit Court of Appeals.

The courts are underfunded, according to prominent judges.

The Supreme Court of the State of New York is not the highest court in the state.

The point is, do not randomly capitalize nouns. Not only is it incorrect, it can cause problems in legal practice, where capitalized words are often used as defined terms. Reading a lot of contracts will start to confuse your eye, and you may start to think that terms like "net profit,"

---

[9]   You could write "my Uncle Joe" if you were using "Uncle Joe" as his name, but you would not write "my Uncle, Joe Smith," where the word "uncle" described a relationship rather than a name. In that circumstance, you would write, "my uncle, Joe Smith."

"managing agent," and "company" are always capitalized, just because you see them capitalized in the documents you read in your work. Don't be fooled. Those terms would not be capitalized if they had not been previously defined in the contract. If you begin capitalizing terms unnecessarily, you may be creating an ambiguity that could lead to litigation.

Avoid random capitalization.

In the course of your education, you may find that some law books or journals capitalize certain words, such as "State," in violation of the rules of grammar. The editors of those publications have made a decision to capitalize some words to indicate that they are being used as legal terms. While such capitalization is unnecessary and technically incorrect, academics accept the convention. Nevertheless, you should try to avoid random capitalization in your written work, for the reasons stated above.

If, for some reason, you are unclear about whether to capitalize something, do not try to hide your confusion by alternating between capitalizing the term and not capitalizing it. Be consistent. The only exception is if you are at one point discussing a term that is not being used as a proper noun—president, for example—and then go on to refer to President Clark. In that instance, you capitalize the word in one context but not the other precisely because the word is being used differently.

YOUR TURN

When should you capitalize titles?

_____

_____

_____

_____

_____

ii. *Apostrophes*

Apostrophes either denote a possessive or stand in the place of a missing letter in a contraction. A possessive is a word that shows ownership. Not all possessives use an apostrophe (for example, "hers," "his," and "theirs" do not), although most do. Usually, when you have a noun, such as the name of a person or of a company, you make that noun possessive by adding an apostrophe followed by an "s."

LaTonya's car

The school's auditorium

If a noun is plural, in many cases it will already end in "s." In those cases, retain the "s" of the plural and add an apostrophe after it.

a student's book but *all the students' book*
(one book in both cases)

a student's books but *all the students' books*
(many books in both cases)

The noun following the plural possessive may be singular or plural depending on the context: for example, if you have several dogs, all sharing one leash, you would have "the dogs' leash."[10]

Another common mistake concerning possessives involves proper names that end in "s" and that need to be made into a possessive. In this case, you add an apostrophe and an "s," rather than just an apostrophe.[11]

Jones's newspaper

Christopher Columbus's vessel

Although most grammar experts insist that this approach is correct, change may be imminent due to the influence of the popular media. You should adhere to the traditional approach on the assumption that the law will be among the last fields to embrace linguistic change.

Apostrophes are also used to replace missing letters in contractions. A contraction is a shortened word that takes the place of two words. For example:

do not	becomes	*don't*
he would	becomes	*he'd*
I will	becomes	*I'll*

---

[10] Single and joint possession of single or joint items can be tricky. For example, "Hank and Maggie's farms" refers to several farms owned jointly by Hank and Maggie. "Hank's and Maggie's farms" refers to separately owned farms. Rarely will you have to get into this kind of detail, so don't worry about it too much. Remember, if a phrase sounds confusing or is too difficult to figure out, you can always change the sentence structure to avoid the problem altogether.

[11] The exception is when the penultimate syllable ends in an "s," in which case use only an apostrophe to form the possessive singular: Jesus' robe, Moses' tablets, Ulysses' journey, Onassis' yacht.

There are too many possible contractions to list here, but you understand the concept. An exception to the rule involves the contraction and the possessive of "it."

it is	becomes	*it's*	
it (possessive)	becomes	*its*	

NOTE

It's = it is

Its = possessive

Its' does not exist

The error is common but quite confusing. Be sure that you do not mistake the two words.

There is also confusion about the contraction and possessive of "who." Please note:

who's	contraction—"who is" or "who was"
whose	possessive—something owned by "who"

Finally, there are three words that sound alike but are spelled differently and mean different things.

they're	contraction—"they are" or "they were"
their	possessive—something owned by "them"
there	an adverb as to location or to indicate the general existence of an item ("there is" a thing or "there are" things)

While we're on the subject of misspelled words, you should be aware of another group of words that often leads to confusion:

to	preposition (someone is going to a place)
	or part of an infinitive verb ("to play" or "to dance")
too	meaning "also"
two	a number

These may seem like minor errors to you, but these mistakes are made every day. More importantly, such errors will drive certain readers insane and cause those readers to doubt your ability or motivation to avoid errors in the substance of the work.

YOUR TURN

What is the difference between "its" and "it's" and between "whose" and "who's"?

_____

_____

_____

_____

_____

iii. Periods, Commas, Colons, and Semicolons

Periods are discussed briefly above, in the section concerning run-on sentences and sentence fragments. Basically, when a thought has been completed, you should use a period. To begin a new thought, begin a new sentence. While eighteenth- and nineteenth-century writers (both in and out of the law) used long, complex sentences with multiple phrases and clauses, the modern style favors shorter, crisper sentences. You

NOTE

If you make your readers work too hard, they may give up altogether.

may certainly use longer sentences for variety or effect, but never underestimate the power of short, simple prose. Your audience will appreciate your ability to communicate your ideas quickly and simply.

The use of periods is a mandatory rule of grammar to the extent that you must avoid run-on sentences and sentence fragments. Many rules about commas are also mandatory, although there are times when commas can be used in a discretionary manner.

Conventional advice regarding the use of commas is to treat them like a pause in the sentence, similar to a breathing space in spoken communication. While this can be a good rule of thumb, it can lead you astray. For example, many people try to use a comma to join two related but still separate thoughts, leading to a run-on sentence (also called a comma splice). The following example can be described as a run-on sentence or a comma splice, since the comma incorrectly joins two thoughts:

The plaintiff ran to his car, he was attempting to escape.

You should either replace the comma with a period, making two sentences, or add other words to make the second clause dependent in some way. Better alternatives would include:

The plaintiff ran to his car as he attempted to escape.

The plaintiff, attempting to escape, ran to his car.

The plaintiff ran to his car in an attempt to escape.

There are several proper uses of commas. When you have a list of things or activities, separate them by commas. For example:

Naseem owned a bracelet, two watches[,] and six pairs of earrings.

The brackets indicate that a comma between "watches" and "and" is optional. If used, this sort of comma is referred to as an Oxford comma or serial comma. Use of the Oxford comma can increase clarity. However, whichever style you use, you must be consistent. It is never correct to switch between the two styles.

You can also use commas to separate different activities.

Tai left his house, ran to the gym, lifted some weights[,] and returned home.

WRIT-ING

When listing several items, make sure they are in parallel form.

Notice that each of the groups of words adopt a parallel structure, meaning that they are all past tense verbs constructed in a similar manner. You must keep your lists in parallel form so that your reader can follow your meaning without working too hard. Again, you can either use the Oxford comma construction or not, but you must be consistent throughout your document.

Do not mix different types of word groups or nouns. For example, the following sentence grates on the ear and the eye:

Melanie enjoys skiing, swimming, and a good run.

Instead, all the activities should follow a similar structure:

Melanie enjoys skiing, swimming, and running.

Melanie likes to ski, swim, and run.

Any time you have a list or a comparison, be sure to use parallel structure.

Sometimes lawyers construct long lists of activities or word phrases that contain commas within individual phrases. In those circumstances, you should use a semicolon, rather than a comma, to separate the different items. For example:

The court requires the plaintiff to produce the following items: all personnel records, whether printed or electronic, relating to the defendant; all telephone logs mentioning the defendant by name; all daily calendars for the years 2007 to 2012, inclusive; and all reports produced by the defendant during his tenure at the company.

When constructing lists like these, you should include a semicolon before the "and" preceding the final entry in the list.

You should also use semicolons when you are listing a complex series of items by number. For example:

The court requires the plaintiff to produce the following items: (1) all personnel records, whether printed or electronic, relating to the defendant; (2) all telephone logs mentioning the defendant by name; (3) all daily calendars for the years 2007 to 2012, inclusive; and (4) all reports produced by the defendant during his tenure at the company.

You can use commas in shorter lists, although some lawyers prefer to use semicolons.

The plaintiff undertakes not to (1) sell, (2) transfer, or (3) otherwise encumber the property until the lien has been paid.

Do not look to judicial opinions, particularly older opinions, as a guide to proper punctuation.

You may notice that some older judges and lawyers do not use commas when listing a series of items or activities. This is a holdover from older days, when the prevailing practice was to avoid using internal punctuation. This convention was adopted to limit courts' ability to construe the terms of a document in a specific manner based solely on the punctuation. Such interpretive canons have now largely disappeared, and you should follow the standard rules of grammar unless otherwise instructed by your employer.

iv.   Parenthetical Information

Parenthetical information is information that can be deleted from a sentence without destroying the sense of the phrase. Be careful, however. Parenthetical information requires two commas, one on either side of the phrase. It is improper to use just one comma unless the sentence begins or ends where the second comma would be. For example:

Tyrell, a tall, striking man, entered the room.

The judge, surprisingly, ruled for the defendant.

The company, by and large, complied with the tax laws.

Of course, Frederick was busy washing the windows.

Law books, for example, can break a student's budget.

In each of these examples, the phrase set off by commas can be eliminated without destroying the meaning of the sentence. However, you must use two commas to show the beginning and the end of the parenthetical phrase (unless the phrase appears at the beginning or the end of the sentence). Use of a single comma would be incorrect and confusing.

v. **Introducing Quotations**

Students often have many problems regarding the proper use of commas when introducing quotations. Most people know the rule that commas should be used to introduce direct speech. While this rule is most often exemplified in fiction, it can be used in legal writing as well. For example:

The judge said, "The duty of care was not established by the plaintiff."

Note that there is a comma introducing the sentence and that the quote, which is a sentence unto itself, begins with a capital letter. You could also write:

The judge disagreed with counsel, saying, "The duty of care was not established by the plaintiff."

If you were only quoting part of the judge's statement, you might write:

The judge said [that] "[t]he duty of care was not established."

Here the quoted phrase is not a complete sentence and thus cannot support an introductory comma. Note also that the use of "that" is optional: the sentence makes sense with or without it. Some writers prefer always to use "that" in these sorts of cases, whereas other people are not so strict. Follow the style that is preferable to you, remembering that clarity is your ultimate aim.

However, you should not use a comma following "that," even if the quotation that follows is a complete sentence. For example:

The judge said that "the duty of care was not established by the plaintiff."

> **WRITING**
>
> Quotation marks always go outside of periods and commas, at least in U.S. publications. However, quotations marks go inside semicolons.

Some questions may arise regarding whether to capitalize the first letter of the quoted material in this example, assuming that the first word was capitalized in the original. The standard rule is that you do not need to capitalize the first letter of a quoted phrase following "that." However, the more important rule, and one that you cannot deviate from in legal practice, is that you cannot change any aspect of quoted material, including capitalization and verb forms, unless you indicate the changes with square brackets. Therefore, if the first letter was capitalized in the original and the tense of the verb was something other than what you wanted, you should write:

> _The judge said that "[t]he duty of care [was] not established by the plaintiff."_

The square brackets indicate that you have altered the original text in some way. While the changes in this case are largely cosmetic, you still cannot take liberties with quoted material.

Make your quotes perfect. Alter nothing from the original, including punctuation, without indicating the change.

The other way of indicating changed text is through the use of ellipses (three periods (. . .)). You must use ellipses if you delete any text, even a single word. Be sure not to change the meaning of the quote through your amendments. If your sentence ends with an ellipsis, then use four periods (three for the ellipsis and one to end the sentence), as in the example, "Congress shall make no law . . . abridging the freedom of speech . . . ."

Direct quotations can be introduced with a colon, although that convention is usually reserved for large blocks of material that are offset by indentations on both the left and right. In such cases, quotation marks are not used because the colon and indentations signify the quote. For example:

> A long quotation, usually numbering 50 words or more, is offset by indentations on both sides. This is called a "block quotation." Often the text is single, rather than double, spaced, and is introduced by a colon. If the quoted material begins in the middle of a sentence, the lead-in phrase may end in the word "that," followed by a colon, despite the rule that quotations introduced by the word "that" should not be preceded by a comma.

The text that follows a block quotation is either set flush left, if it continues the same paragraph, or is indented once, if it begins a new paragraph. A citation for a block quote should always be flush left.

Commas may be used in other circumstances as well as the ones listed above, but these are the three major problem areas. If you want to read more about the proper use of commas, consult one of the many books on grammar.

Students also tend to misuse colons and semicolons. In addition to the uses noted above, a semicolon can be used to separate two independent clauses that are closely linked in subject matter; in such cases, a semicolon falls somewhere between a comma and a period. Be sure that independent clauses exist on both sides of the semicolon, and do not capitalize the first word following the semicolon.

Use semicolons sparingly. Someone reading your text quickly may not notice the semicolon and may think you have written a run-on sentence.

Colons can be used to separate two independent clauses, but they are rarely used this way today. The link between the two clauses would be similar to a premise followed by a conclusion. For example:

> *The plaintiff stated that there was a simple reason why he did not have the requisite mental state to commit the crime: he had been drugged at the time.*

Nowadays, colons are generally used only to introduce a block quotation (as described above) or a list of items. For example:

> *The thief took everything of value from the house: the jewelry, the electronic equipment, the antique silver, everything.*

Remember, do not capitalize the first word following a colon unless that word is a proper noun.

Finally, try not to use dashes in any sort of formal legal writing. For the most part dashes—which can be used to offset parenthetical information as in this example—can and should be replaced with commas. If you use dashes, use them sparingly, since they tend to give an informal feeling to your writing.

YOUR TURN

When should you capitalize the first letter of a quotation?

_____

_____

_____

_____

_____

2. Matters Purely of Style

Everyone has their own unique writing style, but some styles are more accessible and appropriate to legal writing than others. While it is

TIP

Don't take it personally if you're asked to change your writing to take a client's or senior lawyer's stylistic preferences into account. The goal is to draft a document that is clear and suitable to its purpose, not to fight over an adjective or two.

difficult, and in many cases undesirable, to give up your own style of writing completely in favor of another approach, you can and should think about ways to improve your writing. Younger lawyers, in particular, need to be flexible in their writing style, since their supervisors may have very strong ideas about how certain documents should be written. You may need to adapt your style to match that of the person with whom you are working.

It is altogether possible that you will occasionally be given conflicting instructions from senior lawyers. You probably have run across this phenomenon already in college or law school: one professor tells you one thing while another professor tells you the exact opposite. When considering what to do, you first need to determine whether the corrections you have been given concern mandatory rules of grammar or discretionary matters of style.

If the proposed edits concern mandatory rules of grammar, you need to do what is objectively correct, regardless of what others say. Remember, many people do not know the rules of grammar. However, you will need to convey this information tactfully to your supervising attorney.

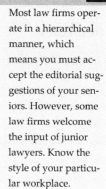

NOTE

Most law firms operate in a hierarchical manner, which means you must accept the editorial suggestions of your seniors. However, some law firms welcome the input of junior lawyers. Know the style of your particular workplace.

If the proposed edits address a discretionary matter of style, you need to consider whether to follow that advice and to what extent. In some cases, you need to make the change only once, on one particular assignment. In other cases, you may need to consider making a permanent change to your writing style if the corrections deal with a firm-wide rule of style. Remember, you can learn something from almost everyone—some lawyers are good at writing opinion letters, others are better at writing memoranda of law, still others are better at writing appellate briefs. If you adopt the best aspects of each person's writing style, you will be well on the way to becoming a better writer yourself.

Below are a number of suggestions on how to improve your writing. Adopt or discard these suggestions as you wish, realizing that none of them reflects a mandatory rule that cannot be broken. For ease of discussion, the advice has been broken down into three major points:

- word choice;

- sentence structure; and

- formatting.

a. Word Choice

Under the heading of "word choice" lies a multitude of issues, including:

(1) beginning sentences with "and" or "but";

(2) ending sentences with prepositions;

(3) using gender-neutral language;

(4) using "as" or "since" instead of "because";

(5) splitting infinitives;

(6) using contractions and hyphens;

(7) spelling out numbers;

(8) using jargon, acronyms, and "legalese," as opposed to terms of art;

(9) using passive, wordy, or verbose language rather than simple, direct phrases; and

(10) differentiating advocacy from inflammatory prose.

We will deal with each of the points in turn.

(1) Some people believe that it is technically correct to begin a sentence with "and" or "but." However, many readers, particularly those in the legal field, find such constructions sloppy or overly colloquial. If you feel you must begin a sentence with one of these words, do so with the understanding that you may put off at least part of your audience.

(2) Just as the beginning of a sentence can cause problems, so too can the end of a sentence. The major concern in this regard involves prepositions. While it is perfectly acceptable for novelists and journalists to end a sentence with a preposition, lawyers do not have the same freedom. Legal writing remains much more formal than fiction and journalism. When you find yourself faced with a sentence that ends in a preposition, you have three possible solutions: (1) place the preposition

earlier in the sentence; (2) find some phrase to tack onto the end of the sentence, thus embedding the preposition in text; or (3) rephrase the sentence to avoid the offending construction. For example:

Kamala wondered whom[12] the letter was from. (ending in preposition)

(1) Kamala wondered from whom the letter was.[13]

(2) Kamala wondered whom the letter was from and glanced at the return address.[14]

(3) Kamala wondered who wrote the letter.

All of these techniques can work well, depending on the context. However, the third sentence appears the best of the three options, since it is the simplest and most direct construction.

(3) Certain problems associated with gender-neutral language have been discussed in earlier sections concerning subject-verb agreement. For the most part, you should avoid using singular pronouns to refer to unknown or unascertained individuals so as to avoid problems with he/she/them. Instead, just change the sentence so that all references are to persons in the plural, thereby avoiding the need to designate gender.

(4) It is quite common to see people use the word "as" or "since" instead of the word "because." For example:

As Pat was a plumber, repairing the drain was a simple task.

She volunteered to join the finance committee, since she had a degree in accounting.

While close inspection of the dictionary suggests that "as" may be used in this way, some readers object strongly to the use of "as" instead of "since" or "because." Again, if your aim is to avoid alienating your

---

[12] Note that the proper word here is "whom," not "who." "Whom" refers to the object of a clause, while "who" refers to the subject. Generally, you should use "whom" whenever you could use the words "him" and "who" whenever you should use "he." It's easier to remember this trick if you use male pronouns rather than female pronouns because the male pronouns demonstrate the he/who, him/whom parallel most clearly.

[13] Although this may sound a bit formal, particularly in the context of this simple sentence, lawyers quickly become used to phrases such as "from whom," "to whom," "of which," etc.

[14] This example reads somewhat awkwardly due to the simple sentence construction, but that will not be the case in all circumstances. However, if tacking on an additional phrase does result in a wordy or unwieldy sentence, you should consider using one of the other techniques instead.

readers, you may want to consider avoiding this type of construction, even if it is technically correct.

Debate also exists regarding the distinction between "since" and "because." Some people take the view that "because" should be used whenever you want to convey a causal connection and "since" should be used only in cases where there is a temporal issue. However, other authorities consider the two terms synonymous with respect to causality, though not with respect to time (only "since" is appropriate in the latter context). Again, when considering which term you use, be aware that some constructions are more controversial than others.

NOTE

Split infinitives involve the improper separation of the infinitive form of a verb ("to (something)"). However, it is also incorrect to split other complex verb forms with an intervening word.

(5)   Most of you have heard that you're not supposed to split an infinitive (the basic "to do something" form of the verb, such as "to go," "to sleep," or "to eat"), with another word. No matter how much you like phrases such as "to boldly go where no one has gone before" (the famous *Star Trek* introductory narrative), be very careful about splitting infinitives in legal writing. While journalists may ignore the rule regarding split infinitives, lawyers should adhere to the traditional form, saying either "to go boldly" or "boldly to go." Although you may technically be correct in splitting an infinitive, you should error on the side of caution.

(6)   Contractions are often discouraged in legal texts and documents. Although the plain English movement has led some lawyers to adopt a less formal approach to language, legal writing is still much more conservative than other types of communication. As a result, contractions should be avoided when you are writing for a legal audience.

WRITING

Do not use contractions in legal writing.

Contractions refer to shortened words. However, words can also be lengthened through the use of hyphens that are used to turn two words into one in order to show how the words relate to one another. These hyphenated words are known as either "compound adjectives" or "complex nouns," depending on how the words operate.

Hyphens are used to combine words so as to increase clarity. For example, there is a significant difference between the phrase "man eating tiger" and "man-eating tiger."

At one time, complex nouns and complex adjectives were quite common. However, the rules about hyphenation have changed. For example, people used to write "decision-maker" rather than "decision maker." Further, some words that used to be hyphenated have now become single words: for example, "life-like" is now "lifelike." Use your common sense and consult a dictionary if you run into trouble.

(7)   Students often question whether to write out numbers. In all cases, you should always spell out numbers zero through ten. Some grammar experts say that you should spell out numbers zero through one hundred, but there is not as much consensus on that particular convention. Unless you have a long series of numbers, fractions (three-quarters, two-fifths, etc.) and rankings (first, second, twenty-seventh) are best in spelled-out form. You should also write out large rounded numbers, such as one million or ten billion. However, if you refer to several different numbers in the course of a discussion, you should be consistent: either spell out all of the numbers or none of them.

(8)   The most difficult thing to contemplate in the abstract is the overall tone of your prose. For the most part, you should avoid excessive use of jargon or acronyms, unless those terms are used universally. You know how difficult it is reading legal opinions that are so overburdened with acronyms and abbreviations that the text is virtually unreadable. The same is true of student essays. Excessive use of acronyms can become confusing or lessen the persuasive power of the work.

Whenever you use an abbreviation, you must be sure to define your terms. If, for example, you throw CWA into an essay without further explanation, it may take your reader a while to understand that you are referring to the Clean Water Act. Similarly, you can abbreviate party names in a problem question, but only after you have defined those terms.

WRITING — Always define your terms before using an abbreviation.

The difference between legal jargon and terms of art can be difficult to define. There are some legal terms that cannot be properly translated into plain English. Some of these terms are in Latin—for example, *res ipsa loquitur*—whereas others are in English—for example, duty of care. You must be able to use these terms correctly and precisely if you wish to convey your meaning. Failure to use the proper legal terminology can lead a professor to conclude that you simply don't know the correct language and therefore don't know the underlying legal principle. Don't worry about repeating the term too much; if it is the correct term, use it whenever it is appropriate. While college-level writing instructors may have encouraged you to use "elegant variations" rather than repeat the same phrase over and over, legal writing is different in that too much variation can lead to confusion, particularly when you are describing a legal principle or a contractually defined term.

NOTE — Legal terms must be repeated verbatim. You cannot use a thesaurus to find a different term meaning "duty of care."

Legal jargon refers to the type of overused legalese that adds nothing to the discussion. For example, referring to "the aforementioned" or "the *res* in question" is pompous and unnecessary. Just name whatever it is you are discussing. Including unnecessary Latin phrases also puts the reader off—for example, there really is no reason to use the terms *qua* or *ex ante*.

The difference between legal jargon and a proper term of art is whether the word or phrase carries a specific legal meaning or is part of a legal test. If the term has acquired this type of official legal value, then it is usually a term of art. It is difficult to describe a fee simple or a constructive trust except as legal concepts. Fraud and misrepresentation are more difficult, since those terms can be used in both a legal and popular context. Be careful how you use those types of "mixed" terms.

If, however, a term is merely used as a matter of tradition and does not carry a particular legal connotation—for example, "heretofore" carries no legal meaning[15]—then there's no real need to use it. Use your judgment, and remember that just because you've seen the phrases used in reported opinions doesn't mean that you should use them in your own work. Many of the cases you read are relatively old, and legal writing has changed a lot in recent years. Similarly, not all judges can be considered good writers.

(9)   Another misconception that students have is that hesitant or equivocal language is more objective and lawyerly than bold, unambiguous statements. Students therefore litter their essays with terms such as "it would seem" or "it appears to be the case that." Avoid these and any other phrases that demonstrate uncertainty. You are the expert. These are your conclusions and arguments; don't weaken them with waffle words. If there is a split in the law or a debate about the wisdom of a particular course of action, then discuss both sides and offer your conclusion. In the end, you may not be able to bring your reader around to your point of view, but if you don't appear to believe in the strength of your own statements, the reader won't, either.

Avoid waffling in your essays.

This is not to say that you should ignore real instances of uncertainty. There are times when you need to say that something "appears" to be true or that one party will "most likely" prevail. However, real splits in authority occur far less often than students think.

---

[15]   There are occasional exceptions. Some contracts use "heretofore" as part of the formula introducing terms and conditions or a party's warranties. For example, "it is heretofore agreed between the parties that . . . ." While you should not introduce this kind of language into your essays, be aware that some practitioners you work with may require you to use these terms in formal documents. You would not need them, nor should you use them, in less formal documents such as client letters.

Instead, students seem to believe that by appearing hesitant about their conclusions, they will hedge their bets and win more points in case they are wrong. In fact, the opposite is true. Your conclusions are your conclusions; stand by them.

Another student habit is to precede statements with the phrase "I believe" or "I think," occasionally tossing in the more formal "this author believes." This type of phrasing is unnecessary. The reader knows that your entire essay constitutes your own thoughts. The only time you might need to identify a thought or conclusion as your own is if the idea stands in close proximity to the report of another person's beliefs. Then you can say "I believe" to differentiate your thoughts from the other person's.

Another problem is using too many words to convey a relatively simple idea. One practitioner who was known for his powerful written communication, advocated the KISS rule: Keep It Simple, Stupid. Don't try anything fancy. Just say what you have to say and move on.

WRITING
When in doubt, apply KISS.

Students often use passive, wordy prose when they don't really know what they're saying. Someone who is overflowing with things to say writes in a tight, energetic manner. If you find yourself becoming passive and wordy in your prose, stop. Do you really know what you're trying to say? If you don't, neither will your reader. Think about what you want to communicate before continuing to write. A short essay that speaks directly to the question is often far better than a long, meandering discussion that never really gets to the point.

Sometimes students become confused by what is meant by the term "passive voice" or "passive tense." In the active voice, the subject of the sentence appears before both the verb and the object. For example, the sentence "John threw the ball" can be analyzed as subject (John), verb (threw), object (ball). Furthermore, the subject (John) is "acting" (i.e., throwing). The passive voice, on the other hand, exists when the object acts upon the subject. For example, the sentence "The ball was thrown by John" is passive because it begins with the object of the sentence (ball), followed by the verb (was thrown) and the subject (John).

WRITING
Do not confuse passive voice with writing in the past tense, which is of course acceptable.

Sometimes it is good to use the passive voice. For example, if you don't know who did something, use the passive voice. Similarly, if you want to try to diminish the involvement of a particular party (such as your client), you might use the passive voice to avoid suggesting that the party in question is to blame. Therefore, a defense lawyer might say that "the funds were removed from the bank account" rather than "my client removed the funds from the bank account." However, in these sorts of cases the passive tense is being used for a highly specific purpose. Feel free to use the passive voice in these sorts of situations. However, use the active voice elsewhere.

Wordiness can also result when the writer characterizes something or some action by using the verb "to be" plus a gerund (a verb acting as a noun) or an adjective. Instead, try using the gerund in its verb form or turning the adjective into an adverb. For example:

Weak Form	Strong Form
Kimiko is advocating reform.	*Kimiko advocates reform.*
Jake was nervous when writing his examination.	*Jake nervously wrote his examination.*

Don't waste your time characterizing a legal event or fact. Instead, describe what is important about that event or fact.

Essays also become wordy when the writer spends too much time characterizing an action or event rather than simply saying what happened and why that event is important. For example, a student may classify a particular case as "radical" or "groundbreaking." These are empty phrases that add little to the discussion. Unless those adjectives are immediately followed by the word "because," you should eliminate them from your essay.

Even worse is the word "interesting," which students have overused to the point that the word has lost its descriptive force completely. Your characterization of the case, statute, or event is not what is important: it is the content and/or impact of the case, statute, or event. Move past vague, introductory language and say why you are discussing the matter. If you show your readers what you're thinking, they will form the same conclusion that you have. If you do not show them what you're thinking, they will not believe or understand your characterizations.

Show, don't tell, in your writing. Use strong verbs and examples instead of adjectives and adverbs.

A similar problem arises when students are overly verbose. Verbose phrases may be correct, but they are wordy and confusing. Consider replacing longer phrases with something more direct. For example:

Verbose	*Direct*
in order to, for the purpose of, with a view to	to

as a consequence, for the reason that, on account of, on the grounds that, in light of the fact that	because
in the event of, in case of	if
in spite of the fact that irrespective of the fact that	although or even though
notwithstanding the fact that	even if
there can be little doubt that,	clearly or undoubtedly[16]
until such a time that	until

Other phrases can be deleted altogether without losing the sense of the sentence. For example:

Weak	Strong
One should note that criminals often regret their actions.	*Criminals often regret their actions.*
The fact was that Kelly didn't want to go cycling that day.	*Kelly didn't want to go cycling that day.*

Some well-known but extremely wordy phrases include:

one should note that

it is important to note that

the fact that

---

[16] Be aware that many writers believe that the use of the word "clearly" or "undoubtedly" actually signals a fact or opinion that is anything but clear or undoubted. It is always better to show the reader something rather than tell the reader something. If the fact or opinion is clear or undoubted, demonstrate that truth with legal authority or a summation of the facts. Showing your reader how you have arrived at your conclusion is more powerful than merely assuring him or her that you are correct.

it is true that

There may occasionally be times when you need or want to use these phrases to add emphasis or to alter the tempo of the paragraph. However, you should use these terms sparingly.

Finally, some people think that unusual, literary, or polysyllabic words impress readers and demonstrate greater knowledge. Not true. Often these words slow the pace or confuse the meaning. Remember KISS—Keep It Simple, Stupid. Don't use a long word if a short one will work just as well. You can be an effective writer without wearing out your thesaurus.

(10) Sometimes the issue is not that a student's prose is too deferential or wordy; it is that it is too one-sided. Strong language is fine as long as you do not exaggerate the claims you make on either the facts or the law. Learn to differentiate between advocacy and inflammatory prose.

Sometimes students think that being persuasive means ignoring or belittling an opponent's argument. Instead, you should strive to make your case as persuasively as you can while still retaining some objectivity. If the other side has a valid point to make, acknowledge it. If you appear to be too one-sided, you will lose credibility with your reader and lose much of your power to persuade. Readers trust objective analysis much more than one-sided rhetoric.

As a result, your essays need to address any gaps or weaknesses in your own arguments while also dealing with any valid points that can be raised by your opponent. You can persuade a reader to adopt your point of view by demonstrating how your argument is more logical, more just, or more in line with the authorities. Dismissing your opponent's argument out of hand or failing to address it at all does not help your case. Practicing lawyers must recognize points of weakness as well as points of strength. You need to do the same in your law school examinations.

As a lawyer, you must zealously advocate for your clients. However, you must also be reasonable and logical to avoid losing credibility with the court.

b.   Sentence Structure

The previous subsection concentrated primarily on issues relating to word choice. However, the type of sentence structure you choose also affects the strength of your writing.

The most common structural error involves excessive use of the passive voice, as discussed earlier. When you write in the active voice, the subject of the sentence is the actor. When you write in the passive voice, the subject of the sentence is acted upon. Compare the following sentences:

Passive	Active
Marcus was treated by the doctor for influenza.	*The doctor treated Marcus for influenza.*
The roses were dug up by the neighbors' dog.	*The neighbors' dog dug up the roses.*

Generally, the active voice is better because it is more direct and engaging to the reader. However, there are times when the passive voice should be used, particularly by lawyers. For example, if you do not know who did something or if you want to emphasize that the act was done, rather than that it was done by someone in particular, you may want to use the passive voice. For example:

The apartment was broken into at approximately 3:00 a.m. (you don't know by whom)

The defendant was found guilty. (the emphasis is correctly on the defendant, not on the jurors who found the defendant guilty)

Unfortunately, the passive voice is often overused in legal writing. Many students and lawyers operate under the mistaken assumption that the passive voice is more objective and lawyerly than the active voice. While the passive voice is one of the many tools available to a good writer, it should be used sparingly and only in suitable circumstances. The active voice will be more useful in most circumstances.

Avoid rhetorical questions in your writing.

Another sentence construction that should be used sparingly is the rhetorical question. Although rhetorical questions can be effective in oral argument, they often fall flat in an essay or exam scenario because they conflict with the author's primary purpose. Rhetorical questions are not meant to be answered: the purpose of an essay, however, is to answer the question given. You see the dilemma. Avoid rhetorical questions as a general rule.

c. Formatting

Finally, it may help to include a few words about how to format your exam. Generally, you should be guided by your professor and your own preferences. For example, most professors prefer typed exams, although they will permit handwritten submissions. Some people may find it easier to type their exams, since they can revise their answers more easily than with a handwritten essay, but not everyone types quickly enough to make this process time effective. Regardless of whether you plan to type or handwrite your essay, you should do a few timed practice tests so that you can make sure that the method you have chosen works best for you and that you are aware of how quickly (or slowly) you write in an exam scenario.

Students who use computers to write their exams sometimes go to great pains to italicize or underline case names and/or quotations and to include full case or statute citations in footnotes. Neither technique is

You must use quotation marks when quoting a source. An unattributed quote constitutes plagiarism.

necessary unless your professor makes it a requirement, which is highly unlikely. You can put case names in the text just as you would in a handwritten essay. Just be sure your references are clear and be sure to use quotation marks to indicate when you are quoting an outside source. Not only are quotation marks necessary to avoid plagiarism, but quoting other authorities can actually win you points, as discussed in chapter four, so you want to draw attention to that aspect of your essay.

Finally, be aware of the visual layout of the page. Most of you have read older decisions that seem to be one long, never-ending paragraph. Nothing is more daunting than facing an unbroken page of type, and few things are harder to read. Normally you should begin a new paragraph every time you begin a new idea, but there are times when, in the heat of the exam, you end up with one very long paragraph. While the absence of paragraph breaks will not by itself affect your grade, you should consider breaking up particularly long paragraphs to increase the amount of white space on the page. Doing so will increase your reader's understanding of your substantive argument and could therefore increase your grade.

The term "white space" refers to the amount of blank page left after hard breaks and before in-dented sentences. Keep an eye on the amount of white space in your writ-ten work—too much text can be off-putting to the reader.

E. Writing Techniques: Self-Examination

You may wish to run through the following self-examination to see how well you know the mandatory and discretionary rules of writing. The answers can be found following the quiz.

1. Part One: Multiple-Choice Questions

Select the correct answer from the options shown.

1. The contraction of "it is" is:

    a. its

    b.   it's

    c.   its'

2.   The possessive of "they" is:

    a.   there

    b.   they're

    c.   their

3.   A sentence fragment can be:

    a.   a sentence without a verb

    b.   a sentence without a noun

    c.   a sentence without an object

    d.   none of the above

    e.   all of the above

4.   A comma splice results when:

    a.   you use one comma instead of two to set off parenthetical information

    b.   you join two independent clauses with a comma

    c.   you use a comma to combine a dependent and independent clause

    d.   you introduce a quotation with the word "that" followed by a comma

5.   You should end a sentence with a preposition:

    a.   sometimes

    b.   always

    c.   never

    d.   it depends

6.   A dangling participle is incorrect because:

    a.   a sentence should never end in a participle

b. it modifies the wrong part of the sentence

c. both (a) and (b)

d. neither (a) nor (b)

7. In legal writing, you should use contractions:

a. sometimes

b. always

c. never

d. it depends

8. Which of the following numbers should be spelled out in text? (circle all that apply)

a. 102

b. 7

c. 17

d. 1/2

e. 3/16

f. 3rd

g. 14th

h. 1,000,000

9. You may use a colon:

a. to introduce a list of items

b. to introduce a quotation

c. both (a) and (b)

d. neither (a) nor (b)

10. Which of the following terms should be capitalized? (circle all that apply)

a. President Nieto of Mexico

b. the President of Acme Food Co., Ltd.

    c.   Edith's Aunt

    d.   the Ninth Circuit

    e.   the Trial Court

    f.   the Agreement between Supply Co. and Builder's Co. (the "Agreement")

    g.   a Legislative decision

11.   You should use the passive voice:

    a.   to sound more lawyerly

    b.   to draw attention to the person doing the action

    c.   to make your prose tighter and more energetic

    d.   to focus the reader's attention on the act itself

12.   Use rhetorical questions only when:

    a.   you are sure the reader knows the answer

    b.   you follow them with words such as "because"

    c.   you want to emphasize a certain point

    d.   you need to speed up the pace of your writing

13.   A block quotation does NOT:

    a.   have fewer than 50 words

    b.   have quotation marks at the beginning and end of the quoted material

    c.   have quoted material within the larger quote

    d.   have a colon as its introductory punctuation

14.   The word "its" is:

    a.   the possessive of "it"

    b.   the plural of "it"

    c.   the contraction of "it was" or "it is"

    d.   "its" is not a word

15. When altering a quotation, you should:

    a. indicate changed letters or words with brackets [ ]

    b. indicate deleted words with ellipses (three periods)

    c. both (a) and (b)

    d. neither (a) nor (b)—you should never alter a quotation

16. Parenthetical information can be:

    a. set off by two commas

    b. set off by one comma

    c. set off without a comma

    d. none of the above

17. Which of the following is NOT correct?

    a. a group of squirrels eats

    b. Mavis's apple cart

    c. the girls' book

    d. a herd of horses drink

18. A good writer:

    a. never acknowledges the merits of an opposing argument

    b. directs the reader's mind by characterizing legal authority and arguments as "strong" or "persuasive"

    c. uses the active voice when at all possible

    d. uses lots of jargon to indicate an insider's knowledge of the law

19. An appropriate gender-neutral variation on "he says" would be:

    a. one says

    b. he or she says

    c. people say

    d. they says

e.   (a) and (b) only

f.   (a), (b) and (c) only

g.   (a), (b) and (d) only

h.   (b), (c) and (d) only

20.   When you begin a new thought, you should:

a.   begin a new sentence

b.   begin a new paragraph

c.   use an appropriate transition sentence

d.   all of the above

ANSWERS

1.	b	8.	b, d, e, f, g, h	15.	c
2.	c	9.	c	16.	a
3.	e	10.	a, d, f	17.	d
4.	b	11.	d	18.	c
5.	c	12.	b	19.	f
6.	b	13.	b	20.	d
7.	c	14.	a		

2.   Part Two: Spotting and Correcting Errors

The following discussion comparing U.S. and Canadian legal structures contains numerous errors. Numbered questions relate to different parts of the text. See if you can spot the errors and improve the language.

TEXT

Before undertaking any comparative analysis of the United States and Canadian class-actions;[1] it is important to outline the differences and similarities between the legal systems at issue. In many ways, the U.S. and Canada has[2] a great deal in common, thus facilitating cross-border comparisons. Both are primarily English-speaking countries, strongly influenced by the English common law tradition, with one civil law territory (Quebec in Canada, Louisiana in the U.S.) standing as the sole representative of continental Europe's influence on it.[3] Both are also Federal States[4] that give considerable authority to the national government while nevertheless still[5] retaining significant power for state, provincial[6] and territorial governments.

Despite these similarities, several distinctions can be made by this author.[7] First, important differences arise with respect to[8] the relative ability of parties within each nation to assert national (or, better stated, multijurisdictional domestic) class actions as a result of vitally important and clearly significant[9] distinctions in the way each nation implements principles of federalism and jurisdiction. For example, an expansive ability to intervene in a variety of matters, including those involving class actions, is possessed[10] by U.S. federal courts.[11] The wide-ranging competence of the federal judiciary is a direct result of the broad interpretation of the concept of interstate commerce under the Commerce Clause of the U.S. Constitution[12] which has arisen despite the jurisdictional limitations explicitly reflected in Article III of that document. As a result, multijurisdictional class actions can be brought in U.S. federal court with relative ease.[13]

The situation is very different in Canada because, there, the Federal Court[14, 15]

> is a statutory court, and its statutory jurisdiction does not include most of the topics that typically give rise to class actions. As the Court's statute now stands, its jurisdiction over claims against the Crown . . .[16] would be the most promising avenue . . . .[17] But the Court does not have jurisdiction over claims in tort or contract against defendants other than the federal Crown.[18]

Peter W. Hogg & S. Gordon McKee, *Are National Class Actions Constitutional?*, 26 NAT'L J. CONST. L. 279, 283 (2010).[19]

These limitations on the jurisdiction of the Federal Court of Canada would be of scant significance[20] if provincial courts in Canada were able to hear multijurisdictional classes. However, provincial courts experience difficulties when attempting to assert jurisdiction over certain people.[21] As territorially-restricted[22] institutions, the only time that provincial courts may assert jurisdiction over a party is[23] (1) if the party is present in the jurisdiction, based on service of a writ on the defendant in the province,[24] (2) if the party consents to jurisdiction; or (3) if the court can assume jurisdiction, as in cases where there is service of the writ outside the province supported by a[25] "real and substantial connection between the litigation and the province." PETER W. HOGG, CONSTITUTIONAL LAW OF CANADA 13–22 (5th ed., 2011 supp.).

Although there is no conceptual reason why it[26] could not be met in cases involving multijurisdictional class actions, the difficulties associated with asserting jurisdiction over non-residents has[27] severely limited the development of multijurisdictional classes in Canada.

The problems experienced by Canada regarding jurisdiction over multijurisdictional classes involving persons from different Canadian provinces and territories also extends to international classes involving persons from Canada and elsewhere. Canada is not alone in this,[28] the United States has also experienced difficulties. The United States, however, has had some limited ability to assert jurisdiction over international classes[29] and Canada has likewise[30] been able to assert jurisdiction in limited cases.

QUESTIONS

1. What's wrong with using a semicolon here?

2. What's wrong here?

3. What's wrong with this sentence?

4. Should these words be capitalized?

5. What's wrong with the phrase "nevertheless still"?

6. What is missing?

7. Is the phrase "by this author" appropriate?

8. How could the phrase "with respect to" be improved?

9. What problems exist with the phrase "vitally important and clearly significant"?

10. Is there a problem with this verb construction?

11. Should "federal courts" be capitalized?

12. Should there be a comma here?

13. Is this sentence correct?

14. Should these words be capitalized?

15. Should there be a colon here?

16. Why are there three periods here?

17. Why are there four periods here?

18. What happened to the quotation marks?

19.   Should this citation be indented as part of new paragraph?

20.   What do you think of the phrase "scant significance"?

21.   Is this sentence correct?

22.   Is a hyphen necessary here?

23.   What is missing here?

24.   Is this comma correct?

25.   Should there be a comma here?

26.   To what does the word "it" refer?

27.   What's wrong with this verb?

28.   Is the use of a comma proper in this sentence?

29.   Should there be a comma here?

30.   Is this phrase correct?

ANSWERS

1.   The author should not have used a semicolon here because the first clause of the sentence is dependent. A comma would have been correct.

2.   The subject-verb agreement here is incorrect. Because there are two subjects, the U.S. and Canada, the author needed to conjugate the verb as "have."

3.   The word "it" here refers to "influence" as the antecedent noun, which cannot be what the author means. The author needs to make the reference clearer or delete the words after "influence."

4.   The words "federal states" should not be capitalized here because the words are not being used as proper nouns.

5.   The word "still" is repetitive following the word "nevertheless." One of these words should be removed.

6.   There should be an Oxford (serial) comma after the word "provincial," since the rest of the piece uses Oxford commas.

7.   The phrase is unnecessary. It slows the reader down and softens an otherwise crisp sentence. The author should simply delete those words.

8. The phrase is technically correct. Still, it might be better to replace "with respect to" with "regarding," which is somewhat more succinct.

9. The author's characterization of U.S. and Canadian differences as "vitally important and clearly significant" is unnecessary. The author would be better served by showing how those attributes are true rather than simply stating that such features exist. This type of heavy-handed commentary is seldom successful.

10. This author wrote this sentence using passive voice. How could you make this sentence active?

11. The words "federal courts" should not be capitalized here, since the words are not being used as proper nouns.

12. Yes, there should be a comma here. The word "which" indicates the following clause is nonrestrictive. Commas (or a comma and a period) must offset nonrestrictive clauses.

13. Although this sentence is in the passive voice, the construction is intentional and works perfectly. While the author could write that "plaintiffs can bring multijurisdictional class actions," the true focus of this sentence is not plaintiffs. Rather, the author wants to concentrate on multijurisdictional class actions.

14. Yes, the words "Federal Court" should be capitalized here, since the words are being used as part of a title or official designation and are thus operating as proper nouns.

15. A colon is necessary to introduce the block quote that follows.

16. The author correctly used three periods to indicate the omission of quoted material.

17. The author correctly used four periods, three periods for the deleted material and one to signify the end of the sentence.

18. Quotation marks are unnecessary with block quotes.

19. The citation's placement is correct. Because the citation is flush against the left margin, the reader knows this is the citation for the block quote.

20. The phrase "scant significance" is technically correct but is a bit stilted. How would you improve this sentence?

21. While this sentence does not violate any mandatory rules of grammar, the phrase "certain people" is somewhat imprecise, which makes this sentence confusing.

22. Yes, the hyphen is correct here. "Territorially-restricted" is acting as a compound adjective.

23. This list should be introduced with a colon.

24. The author should have used a semicolon, not a comma, so as to be consistent with punctuation found elsewhere in the sentence.

25. A comma would be incorrect because the quoted phrase is not a complete sentence.

26. The word "it" does not have a clear antecedent. The author should revise this sentence.

27. The verb must agree with "difficulties," which is plural, not "jurisdiction," which is singular. Therefore, the verb should be conjugated as "have."

28. This is a comma splice. Because the sentence contains two independent clauses, a comma is too weak to join them. The author can keep the wording as is by replacing the comma with a period or a semicolon, or the author can change the sentence slightly by adding a conjunction and retaining the comma.

29. Here, a comma is the solution. Because this sentence contains two independent clauses and a conjunction, the author needs to include a comma before the word "and" to separate the two stand-alone clauses.

30. The author here has improperly split the verb. The author should have written either "likewise has been" or "has been likewise."

This concludes our discussion of general tips on legal writing. Although there is a lot of information contained in this chapter, it can be simplified to two basic rules:

(1) If you confuse your reader, you will not earn a top grade, no matter how brilliant you are.

(2) If you can't figure out what the rules of grammar would require in a particular circumstance or if a certain phrase just looks strange, the best and fastest solution is often to change the sentence structure. There's no reason why you have to retain your original approach.

As mentioned before, there are numerous books on writing, including some concerning legal writing in particular, and you should consult them if you have further questions. At this point, however, we will turn to the question of how to adapt the IRAC method for use in legal practice.

CHAPTER 9

Adapting IRAC for Professional Practice

Many students worry about the transition from law school to professional practice. Although that fear is perfectly understandable, you should take comfort knowing that your supervising attorneys will give you lots of very specific guidance on how to write letters, memoranda, risk assessments, motions, briefs, judicial opinions, and other types of legal documents once you enter practice or start a clerkship. In fact, it is helpful not to get too wedded to one particular model before you start on your first job, since most firms have their own particular way of doing things.

You are also well prepared to make the transition because you are now familiar with the way practitioners analyze the law and present their arguments in writing. Although you will have to adapt the IRAC method to some extent when you get into practice, you have a solid foundation from which to work. Many students arrive at their jobs without having anywhere near as strong an idea about how to begin.

Although IRAC techniques will be helpful to you in numerous areas of professional practice, some types of written assignments require you to work with model documents (also known as boilerplate documents) that provide much of the basic form and content. Model documents can be transactional in nature (such as a model contract for the sale of goods or services) or litigation-oriented (such as a model complaint). Your supervising attorney will usually give you the necessary documents with which to start, but you can also find helpful forms in various types of practice books. Make sure you are using a form book for your jurisdiction, since legal requirements for particular types of documents can vary significantly across state lines.

Model documents are used in situations where it would be impractical to create an entirely new document from scratch every time a particular matter arose. However, no matter how routine a legal issue may appear or how credible the source, you should never reproduce any boilerplate document without carefully considering whether and to what extent it needs to be changed. Every case or transaction is different, and you must review your models each and every time you use them to make sure that the final document addresses all of your client's needs and desires.

Do not use model documents by rote. Think about what you're doing.

Some lawyers operate on rote, merely filling in the blanks of a model document without thinking about content or consequences. That is the road to malpractice and disciplinary proceedings. Engage your brain and independent judgment each and every time you sit down to draft something, even if a more senior lawyer assures you that this is just a routine matter that doesn't need any special attention.

This chapter does not discuss the art of adapting model documents because those skills will be taught by senior attorneys or judges once you graduate. Adapting model documents is also very case- and transaction-specific and therefore difficult to discuss in the abstract.

Instead, this chapter focuses on how to draft original documents in professional practice and how to adapt the IRAC method to help you create those documents. This chapter therefore discusses:

(1)　what types of documents you will encounter in legal practice;

(2)　how to find the question in legal practice;

(3)　how to answer the question in legal practice; and

(4)　how to approach formatting issues in legal practice.

A.　Types of Legal Documents

Although professional legal documents bear some similarity to the types of essays that you write in law school, there are significant differences, in both style and content. These differences will be discussed in greater detail once you begin practice. However, IRAC principles can be helpful when you're drafting:

(1)　letters and electronic mail (email);

(2)　attendance notes;

(3)　memoranda; and

(4)　risk assessments.

Each of these four documents serves a different purpose and requires a different focus. Letters, for example, are used to communicate with parties outside the author's own firm. Legal practitioners write letters that go out not only under their own or their firm's name but also under their clients' names. Any or all of these letters can end up as exhibits in a litigation or arbitration, so you want to be sure that they are as accurate and precise as possible.

WRIT ING

To some extent, your firm will have a standard style that you should adopt in correspondence. Similarly, there are certain conventions regarding formats, including the proper greetings and salutations. If you have any questions on how to proceed, seek guidance from your supervisors or refer to books that deal specifically with legal writing in professional practice.

Draft all of your docu- ments as if they will end up in court as exhibits. Who knows, they might.

Many lawyers now conduct much of their correspondence by email rather than through formal letters. You must be very careful about what you say in an email, even if it is only sent internally. Email can be forwarded to other parties very easily, and what you thought was only going to be seen internally can suddenly be sent to any number of people, intentionally or unintentionally.

Be sure to use proper spelling and grammar, even in email. Do not confuse a professional email with a tweet or text message.

Emails are problematic not only with respect to distribution methods but also with respect to content. Because email is more informal than conventional correspondence, people tend to write more colloquially and spend less time thinking about what they are saying. As a result, mistakes can occur more readily. People also feel free to include jokes in their emails. Again, be careful. What you intend as a joke may not be read by the recipient as one. Even if the person who initially reads your email sees the humor in what you have said, the message may not seem as appropriate two or three years down the line when the email appears as an exhibit in a court case.

Computer records, including email records, are discoverable under the rules of civil procedure, so don't be fooled into thinking that just because there is no hard copy of an email no one will ever see it. Courts routinely require disclosure of electronic files, including back-up copies of documents or emails that were never communicated to others.[1] Essentially, everything that you type into your computer is recoverable by experts, no matter how hard you try to delete it or overwrite it.

Attendance notes differ from letters in several significant ways. An attendance note (sometimes referred to as a note to file or memo to file) memorializes conversations and meetings by describing who attended the event, what was said, what was agreed, and whether any documents

---

[1] In the coming years, disclosure and analysis of metadata will become increasingly important in litigation.

were exchanged. An attendance note can be quite short or quite long depending on the circumstances. Sometimes it is good practice to make a note of attempted telephone calls or in-person visits that did not result in any sort of conversation, just so that you have a record of your various attempts to make contact. As with letters, attendance notes can end up as exhibits in a court case. Attendance notes are generally not sent to anyone in particular but simply reside in the file as a record.

Memoranda involve communications within an organization such as a law firm. Memoranda may convey the results of legal or factual research or provide a status report on an ongoing project. Because memoranda often involve legal analysis and are not disclosed to

Even privileged documents can sometimes end up in court.

outsiders, such documents can sometimes be excluded from discovery on the grounds of some form of legal privilege. However, legal privileges can be lost (for example, if a confidential document is shown to a third party) or waived (for example, if a client wishes to sue his or her lawyer), and not every memorandum can be considered privileged in the first place. Therefore, you should be cautious about what you say in any sort of memorandum, even if you believe that the document will be never be produced in discovery.

Risk assessments are yet another type of document that you may be asked to draft once you get into practice. Risk assessments are formal documents intended to identify advantages and disadvantages of a possible course of action. Risk assessments are used in a variety of circumstances, including large corporate transactions where the parties need a high level of assurance about a particular legal issue before the deal is completed. In these documents, an attorney provides an opinion asserting the legal propriety or status of a certain aspect of the client's business, which may give another party sufficient confidence to proceed with the transaction.

B. Finding the Question in Professional Practice

One of the most difficult aspects of professional practice is figuring out what question you need to answer. Students have it easy: not only are they given the question that they must answer, but they are given a discrete amount of time in which to work. Practitioners not only have to identify the question themselves, they have to determine when the question has been answered sufficiently.

"Running out of time" can mean coming up against a hard deadline or can mean reaching the end of the budgeted amount of hours for that particular task. Cost-conscious clients do not want endless research on minor points of law.

Students and junior practitioners often wonder when is the right time to stop researching a particular matter. The short answer is: when you have found the answer or run out of time. The long answer is: when you have found the answer, run out of time, or reached the point of diminishing returns on your investment of time and money. After a certain point, you will find yourself spending a lot of time without finding anything new. That is probably the point when you can stop, since your client will probably not want to pay for you to continue past a reasonable point.

The problem of when to stop researching a question is something that you need to work out as a practical matter on each assignment. The more important issue, in terms of adapting your IRAC methodology, is how to identify the relevant question once you get into professional practice.

Legal research is an iterative process. Adjust your analysis as you gather new law and new facts.

One of the things you will learn early on is that you must be flexible when identifying the legal question, since the question can change as a result of new factual discoveries or legal research. Therefore, you need to re-evaluate the scope and direction of your analysis on a regular basis to take new information into account. Do not be afraid of abandoning a line of questioning and adopting a new approach halfway through the project; the truth is that no work is ever lost or wasted.[2] Often that information will become useful later. Keep your materials so that you can refer to them later or draft a quick note to file.

Often you cannot identify the legal question definitively until you have a full (or relatively full) set of facts. As you know from law school, the addition or deletion of a single fact can change the entire analysis. For example, all the facts may point to your client having committed a battery on another person. All of your legal analyses may point in one direction until you learn that the other person shoved your client before the alleged battery. That shove changes the entire analysis: instead of a simple battery, you are now dealing with self-defense. You could have learned about the shove as a result of good factual analysis (such as a rigorous question-and-answer session with your client regarding all the events leading up to the alleged battery) or as a result of good legal analysis (for example, if your research identified self-defense as a potential legal defense to battery, you could then ask your client about the events leading up to the alleged battery). Either way, you need to know how the facts and the law interrelate.

---

2   One of the questions young attorneys ask is whether they should bill the client for abandoned lines of research. Consult with a more senior lawyer at your firm to find out your firm's billing conventions before you delete that time from your records. Different firms approach the question differently, and some may want you to account for all of your time, regardless of the outcome, since, as stated above, no research is ever truly wasted.

Few law schools teach students how to investigate facts, although that is a very important aspect of legal practice.

Much of law school focuses on providing you with the knowledge about basic legal principles so that you can spot relevant issues once you get into practice. Law school also teaches you the basic rules of legal research. Although law school provides you with a foundation in both the content of the law and the means of discovering more detailed information, you need to continue to work on these skills once in practice. You also need to learn how to undertake factual research, since the facts will help you identify the legal question at stake.

Problem questions in law school are somewhat misleading in that they encourage you to think of legal issues as differentiated by subject matter. In real life, a single set of facts can give rise to claims in several different areas of law.

As you conduct your factual analysis, you need to keep the potential legal issues in the back of your mind and vice versa. This process is similar in ways to the second step of your IRAC analysis, where you were required to keep the facts in mind as you answered the legal aspects of the question. You had to be aware of the relevant facts, since you would later be evaluating the law in light of the facts during the "A" step of the essay. However, problem questions in law school were relatively easy because you were given a discrete set of facts and law, and because you knew which area of law (tort, contract, etc.) was at issue. Professional practice is more challenging because you have to identify the relevant law and subject matter area(s) at the same time that you are discovering the relevant facts.

All types of lawyers have to learn how to conduct factual inquiries. For example, transactional lawyers have to do due diligence into the financial and legal condition of the company or companies that are being traded. Family lawyers have to learn about all the facts affecting the case at hand, whether it is a divorce or the drafting of a will. Litigators have to gather all of the facts relevant to the dispute.

Your internships and first years as an attorney should help provide you with the skills you need to carry out a factual investigation. Because every investigation is carried out for a different purpose, it is impossible to identify, in the abstract, what questions you should ask and what documents you should seek. However, as a general rule, you should start with a relatively broad investigation, since you don't want to foreclose any potentially relevant issue too soon.

1.   Asking the Right Questions

One of the hardest things for a young practitioner to do is focus a factual investigation. However, this is an area where your training in the IRAC method can help you.

As you recall, the issue in the IRAC system can be analogized to the cause or causes of action that your client may want to pursue or may need to defend against. If your professional practice involves litigation, you can do the same thing: figure out all the potential causes of action that may arise in your particular action and start identifying what elements need to be established as part of the plaintiff's *prima facie* case. Of course, you should also consider what defenses may exist and what elements must be established for any particular defense to prevail. After that, you simply need to search for facts to support or eliminate each of those elements.

You don't have to be working in litigation to use the IRAC method to help your fact-finding process. You can still think of what you wish to accomplish in terms of an IRAC-type issue, even in other areas of legal practice. For example, your client may want you to draft a will. If you think about your "issue" in terms of what your purpose is in representing this client, you will see that you need to identify all of the facts that will affect the shape and content of the will. Failure to do so will result in a will that is incomplete or that doesn't properly reflect your client's wishes. Therefore, you need to find out about your client's assets, dependents or other beneficiaries, charitable interests, and tax status, among other things. Only then can you give solid legal advice and carry out your instructions.

To adapt the IRAC method to professional practice, you need to modify the first step of the IRAC analysis (identifying the issue) to include both factual and legal concerns. Therefore, the process of identifying the issue requires you to gather all the relevant facts while keeping in mind all the matters that have to be addressed as a matter of law. If you are working in a litigation context, the legal issues can be equated to the possible causes of action and defenses. If you are working on a will, the matters are the legal elements required to make a valid will and carry out your client's wishes. As difficult as this proposition sounds, you are well prepared to consider both legal and factual matters simultaneously, since you have written numerous student essays in which you presented the law in one part of your essay while keeping the upcoming factual evaluation on hold. All that you need to do now is pull back one step and carry out that balancing act as part of the process of identifying the question that you need to answer.

Remember, the process of determining the issue is a continuing one. You cannot be expected to anticipate every possible contingency in your first interview with your client, nor will you be able to conclude all your legal research in one attempt. Obviously you should try to identify the legal and factual issues as quickly as possible, but you must remain open to the need to shift to accommodate new developments.

2. Drafting the Facts

In law school, you are given a fact pattern as part of a problem question. As a practitioner, you must draft your own factual summaries. The style that you use to outline the facts will depend on the purpose of your document. For example, if you are drafting a traditional memorandum of law to a senior lawyer, you will not relate each and every fact known; you will only mention those facts that you believe are important to the legal issue.

Memoranda only include the facts relevant to the legal issue at hand. Other documents may require a broader approach to facts.

Other kinds of documents may require you to be more expansive in your discussion of the facts. For example, you may need to draft a memo to file outlining all of your factual findings. Since this document is intended to constitute the definitive description of the facts as known at that particular point in time, you should include virtually everything you have discovered, even if you have decided that a particular fact is ultimately irrelevant to the legal issue at hand. Your analysis may change down the road, and you don't want to forget a certain piece of information that might be relevant to your revised theory of the case.

Regardless of whether you are drafting a narrow or broad summary of the facts, you must proceed in a logical manner. A chronological approach is often best when dealing with facts. Use the same kind of strong, decisive language that you used in your student essays and avoid characterizing the facts or drawing unnecessary conclusions. Simply state what happened and move on. Put your conclusions in a separate section so that your reader knows what is fact and what is conjecture.

C. Answering the Question in Professional Practice

Although the content of your legal document matters more than its physical layout, some senior lawyers become irate if a particular item does not look the way it is supposed to look. Since nearly every organization has its own way of doing things, rely on the advice of your colleagues about the visual format of your documents. This subsection will instead focus on matters of content.

As you can anticipate, you will be asked to draft a variety of documents once you begin legal practice: letters, attendance notes, memoranda, risk assessments, etc. Each of these documents has a separate purpose and therefore contains slightly different types of information. Letters and attendance notes do not need to be mentioned here, since there is no need for you to apply a rigorous IRAC-type analysis in those types of materials. However, some of the more complex documents such as legal memoranda can benefit from an IRAC analysis. Although you should be guided by the senior lawyers at your organization, you can anticipate that these types of complex legal documents will contain all or most of the following elements:

(1)   questions presented;

(2)   brief answers;

(3)   fact summary;

(4)   discussion;

(5)   conclusion and advice; and

(6)   methodology and further questions.

We will discuss each of these elements in turn.

1.   Questions Presented

As discussed earlier in this chapter, identifying the question is an important feature of nearly every written assignment you will receive in practice. Going through the analysis can take some time and effort, but once you have figured out what the question is, the hard work is done. Once you have identified the question, writing up your answer is almost mechanical in its simplicity.

When you move into professional practice, you should begin every document by identifying its purpose. Most pieces of writing have a dual purpose, one logistical and one substantive.

The logistical purpose of a written document can be determined by its role in the litigation or transaction. For example, the logistical reason for writing a letter may be to respond to another letter. An attendance note may be created to summarize the content of a telephone call or in-person meeting, and a memorandum of law may be meant to answer a particular question given to you by a senior lawyer. It is good practice to identify the logistical purpose of your document at the outset so that your reader understands what you are doing and why. This technique may seem unnecessarily pedantic at first, but you will see how useful it is when you look back at a piece of your writing two years later, with fresh eyes. The clarity of this approach will amaze you.

You should not only know why you are doing what you are doing, you should say clearly what your purpose is in writing a particular document.

How you go about stating your logistical purpose is a matter of style and can vary according to the type of document. For example, a letter may begin, "This is in response to your letter dated X," although some people now consider that a rather old-fashioned convention. An attendance note may begin, "This is to summarize the meeting of May 23, 2019, between Sandra McClintock, Josefa Morales, and Ezume Sato." Both of these examples succinctly describe the purposes of the document. Take guidance from your colleagues as to how things are done in your workplace, but try to remember to set out the purpose of every piece of writing. In terms of language, be as clear and as concise as you were when you identified the issue in your IRAC essays. As you now know, there is no need to ease your reader into the discussion.

You also need to identify your substantive purpose in writing the document. This is the legal question that you are attempting to answer and is equivalent to the issue in IRAC.

Now that you have experience writing IRAC essays, you should have no difficulty in melding these two purposes into a succinct introductory sentence. For example, if a senior partner at your law firm asks you to draft a memorandum of law relating to a particular question that he or she has identified, you can frame your memorandum as either (1) a response to the partner's question or (2) a response to the legal question. You could begin your document in one of two different ways:

Option 1: answer the partner's question

EXAMPLE

I was asked by Eion O'Connor to research the boundaries of the doctrine of "piercing the corporate veil" to determine whether our client, Marianne Trudeau, can be held personally liable for actions taken in her capacity as director of Acme Food Company from May 2014 to August 2019.

NOTE

You should indicate clearly on the face of the document if any sort of legal privilege exists. Your designation of something as privileged is not determinative, but it will raise a red flag later and help avoid problems with inadvertent production.

This approach addresses both the logistical and the substantive question. As a result, you can use this opening sentence with confidence in a number of situations. This method is particularly useful when you are writing an internal document, since you want to highlight the fact that the boundaries of the question have been set by a senior lawyer. You can also use this technique when you want to indicate that the work is being done at a client's request. By referring to the client in the opening line, you are making it clear for later readers that the document may be protected by some sort of legal privilege.

Option 2: answer the legal question

EXAMPLE

This memorandum defines the boundaries of the doctrine of "piercing the corporate veil" and discusses whether Marianne Trudeau can be held personally liable for actions taken in her capacity as director of Acme Food Company from May 2014 to August 2019.

This second approach is somewhat more limited, since it really only addresses the substantive question. This method may be appropriate in situations where you are creating a document that will be shared with a client, since you are speaking on behalf of your firm. In that case, it is not as important to identify the request as originating from a particular lawyer, although you could refer to the client's original request if you wished to do so.

One of the benefits of indicating that you are responding to a request from a client or a senior lawyer is that this approach helps identify the scope of information that you have been given. Remember, there could be other relevant facts that could affect your analysis. Limiting your discussion to the question asked helps minimize the possibility that your conclusions will be given more force than they merit.

Sometimes, in a very formal document, you will phrase the purpose of the discussion in the form of a question. Again, the question will resemble the issue in an IRAC analysis.

EXAMPLE

Under New York law, does the doctrine of "piercing the corporate veil" support an argument that Marianne Trudeau should be held personally liable for actions taken in her capacity as director of Acme Food Company from May 2014 to August 2019?

Whichever way you decide to proceed, remember that a quick, concise statement describing the aim of your written work — i.e., the question that you are seeking to answer — is as important in the professional realm as it is in the academic realm. Doing so defines the scope of the discussion and helps your reader know what to expect from the document.

Although "twists" can be great in stories, always ensure your reader knows what is coming next in a legal document. Nothing should come as a surprise.

2. Brief Answers

The term brief answer refers to a single paragraph that provides the response to the question presented—the "yes" or "no" answer—as well as an overview of why the question has been answered in that way. Notice that this technique contradicts what you need to do in an academic setting. When you write your IRAC essays, you should avoid conclusory remarks, meaning phrases that omit the intermediate analyses and go straight to your conclusion about how a matter of fact or law will be decided. In law school, you must walk your reader through your analysis, step by step, and support every statement of law with some sort of legal authority.

NOTE

Sometimes a "brief answer" is referred to as an "executive summary." Corporate clients often appreciate the term "executive summary," since that phrase is routinely used in commercial practice.

In practice, you also need to demonstrate your analysis and show legal support, but you do that in the body of the document—the discussion. The brief answer gives the reader a short outline of your discussion. While this kind of summary is a helpful tool in any piece of writing, the time and space restrictions on academic writing—particularly in a timed essay situation—preclude students from using this device.

The length and content of a brief answer varies according to the type of document. For example, a short letter may not need a separate section for the brief answer but can instead summarize the conclusion in one sentence.

EXAMPLE

This letter is in response to your letter dated August 24, 2020, which requests our client provide your client with information relating to all company directors' meetings from May 2014 to August 2019. For the reasons set forth below, we believe your client is not entitled to that information.

Often a letter such as this would go on to describe the reasons why the information will not be produced, but you should be aware that writing in a professional context is somewhat different than writing in an academic context. Sometimes, for tactical reasons, you may not want to provide the type of full and frank discussion that is expected in an academic setting. There may even be times when you will be purposefully vague when communicating with an opponent or third party. You should take guidance on these matters from more experienced lawyers, while always keeping in mind the relevant rules of responsible professional behavior. Tactics should never outweigh ethics.

On the other hand, an internal memo or client document would likely contain a longer brief answer, since the document itself would be longer. The brief answer or executive summary would note the key legal or factual issues as well as the anticipated outcomes. You can even use explicit headings to separate each section of your work.

NOTE

The longer the document, the higher the need for headings.

EXAMPLE

Question presented

Under New York law, can the doctrine of "piercing the corporate veil" support an argument that Marianne Trudeau should be held personally liable for actions taken in her capacity as director of Acme Food Company from May 2014 to August 2019?

Brief answer

No. New York courts hesitate to pierce the corporate veil and treat a director as the "alter ego" of a company unless a high degree of impropriety exists. The ability to pierce the corporate veil is extremely limited in New York law and the motive of the alleged wrongdoer is highly material. The appropriate test is whether special circumstances exist, making the company a mere façade for the wrongdoer. The company must be used as a puppet of the sole director before courts will go behind the corporate structure to hold the director personally liable. Because our client's activities do not rise to this level of wrongdoing, it is unlikely that she will be held personally liable for her actions as a director of Acme Food Company.

3. The Fact Summary

As the title suggests, the fact summary contains an outline of the relevant facts. Of course, the scope of the discussion depends on the nature of the document. A memorandum summarizing a witness interview or describing your review of documents will need to relate everything you have learned in its entirety, whereas a memorandum of law or a letter to a client or third party will be much more limited.

When considering how to draft a fact summary, you should think about how problem questions were drafted when you were in law school. Every sentence bore some relation to the legal issues that you then discussed. While your recitation of the facts may be longer than that found in a problem question, you should strive for a similar level of clarity and relevance. Remember, you are the expert on the subject matter of your document; you know what is relevant and what is not. If you are unsure about whether a particular fact will become relevant, put it in a separate "questions" section.[3]

Putting potentially irrelevant information in the facts section gives rise to two problems. First, you expand what should be a short summary into a longer, less straightforward section. Sometimes people who are (or who think they are) familiar with the facts will skim quickly through a fact summary, particularly if it is on the long side. Other people will skip it altogether (always dangerous and not to be recommended, since the reader may not know certain key facts disclosed in the summary or may, on the other hand, be able to correct the author on certain points). If you keep the fact summary short, you are more likely to keep the reader's attention.

When drafting exam answers using the IRAC system, you demonstrated legal judgment not only by what you included in your essay, but by what you excluded. The same is true in practice.

Second, putting extraneous information into your fact summary can end up hiding potentially important points. If you think something is critical to your analysis, make sure it stands out. Don't clutter your discussion with irrelevant detail. Not every fact is of equal value; use your discretion and omit those items that are not of great weight, just as you omitted minor arguments and legal authorities in your IRAC essays. The result will be a stronger and more readable fact summary.

4. Discussion

At this point, you are ready to undertake your normal IRAC-type analysis. The substantive question presented at the beginning of the document stands as your IRAC issue. Now you need to proceed to the "R" and "A" steps of the analysis, remembering always to keep your discussion relevant to the question you are addressing. You typically have more scope for discussion in a professional document than in an academic essay, but you should still apply the same analytical method. For example, a strong IRAC essay always puts case references into context rather than just dropping a case name in at the end of a sentence. The same is true in practice. Take your time and explain what you are doing and why. Keep the length of your analysis within reason, but realize that you may be covering legal points that your reader has not considered since he or she left

When writing a memorandum, remember that your reader has not had the benefit of reading all of your research. He or she still needs to be informed about the weight and scope of the relevant authorities.

---

[3] Recall that you had a "comments" section in your case briefs in law school. That technique prepared you to draft a "questions" section in your professional documents.

law school. Alternatively, you may be parsing through a very detailed statutory provision or judicial opinion. Take as much time as necessary to convey your meaning.

One reason you can and should spend sufficient time discussing the details of the cases and statutes that you cite is because those authorities will be even more relevant to your particular issue than the materials you used as support in your academic essays. When you are in law school, you have a limited number of relatively general legal authorities that you then use to support your arguments. Once you move into professional practice, however, you have access to a much wider range of cases and statutes and will only introduce those materials that are extremely relevant to the problem you are discussing. Because these authorities bear directly on the question you are answering, you want to discuss those materials thoroughly and identify how they relate to the issue you are researching. Furthermore, you want to show your reader how you came to your conclusion just in case your reader interprets the information differently or draws different insights from the materials. Although you may be disappointed if one of your readers does not adopt your conclusions, disagreements can lead to fruitful discussions and a better analysis.

Although you should be sure to include both "R" and "A" steps in your analyses, you need to adapt your writing style to conform to the needs of the document. Lengthy analyses are most likely to be found in memoranda of law and similar documents, although the format and approach can vary greatly even among this group of documents. Again, the best way for you to learn how to write a good analytical section is to ask senior colleagues to lend you some of their old papers as samples. While you must adapt the samples to suit your own particular needs, these samples can give you a good idea about how to put different types of documents together. You can also get good ideas from documents received from your opponents in the course of your practice. However, firms often have their own way of doing things, both substantively and stylistically, and you should conform your writing style to match that of your supervisors, not that of your opponents. Sometimes there will be great variation in approach even within the same firm, so you should ask each person with whom you work how he or she wants a document to appear. Again, ask for samples whenever possible.

NOTE

You need to adapt your writing style not only to suit the type of document that you are creating, but also to accommodate the individual quirks of the person requesting the document.

5. Conclusion and Advice

In your IRAC essays, you were told to provide a short conclusion at the end of your analysis. Not only did that approach mirror what is done in litigation, it also suited the restricted format of an academic essay.

Once you are in professional practice, you can take slightly more time to describe how you envision a particular problem playing out. Very often, you will be asked not only to anticipate the resolution of a particular question, but to provide advice on how to proceed. For example, you might be expected to describe how to remedy or mitigate the client's problem. You might also need to suggest further legal or factual research. How you phrase your conclusion depends, as always, on the type and purpose of your particular document, but you need to remember that you are now acting as a professional. While you will still have to analyze a question, as you did in law school, you are now being asked to go beyond simple analysis and use your best professional judgment to advise your reader about the appropriate measures to be taken as a result of the analytical process.

Lawyers are problem solvers. Consider including suggestions on how to proceed next, if appropriate.

You should put your conclusion and forward-looking advice in a separate section, so that anyone who is in a hurry can flip to it immediately. As always, be clear and concise, and separate different types of actions.

EXAMPLE

V. Conclusions and Advice

As the above analysis suggests, it is unlikely that a New York court will pierce the corporate veil to hold Marianne Trudeau personally liable for her actions as director of Acme Food Company. However, this analysis is based on the facts set forth above. As suggested in section III, there are several areas that require further investigation before the threat of an action based on "piercing the corporate veil" can be dismissed.

There are also a number of questions that need to be answered going forward. For example:

- Are there any contemporaneous documents showing that Ms. Trudeau suggested Resolution 115 as a means of reducing taxes to the company, rather than a means of increasing dividends paid out to shareholders, including himself?

- Is there any truth to the allegation that Ms. Trudeau's personal stock portfolio had just suffered a large loss at the time she suggested Resolution 115?

- Did Ms. Trudeau the proper corporate formalities when introducing Resolution 115?

There are also several additional steps that should be taken to minimize the likelihood that Ms. Trudeau will find herself subject to these kinds of charges in the future. For example:

- We should advise Ms. Trudeau of the importance of following proper corporate formalities when acting as a director.

- We should look into whether the corporate charter or bylaws should be amended to clarify the procedures that need to be taken when introducing resolutions regarding dividend distribution.

- We should look into whether additional director positions should be created to ensure a measure of objectivity in the decision-making process.

6. Methodology and Further Questions

Because many legal matters stretch out over several months or years, it is often useful to explain your research methodology in certain types of documents. For example, in a formal opinion letter you will want to list which documents you reviewed so that someone cannot come back later and claim that you overlooked an important fact contained in a particular letter or report. Conversely, if you were not given the document, you cannot be held responsible for not knowing any facts reflected therein. A similar situation exists with respect to legal research. Identify what types of searches you have done in case questions arise now or later about the scope of your work.

Laying out your methodology helps you remember what you've done so that you don't accidentally repeat the same steps later.

Some people believe that the methodology section should appear at the beginning of a document rather than at the end. Ultimately, where you put this information is a matter of personal choice, as long as your approach is logical and easily understandable to the reader. Just remember to include the information somewhere if your document is of a type that would benefit from a methodology section. If it is not appropriate to include this kind of information in the document itself, you can always outline your research methodology in a note to file.

EXAMPLE

The preceding research involved an all-text search on Westlaw and LexisNexis for the phrase "corporate veil" and "director's liability" in Second Circuit case law over the last fifteen years. I did not have time to review journal articles or treatises, although I believe some follow-up in this area would be helpful. No statutes appeared to be relevant to this analysis.

D. Formatting Issues

Earlier chapters discussed the use of footnotes and case citations in law school exam essays. The suggestion there was that you did not need to include either footnotes or full case citations in an exam scenario unless your instructor required you to do so. The brevity of academic essays, as well as the problems associated with remembering case names in an examination scenario, removed the need to use formal citation methods.

NOTE

If you haven't learned the rules of Bluebooking already, do so now. You should be able to create perfect citations for all standard authorities without looking at a form guide. Know the difference between state and federal practice in your jurisdiction.

The situation is very different in professional practice. Once you have started to work as a lawyer, you will need to use proper citations, including the full names of cases and statutes, even in internal documents. While perfect citations may seem pedantic, or like some sort of academic exercise, nothing could be further from the truth. Citations are vital. Make them perfect each and every time.

Formatting generally follows the rule of common sense. Practitioners are busy people and appreciate the use of standard formatting devices to organize written material visually. Therefore, long document should use numbers and letters to break the text into sections. Shorter documents can be organized through various headers, set off by different fonts. Bullet points have also become common in business documents and correspondence—especially emails—although they are not routinely used in formal legal documents such as court filings or contracts. Always be aware of how white space can be used to assist the reader.

WRITING

Breaking a long discussion into subparts not only helps you organize your thoughts, it helps readers follow your argument.

While you should not get too elaborate in your text design, many readers appreciate the use of **bold** type to highlight different section headings. Practitioners often use *italics* for emphasis. However, if you use italics to draw attention to one part of a long quotation, you must indicate in your citation that you have added the emphasis to the quote.

Although the use of special fonts is becoming more common, you should avoid relying on these types of formatting techniques to cure weak writing. If your prose is strong, then you do not need to use fancy fonts to make your point.

You now have an overview of how to adapt IRAC to legal practice. However, making the transition from law student to legal practitioner can be difficult at times. You should not hesitate to ask the senior lawyers with whom you work for assistance, even if you feel awkward doing so. It is part of their job to provide young attorneys with guidance. At the same time, it is not just up to supervisors to anticipate your every need, nor is it their job to proofread or otherwise correct your work. Instead, it is your responsibility to make your documents as good as they can be and seek help when you need it.

Many mistakes happen because of a miscommunication regarding the scope or purpose of the assignment. It's far better to take ten minutes at the beginning of a project to go over the assignment with your supervisor than to show up at the last minute with a ten-page memorandum that fails to address to correct question. At that point, it's really too late to do anything.

NOTE

Know exactly what your assignment is before you leave your supervising attorney's office.

This chapter has focused on issues that arise in professional practice. However, you cannot enter practice without completing law school and passing a state bar exam. Therefore, the following chapter will provide detailed comments on student essays to further solidify your understanding of the basic IRAC method.

CHAPTER **10**

Worked Questions

The preceding chapters should give you a good idea on how to write an IRAC essay in response to either a problem question or a discuss question. However, writing is difficult to learn in the abstract. What students need are examples. The problem with many exam guides is that they only provide perfect, seemingly unattainable writing samples. Students become discouraged when they read essays that they don't believe they can reproduce. Perfect writing samples are also problematic because students don't know why the essays are so good. As mentioned in earlier chapters, good writing is often noted more in its absence than its presence. Therefore, there is little educational value in providing a few samples and saying "just do this."

Instead, it is more helpful to provide you with essays written by current law students along with detailed commentary indicating the essays' strengths and weaknesses. None of these essays are perfect, although some are outstanding. In either case, the commentary indicates how the students' writing could be improved. Read through the essays and the discussion points to learn how to improve your own essays. There are some tips contained in this chapter that are not included in the previous chapters, so it is worthwhile to work through all of the examples.

This chapter contains tips not found in the previous pages.

Remember that not every comment applies to every student. For example, some writers are quite wordy, whereas others are naturally succinct. If you tend toward the concise, don't read a comment aimed at another writer and think that you need to become even terser. Brevity can be taken too far. However, if you fall into the former category, then you should take the suggestions on how to make your writing more concise to heart.

Be judicious in deciding which corrections to apply to your writing. Not everyone has the same issues to address.

You should also be aware that every law school and every professor has their own standards concerning student essays. Some law schools or professors want to see a lot of black-letter law, whereas other law schools or professors prefer to see a deep discussion of policy in response to every question. You need to identify the standards by which you will be judged, since you cannot meet (or exceed) those standards unless you know what they are.

Ask your professors what they are looking for, both in terms of substance and style. The best essays conform to the reader's expectations and desires, not the author's.

This chapter contains six student essays. The first two essays focus on tort law, followed by essays on criminal law and contract law. While these first four examples involve subjects from first year courses, it is also useful to see how upper-level students handle the IRAC technique. The last two student essays therefore relate to estates and trusts law. These are some of the best student essays in the book, so be sure to read all the way to the end of this chapter even if you have not yet taken those courses. Because the comments focus on structure and style rather than substance, you can glean some important tips even if you know nothing about trusts and estates.

The essays are critiqued on a line-by-line basis, in addition to general comments before and after each of the submissions. For the most part, comments do not refer to the discussion of the substantive law, since your syllabus may differ from that given to the students who wrote these essays. Furthermore, this book does not focus on the content of the law but on how to write good essays, so it is appropriate to focus only on the writing style and structure.

Before beginning the line-by-line critiques, it may be useful to provide a visual model of the task that you are aiming to achieve. Following is a representation of Bloom's Taxonomy, which is a hierarchical structuring of cognitive skills that educators use to help guide and assess students in the process of learning.[1] As the graphic suggests, it is necessary to master the earlier steps (i.e., those that appear lower in the pyramid) before moving on to the higher levels.

---

[1] The version used herein is reproduced with the permission of the Vanderbilt University Center for Teaching. The verbs listed under the main headings are simply synonyms for the concept in question.

Bloom's Taxonomy (Revised)

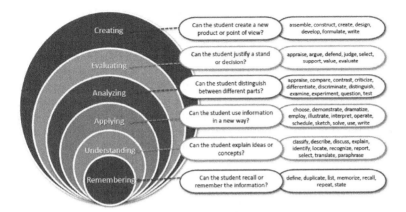

	Can the student create a new product or point of view?	assemble, construct, create, design, develop, formulate, write
Creating		
Evaluating	Can the student justify a stand or decision?	appraise, argue, defend, judge, select, support, value, evaluate
Analyzing	Can the student distinguish between different parts?	appraise, compare, contrast, criticize, differentiate, discriminate, distinguish, examine, experiment, question, test
Applying	Can the student use information in a new way?	choose, demonstrate, dramatize, employ, illustrate, interpret, operate, schedule, sketch, solve, use, write
Understanding	Can the student explain ideas or concepts?	classify, describe, discuss, explain, identify, locate, recognize, report, select, translate, paraphrase
Remembering	Can the student recall or remember the information?	define, duplicate, list, memorize, recall, repeat, state

Bloom's Taxonomy indicates that remembering the relevant information is the lowest level of cognition a student can show. However, this is only the first, most basic element of learning; it is not the final step. This is why students who focus solely on recall do very poorly in law school.

The second level in Bloom's Taxonomy involves understanding the material. Like recall, understanding is a necessary part of law school exams but is not enough to earn high marks. Instead, showing an understanding of the material will only earn a passing or low passing grade.

The third level of the pyramid involves application of information learned during the course to new situations. It is no coincidence that the third level of Bloom's Taxonomy uses the same term—"application"—as the third step of the IRAC analysis, since both IRAC and Bloom's Taxonomy value the ability to see how material learned during the course can be extrapolated into novel circumstances. As a result, "application" is necessary for any student who wants to achieve a median grade or higher in law school.

While law students must master the first three stages of Bloom's Taxonomy, those seeking to excel need to go beyond the application stage. As the graphic suggests, an exceptional law student will be adept at analyzing legal materials, meaning that they can see relevant connections and conflicts between different rules and principles. Indeed, this skill is precisely what is needed when distinguishing case law.

The best student essays in this chapter are found in the trusts and estates section. You should read those essays even if you have not taken trusts and estates, since you will be able to see the strength and the simplicity of the IRAC method even without understanding the substance of the discussion.

The ultimate goal on a law school exam is to evaluate the problem that has been set.[2] However, as Bloom's Taxonomy suggests, evaluation can only occur when four other skills—recollection, understanding, application, and analysis—have been both mastered and reflected in the exam response. For example, it is not enough that you understand the materials from a subjective perspective—you must objectively show that you understand the relevant statutes and cases before you can build an argument that properly evaluates the issue at hand.

As this analysis suggests, drafting an essay that includes all of the necessary elements takes time and practice. The following sample essays will show both what should be done and not be done as you hone your exam-writing skills.

A. A Professor's Model Essay

Students often ask to see how a professor would conduct an IRAC analysis. Following is a sample essay drafted by a law professor to indicate how a tort essay might be constructed using the IRAC method. This sample is somewhat simplified and is by no means the only way to answer this particular question, stylistically or substantively. However, the model shows how to implement each step in the IRAC analysis clearly and concisely.

The author has broken the answer into two sections, one for each major cause of action. This is a good technique to use whenever you have multiple torts, crimes, or similar causes of action. Another way to organize a complex fact pattern is to break your analysis up according to different plaintiff-defendant pairings, if you have more than one.

QUESTION

Kristy paid $20 for a ticket to enter a haunted house attraction called "Doom Mansion." Unbeknownst to Kristy, her ex-boyfriend Dale was the owner and operator of Doom Mansion. Dale, who was disguised as a vampire, immediately recognized Kristy when she walked through the attraction's front door.

Once in the haunted house, Kristy walked into a small room with only one door. Dale then slammed the door shut and shouted, "You can't

---

2   The highest echelon of Bloom's Taxonomy is associated with independent research projects and journal submissions rather than law exams.

get away this time, Kristy." Kristy tried to open the door, but there was no doorknob. Kristy yelled, "Let me out!" but Dale refused. Knowing that Kristy was so afraid of small spaces that she couldn't even ride on elevators, Dale said, "Escape is impossible." Kristy screamed, hyperventilated, and passed out.

Discuss Kristy's potential claim(s) against Dale.

ANSWER

There are two issues here: (1) whether Kristy has a claim against Dale for false imprisonment and (2) whether Kristy has a claim against Dale for intentional infliction of emotional distress.

(1) False Imprisonment

The first issue is whether Kristy can pursue a cause of action against Dale for falsely imprisoning her within the room in Doom Mansion. For false imprisonment, the plaintiff must prove the defendant acted with intent to confine, actual confinement resulted, and the plaintiff was aware of or harmed by the confinement. *See* Rest. 2d, s. 35. However, there cannot be a false imprisonment if the plaintiff consents, *see* Rest. 2d, s. 892, or the defendant is justified. *Parvi v. City of Kingston* (where police were not justified for arresting a man who had not committed a crime). Kristy's case will turn on whether Dale's failure to open the door was an intentional act and whether she can prove she did not consent.

Generally, an act is intentional if the defendant desires the consequences of the act or is substantially certain the act will cause a tort. *See Garratt v. Dailey* (involving a boy who pulled a chair out from a girl, causing the girl to fall). However, an omission can be an intentional act if the defendant has a legal duty to act affirmatively. *See* Rest. 3d, s. 39. Thus, *Whittaker v. Sandford* held that a defendant falsely imprisoned a plaintiff by omission when the defendant invited the plaintiff onto the defendant's yacht but would not let the plaintiff take a boat ashore once reaching port. *See also* Rest. 2d, s. 45.

A plaintiff cannot be falsely imprisoned if consent exists. Section 892 of the Restatement Second of Torts states that a plaintiff can manifest consent by action or inaction and that a defendant may infer apparent consent if a plaintiff's words or conduct are "reasonably understood" as giving consent. However, if a defendant exceeds the given consent, a defendant cannot claim the plaintiff consented. *See* Rest. 2d, s. 892A.

Consent is often an issue in false imprisonment cases. *Meints v. Huntington* involved a plaintiff feigning consent to confinement after an angry mob arrived at his sons' house and assaulted one of his sons. The Eighth Circuit held that the plaintiff was coerced into consenting due to the defendants' words and acts. The Eighth Circuit again held that a plaintiff was coerced into feigning consent in *Eilers v. Coy*, where deprogrammers attempted to rescue the plaintiff from a cult.

These holdings seemingly conflict with the Restatement's approach that a court may find consent if a defendant "reasonably understood" the plaintiff as giving consent. However, the defendants in both *Meints* and *Eilers* should have understood the plaintiffs would feign consent.

Here, Dale acted intentionally when he slammed the door and confined Kristy within the small, dark room. Further, Dale acted by omission when he failed to open the door. Like the defendant in *Whittaker*, Dale had a duty to act because he confined the plaintiff. By stating, "You can't get away this time, Kristy," Dale used words, as in *Meints*, to cause fear and confinement. Kristy was aware of her confinement and even suffered a physical harm by hyperventilating and passing out.

Although intent to confine exists, the question of consent remains problematic. Kristy consented to entering the haunted house and even paid money to do so. Being confined in a small, dark room does not seem atypical for a haunted house. However, screaming "Let me out!" could be seen as an attempt to revoke consent.

Dale will argue that a simple yell at a haunted house is not enough to withdraw consent. Further, unlike the plaintiffs in *Meints* and *Eilers*, Kristy never feigned consent but gave actual consent by entering the haunted house willingly. Kristy will argue that because of Dale's knowledge of Kristy's fears, that under the Restatement, Dale knew that Kristy's pleas truly revoked consent. The stronger argument, however, is that a simple yell is not enough to be removed immediately from a room in a haunted house.

Thus, the claim of false imprisonment fails because, although Dale acted through his omission of not opening the door, Kristy consented. Further investigation would be helpful in establishing the customs of haunted houses and placing patrons in closed rooms.

(2)   Intentional Infliction of Emotional Distress (IIED)

The next issue is whether Kristy can pursue a cause of action against Dale for IIED for when Dale put Kristy in the room and told Kristy that she could not leave. To prove IIED, a plaintiff must prove the defendant, by extreme and outrageous conduct, intentionally or recklessly caused the plaintiff severe mental distress. *See* Rest. 2d, s. 46. In comment d of section 46, the Restatement defines extreme and outrageous as going "beyond all possible bounds of decency" and as "utterly intolerable in a civilized community." The most difficult element for Kristy is whether Dale's conduct was extreme and outrageous.

Generally, extreme and outrageous conduct is judged by an objective standard and mere insults are not enough to meet that standard. For example, *Slocum v. Food Fair Stores of Florida* held there was no extreme and outrageous conduct when a store employee cursed and told a plaintiff that the plaintiff smelled bad.

Conduct will be judged subjectively, however, if the defendant has special knowledge about the plaintiff's hypersensitivities. *Nickerson v. Hodges* held that defendants acted extremely and outrageously when they tricked a known former mental patient into finding and opening a fake pot of gold. Although the defendants' act would not normally rise to the level of extreme and outrageous conduct, the defendants knew about the woman's mental history and her obsession with finding gold. The court was unpersuaded by the defendants' argument that they were merely pulling a prank.

Here, Dale's acts were intentional or at least reckless. He knew Kristy's fear and disregarded that fear. As in *Nickerson*, whether Dale's conduct was merely a joke is irrelevant. Furthermore, Kristy showed a physical manifestation of severe mental distress by hyperventilating and passing out.

The element of extreme and outrageous conduct is also met, since Dale had special knowledge of Kristy's claustrophobia. While, by an objective standard, putting a person in a confined and darkened room in a haunted house would not be "intolerable in a civilized community," this situation is more akin to *Nickerson* because Dale knew of Kristy's hypersensitivities. Dale should therefore be judged according to a subjective standard and should be held to have acted in an extreme and outrageous manner.

Therefore, Dale should be held liable for IIED. Evidence of whether Kristy later experienced additional severe distress resulting from the incident would bolster her case.

B. Torts Question One

Following is the first of two student answers responding to a question in torts. This is an outstanding essay in terms of both structure and analysis, and would likely earn a very good grade, particularly if the professor values robust application of the facts to the law.

As discussed throughout this text, each professor has his or her own preferences in terms of the weight of "R" versus "A" steps. However, this author

This author does an excellent job in applying the facts to the law without simply repeating the facts in a pure narrative. As seen below, any mention of a fact is directly linked to the legal standard adduced in the "R" section. That is IRAC writing at its best.

does a very good job in balancing these competing demands. A professor who wants to see a lot of "application" analysis will appreciate how well this author links each legal element to the underlying facts, while a professor who wants to see a lot of "rule" analysis will value the precision of the legal language and the fact that the author explicitly mentions three different cases. While some students might introduce one or two more authorities and therefore might earn a few more points than this student if the professor puts a high priority on density of cases and authorities, this is nevertheless an outstanding example of the IRAC technique. The author has obviously taken the suggestions outlined in this book to heart and has implemented them beautifully.

QUESTION

Twelve-year-old Scott and thirteen-year-old Logan are best friends and spend most of their free time together, building all sorts of gizmos. One day, they decided to build a tree house in Logan's backyard. The boys placed a ladder at the base of the tree and climbed up to build the floor of the tree house. When the floor was complete, Logan hurried down the ladder and pulled it away, leaving Scott stranded twelve feet off the ground.

Initially, Scott laughed and enjoyed the view, but after five minutes, he tired and told Logan to put the ladder back up. Logan refused, telling Scott that he should "just jump." Scott began to cry, and Logan started calling Scott a "wimp." Logan knew the term "wimp" would greatly affect Scott because it was the same term that Scott's abusive father routinely called Scott. Scott cried even harder, and after continued taunting from Logan, Scott jumped to the ground, breaking his ankle upon landing.

Discuss any potential intentional torts and defenses.

RESPONSE (paragraph one)

There are two issues in this case: (1) whether Scott has a proper claim for false imprisonment against Logan and (2) whether Scott has a proper claim for intentional infliction of emotional distress against Logan.[1] The potential defenses Logan might bring for each tort will also be discussed.

COMMENTS (paragraph one)

1. This is an excellent "I" statement—concise and clear. We see that the author has two different torts in mind, so the reader knows the analysis will be complete. The following sentence regarding potential defenses is similarly reassuring.

RESPONSE (paragraph two)

The first tort to be addressed is false imprisonment.[2] For a claim of false imprisonment to be brought, a plaintiff would need to show (1) that the defendant intentionally confined the plaintiff to a given area, (2) that the restraint was against the plaintiff's will, and (3) that the plaintiff was either conscious of the confinement or harmed by it.[3] The restraint can either be a physical barrier which the plaintiff can't get around or simply words spoken by the defendant which the plaintiff fears to disobey.[4] As we saw in *Whittaker v. Sanford*, where a woman was found to be falsely imprisoned on a boat, actual physical force in keeping the person restrained is not required for false imprisonment to have occurred.[5] In that case, the court decided that any type of refusal to grant the means to overcome a barrier, whether it be a locked door, the taking of someone's car keys, or not providing a way to get from the boat to the shore, qualifies as false imprisonment.[6]

> **TIP** ✓
>
> Try to avoid the unnecessary use of the word "would" in your essays. Though it's occasionally necessary, "would" is often "wooden." Here, it can be deleted with no adverse effect.

COMMENTS (paragraph two)

2.   This is a classic topic sentence setting up the structure of the essay.

3.   This is an excellent introduction to the "R" section of the essay—simple, straightforward and legally comprehensive. The only possible improvement would be to include a legal authority, which could be either a case or the Restatement. Stylistically, putting the three phrases in parallel form makes the sentence flow smoothly. It might also be useful to identify which of the elements of the tort are most in contention, but that ultimately becomes clear from context.

4.   By defining an important term ("restraint"), the author adds useful complexity and precision to the analysis. Note that the definition is not restricted to the element relevant to this fact pattern (i.e., words difficult to disobey) but includes all relevant elements.

5.   This is a very good use of case law. Not only is the decision directly on point, but the author shows why the citation is being used here. Remember that you can use part of the case name if you cannot remember the whole citation. Alternatively, you can simply summarize the facts of the case (concisely, as was done here) if you can't remember the name while working under time constraints.

6.   Again, excellent expansion of the concept of restraint based on legal authority.

RESPONSE (paragraph three)

Here, Logan's act of removing the ladder so that Scott could not safely get down from the treehouse is where false imprisonment is likely to have occurred.[7] It is clear in this case that Logan's act of removing the ladder was an intentional act, as he waited until he was on the ground before pushing it away from the tree, and refused when Scott later asked him to put it back up.[8] By not putting the ladder back up when asked, Logan intentionally confined Scott to the treehouse.[9] As in *Whittaker*, Logan didn't need to use physical force in restraining Scott in the treehouse, but instead restrained him by removing his only way to leave.[10] It's also apparent that this restraint was against Scott's will, as he not only asked several times for Logan to put the ladder back up so he could climb down, but was so eager to get to the ground that he risked hurting himself by jumping.[11] In this case, Scott was also conscious of his confinement and was ultimately harmed by it, meeting the third requirement of false imprisonment.[12] Scott was aware that the only safe way to the ground was by using a ladder, which he knew Logan had removed.[13] He also, because of this imprisonment in the treehouse, had to resort to jumping to the ground, which resulted in a broken ankle.[14]

COMMENTS (paragraph three)

7. This sentence shows that we are moving into the "A" section of the analysis and does a good job of beginning to tie the facts to the law.

8. This sentence is slightly confusing—the "and refused" phrase doesn't really parallel the first half of the sentence—but these types of errors arise in timed essays. Ultimately, the reader gets the gist of the sentence, which involves linking one of the legal requirements of the tort—intentionality—to the facts.

9. This sentence is a bit duplicative, but not problematically so.

10. This sentence nicely links the analysis to the cited case law, showing that the author understands the use and purpose of legal authorities in legal reasoning.

11. The author may be belaboring the point a bit at this stage, but everything he or she says is true and some professors may like this type of extensive discussion. The contraction ("it's") is not technically incorrect, but may be slightly informal for legal writing.

12. This is an excellent point to make and one that might have been overlooked if the author had not described the test for the tort with specificity at the beginning of the "R" section. The word "requirement" is not quite as precise as it could be—"element" might be better—but the meaning is clear.

13. This sentence might usefully be combined with the previous one, but the author is making very sure to tie the legal authority together with the facts, which is very important to some professors.

14. Again, this sentence may not be entirely necessary, since the test for the tort indicates that the third element can be met either by conscious knowledge of the false imprisonment or harm, but it is good to note all the ways that the plaintiff has met the legal requirements.

Some professors prefer that you spend most of your time on the "R" step, whereas others want you to focus more on "A." Find out in advance which your professor prefers. This author addresses both the "R" and "A" elements, but focuses a bit more on the "A" section.

RESPONSE (paragraph four)

Logan could potentially argue that because Scott had the ability to jump down, it wasn't actually an act of false imprisonment, but seeing as Scott ended up breaking an ankle when doing that, it's clear that this was not a safe alternative that Scott could rely on as a means of escape.[15]

COMMENTS (paragraph four)

15. It is unclear whether the author is arguing from legal authority here or simply from common sense, but it would be useful to have a case or other cite if possible. Stylistically, the sentence could usefully be split into two, both to increase clarity (use of the phrase "seeing as" is a bit colloquial and often suggests a problematic sentence structure) and to avoid a single-sentence paragraph. Contractions could also be usefully avoided. However, the intention behind the sentence — to introduce a possible defense and analyze it — is good.

RESPONSE (paragraph five)

Therefore, due to meeting all three of the above elements, it's very likely that Scott would have a proper cause of action were he to sue Logan for false imprisonment.[16]

COMMENTS (paragraph five)

16. This sentence could be shortened a bit and made less colloquial, but successfully acts as a clear conclusion to the analysis of the first tort.

RESPONSE (paragraph six)

The second tort potentially committed here is that of intentional infliction of emotional distress.[17] A claim for intentional infliction of emotional distress requires that (1) the conduct is intentional or reckless, (2) the conduct is extreme and outrageous, (3) there's a causal connection between the wrongful conduct and the emotional distress, and (4) the emotional distress is severe.[18] According to the case of _Harris v. Jones_, determining whether an act is extreme and outrageous is dependent on the facts of the particular case, including the relationship between the parties and the circumstances of the situation.[19] The severity of the emotional distress depends on what a reasonable person would be expected to endure, and as discovered in _Slocum v. Food Fair Stores of Florida_, most slurs or insults don't qualify, as they're typically not outrageous enough.[20]

COMMENTS (paragraph six)

17.   The author here clearly introduces the second IRAC analysis.

18.   This sentence sets forth the initial "R" criteria clearly and completely. The author is becoming slightly more colloquial in his or her writing style, possibly because of the press of time, but it has not yet become problematic. Remember, the more professional you can keep your writing, the more points you will earn because of the "halo effect" generated by the reader's positive perception of your prose.

19.   The author here returns to succinct legal writing, likely because of the citation to the legal authority, which not only provides the content for the analysis but also helps stylistically by assisting with word choice.

20.   This sentence reflects excellent use of authority and foreshadowing of how the case cited will apply to the facts. We have again reverted to a more colloquial style, as seen through the use of contractions, but reliance on the decision increases linguistic precision.

RESPONSE (paragraph seven)

Here, the possible tort of intentional infliction of emotional distress stems from both the act of removing the ladder so Scott couldn't get safely to the ground and Logan's use of the term "wimp" when Scott refused to "just jump."[21] As mentioned above, it's clear that Logan's act of removing the ladder was intentional, as he pushed it away and refused to put it back when Scott asked.[22] It's also clear that Logan's use of the term "wimp" was intentional, especially since he continued to taunt Scott with it even after Scott started to cry.[23] Although most courts have decided that slurs and insults don't qualify as outrageous conduct, as in Slocum, where the plaintiff was told she stinks, there might be an exception here.[24] Because of the relationship between the two boys, and the knowledge that Logan had of Scott's abusive father, it's likely that the use of the word "wimp" would qualify as extreme and outrageous.[25] Although this isn't a term that a reasonable person might find extreme and outrageous,

TIP

Be careful of problems with antecedents. These types of grammatical errors can lead to substantive errors and cause you to lose points.

Logan knew this was a word that Scott's abusive father used often, which he knew would have a severe emotional impact on his friend.[26] The case before us also meets the third element, as the emotional distress was a direct result of the intentional conduct committed by Logan.[27] The final element, however, might not be met.[28] Although the actions did eventually result in a broken ankle, the emotional distress itself did not amount to anything more than crying.[29] If this case were to be brought, the evidence here for severe emotional distress might be too weak to succeed.[30]

COMMENTS (paragraph seven)

21.   This sentence brings the essay clearly into the "A" section of the analysis and does a good job of beginning to link the law and the facts.

22.   This is a good internal cross-reference and a good demonstration of how one of the required elements of the tort is met by the facts.

23.   Again, this is a good demonstration of how the facts line up with the required elements of the tort, although this sentence could have been combined with the previous one to make the analysis even more succinct.

24.   The author does well to mention *Slocum*, which was previously cited (although the reference here is not in italics, as it should be—a small error). Furthermore, it is fine that the author includes some additional facts from that were not mentioned earlier. The "R" and "A" sections are always a bit fluid, so an author needs to use his or her discretion in determining where to place certain elements.

25.   The conclusion here is very good as a matter of substance, and the use of commas is very good as a matter of style.

26.   Here, "he" is misplaced—the term refers to Scott's father rather than to Logan, which is not what was intended. Antecedent errors are extremely common in timed essays, but you should do your best to avoid them, since they can cause significant confusion. What is good here is that the author is demonstrating how the usual standard (i.e., that of the reasonable person) might differ in this circumstance. As a matter of substance, it would be useful in the "R" section (or even here) to have some authority discussing "eggshell plaintiffs" and similar concepts.

27.   Again, the author is doing very well to demonstrate explicitly how each element of the tort in question is met by the facts of the case.

28.   It is absolutely fine to be unsure whether each of the elements is met. The call of this question (as with most exam questions) is to analyze certain legal claims, not to act as an advocate who tries to show that his or her client will win. Of course, you should always be objective in your analysis, since advocates also have to recognize weaknesses in their arguments.

29.   This is an excellent distinction between mental and emotional injury and shows good sensitivity to the requirements of the legal test.

30.   This is a good interim conclusion.

RESPONSE (paragraph eight)

In defense, Logan would likely rely on the idea that a reasonable person would not find his conduct to be outrageous and extreme, and that Scott has little evidence to prove that the emotional distress was severe.[31] As mentioned above, there's a chance that the personal connection between the boys and Logan's knowledge of the abusive father might allow the second element to be met, however, it's likely that there is not enough evidence to show severe emotional distress.[32]

COMMENTS (paragraph eight)

31.   This appears to be a common sense defense based on whether the plaintiff can meet the requirements of the cause of action rather than an affirmative defense with its own elements. Be sure to consider both types of defenses in your essays.

32.   This sentence could be improved by splitting it into two (it is something of a run-on as it currently stands), but the analysis is excellent, since it focuses on whether the behavior in question complies with the legal standard identified in the "R" section of the essay.

RESPONSE (paragraph nine)

Because of the factors discussed above, it's likely that Scott would not succeed if he were to sue Logan for intentional infliction of emotional distress.[33]

COMMENTS (paragraph nine)

33.   This is an excellent "C" statement, concise and to the point. The professor might differ as to whether the case would go the other way, but the author has justified his or her conclusion by reference to the law and facts, which is all that a professor can ask.

As the above shows, this essay excels not only in terms of structure but also in terms of style. Virtually every sentence is clear and concise and adds a new, relevant element to the analysis. There is a general feeling of competence and authority throughout, a perception that is aided by the absence of typos and grammatical mistakes. While the author occasionally lapses into a slightly colloquial tone, as seen by the use of contractions, those are not technically incorrect and are to be expected from a first-year law student writing under time constraints.

C. Torts Question Two

This essay has many strong elements, particularly in its early sections. It is well organized and clearly identifies the legal authority on which the analysis is based. The major problem is in the "A" section. Like many law students, the author appears unclear how to apply the facts to the law and spends unnecessary time speculating or extrapolating on the facts. Although some of the later paragraphs in the "A" section improve on this analysis, primarily by identifying the precise elements of the legal test that are going to be discussed, a number of sentences could be cut without undue effect.

Compare the "A" analysis in this essay to the "A" analysis in the previous essay. Although the fact patterns are different, you will see a significant difference in how the authors approached the process of applying the law to the facts.

One of the ways to determine whether the application section is too wordy is to consider the relative length of the "R" and "A" sections. Here, the application analysis is far longer than the legal analysis, which suggests a problem. The best essays tend to have an "R" section that is longer than a succinctly worded "A" section, though it is possible that a good essay could have the two sections be equal in length.

QUESTION

Sam is employed as a door supervisor at a popular night club, Midnight Madness, where his primary duties include ensuring the safety of the patrons of the club. Door supervisors are required to wear fashionable Midnight Madness t-shirts as well as slightly less fashionable door supervisor identification badges, which are to be worn whenever the employee is on duty.

Employees of Midnight Madness "clock out" at the end of their shifts by using an electronic fingerprinting mechanism that is housed in the employee break room at the back of the club. There is no separate employee entrance at Midnight Madness, which means that employees must use one of several public entrances and exits to enter and leave work.

On the night in question, Sam had clocked out and was leaving through Midnight Madness's main entrance, still wearing his t-shirt but not his door supervisor badge. His fellow door supervisor, Carlos, was having some problems with a pair of drunken men who wanted to come into Midnight Madness. Sam stopped to help Carlos and a fight broke out. One of the drunken men had his nose broken by Sam and now brings an action against Midnight Madness.

Is Midnight Madness liable for Sam's actions? Would your answer change if Carlos called out, "Help me, Sam," just as Sam passed by?

Would your answer differ if Carlos instead said, "It's okay, I've got this, Sam?"

RESPONSE (paragraph one)

(1)[1]   The main issue is whether Midnight Madness is liable for Sam's actions when he left the nightclub and broke a drunken man's nose.[2] In general, employers may be held liable for the torts of their employees under the doctrine of respondeat superior.[3] In order to establish liability under this doctrine, a plaintiff must establish that the tortfeasor is an employee of the employer and that conduct occurred within the scope of employment. *Christensen v. Swensen.*[4] The most important sub-issue is whether Sam was acting within the scope of employment.[5] In addition, the following discussion assumes Sam actually committed a tort, such as assault or battery, and did not act in self-defense.[6]

> **TIP** ✓
>
> Assuming certain requirements have been met can be risky but can also be appropriate given the call of the question.

COMMENTS (paragraph one)

1.   The author has chosen to separate his or her response to each of the sub-questions in the prompt by using different numbers to correlate to each sub-question. This is acceptable and, in many cases, beneficial to both the author and the reader, since it ensures that each element of the question is addressed. If the question has differently numbered sub-parts, you should definitely track those numbers in your essay. Anything you can do to make the reader's job easier is to be encouraged.

2.   Although this statement does not name the tort in question, it is an acceptable "I" statement, given that the author has decided to answer the sub-questions in different sections.

3.   This sentence also acts as an "I" statement by introducing the legal principle that triggers liability.

4.   This sentence uses terms of act appropriately ("tortfeasor"), identifies the general elements of the tort, and provides legal support. While some professors might want a short parenthetical describing the main holding of the case that is cited, that may not be necessary if the case was one that was discussed at length in class and the basic issue at stake in the case is the same as is enunciated in the lead-in sentence.

5.   The author has done well to identify the sub-issue clearly.

6.   The technique of assuming that an underlying element (in this case, a tort committed by the employee) has been fully established is somewhat risky, since the professor might be using this question to test that element as well. Your best bet is to consider the amount of time and

the number of points allocated to the question. If there are a lot of points allocated to the question, the professor probably wants you to run through the elements of the underlying tort in more detail. Certainly, it wouldn't take much to list the basic elements to cover your bases even if you don't go into much depth. However, the author here has done well to avoid the trap of focusing on the assault and battery issue at the expense of the *respondeat superior* analysis, which is clearly the focus of question.

RESPONSE (paragraph two)

In order to determine if an employee acted within the scope of their employment, courts analyze three characteristics of conduct: (1) the conduct must be of the general kind the employee was hired to perform; (2) the conduct must occur substantially within the hours and spatial boundaries of the employee's employment and; (3) the conduct must serve, at least in part, the interest of the employer. *Birkner*.[7] Moreover, determining if the conduct occurred during the scope of employment is a question for the jury and may only be decided by a court if the conduct is clearly outside or inside the scope of employment and reasonable minds cannot differ on the matter.[8] *Christensen v. Swensen* (holding that reasonable minds could differ applying the *Birkner* test when the employee took a meal break and traveled to a nearby café to eat and injured a third party while doing so).[9]

> **TIP** ✓
> If you have discussed two different tests in your course—for example, a common law test and a Restatement test—you should introduce both and indicate how they differ, if at all. Those differences may be key to answering the question.

> **TIP** ✓
> This essay only cites two cases as authority, which is a little sparse. It may be that the author did not introduce information on independent contractors—often a major part of coursework on *respondeat superior*—because he or she thought that was not a live issue. However, it is still useful, if not necessary, to include that information to show that Sam indeed fell into the scope of the doctrine.

COMMENTS (paragraph two)

7.   There are a few grammatical errors here—"if" should be "whether" and the semi-colon after "and" should go before it—and the lead-in to the list is a bit awkward, but the content is very good. The author has succinctly identified the elements of the test, using the language that is closely tied to that used in the case, and has provided legal authority for the proposition. Note that the author here only remembered half of the case name, but that is fine: even a one-line summary of the case facts is enough if the author can't recall the name of a particular decision.

8.   This sentence has the same grammatical error that the preceding sentence did (i.e., the first "if" should be "whether") but again has

excellent content. Notice that this sentence is not technically necessary with respect to the question of liability but does show the depth of the reader's understanding of the legal principle at issue as a procedural matter. For the most part, procedural considerations like the applicable standard of proof are icing on the cake in substantive courses; they cannot act as a substitute for core considerations (i.e., the elements of the main dispute and any sub-issues), but they can help your essay look complete and professional, which can make a reader subconsciously rank your submission higher than others.

9.   It is absolutely fine to cite a case more than once, as the author does here, so long as the decision is relevant to the new point as well. The parenthetical is minimally helpful in that it describes how the *Christensen* court applied the *Birkin* test, but the discussion is marred by some grammatical problems that could largely be solved by putting the *Birkin* phrase first, followed by a comma.

RESPONSE (paragraph three)

Here, Sam's primary duty as a door supervisor is to ensure the safety of patrons, which would include interacting with them.[10] On the one hand, there is no doubt Sam's conduct of getting involved in the matter outside of the main entrance to help Carlos is warranted.[11] Midnight Madness is a popular nightclub where it is likely that people will drink, get into fights, and cause mischief.[12] It is likely Midnight Madness hires door supervisors to keep the main entrance safe, secure, and under control.[13] Because Carlos was having problems with the drunken men about admittance to the club, Sam worked in his capacity as a door supervisor when he intervened.[14] On the other hand, it is unlikely Midnight Madness hires door supervisors to engage in conduct that will harm patrons.[15] Indeed, Sam broke one of the drunken men's nose, which presumably takes a considerable amount of force.[16] As such, while it is likely that Sam's job requires him to get involved with patrons who are causing issues at the main entrance, reasonable minds could differ as to whether using force against a patron is part of his job duties.[17] Further information would be helpful to determine how the drunken man's nose came to be broken.[18]

COMMENTS (paragraph three)

10.   We have obviously segued to the "A" analysis, although this sentence seems more a repetition of facts than an application of the facts to the law.

11.   Actually, this issue is in no way clear. Instead, it is at the heart of the question.

12.   While true, this sentence does not add to the application of law to the facts.

13. Again, this sentence is extraneous supposition and expansion of the facts, with no clear reference to the legal standard.

14. This sentence is not only conclusory, it is at odds with the legal standard identified in the preceding paragraph, which indicated that "the conduct must occur substantially within the hours and spatial boundaries of the employee's employment." Whether Carlos was having problems or not has nothing to do with the test enunciated. This type of approach is common with student essays but does not constitute a real "A" analysis.

15. This is unnecessary speculation and can be eliminated.

16. This sentence has nothing to do with the legal test enunciated in the preceding paragraphs and can be eliminated.

17. This sentence has more of a link to the legal test, but could be improved by tighter language and a clearer connection to the legal test.

18. Suggesting more facts are needed is allowed in essays but seldom necessary. Typically your professor will give you all the facts necessary to answer the question, as is true in this case.

RESPONSE (paragraph four)

Next, we need to determine if the conduct occurred substantially within the hours of employment and spatial boundaries.[19] In this case, Sam definitively clocked out of his shift and was no longer "working." However, Sam continued to wear his Midnight Madness t-shirt when he exited the building, which could have made it apparent to others that Sam was still at work. Although it seems clear that Sam subjectively intended to cease his work when he clocked out, a jury may determine that clocking in and out is not dispositive due to safety concerns. As such, reasonable minds could differ when determining if Sam's conduct was within the hours of his employment.[20]

COMMENTS (paragraph four)

19. This paragraph is better than the preceding one in that it refers specifically to the elements of the legal test.

20. The preceding four sentences are undertaking the proper analysis but can be condensed and made more precise. There may also be legal authorities that consider whether the tortfeasor's subjective mindset is relevant to the analysis. If you only remember those cases at this point, you can still introduce them.

RESPONSE (paragraph five)

In addition, Sam was most likely within the spatial boundaries of his employment.[21] His role as a door supervisor is to ensure the safety of all patrons, which would require him to be near the entrance of Midnight Madness and any other area that would be deemed necessary. Further, the incident in this case took place right where Sam typically works.

COMMENTS (paragraph five)

21.   This paragraph can be condensed to a single sentence noting that the spatial element of the test is met. That is not an issue that is in contention in this question.

RESPONSE (paragraph six)

The final issue to determine is if Sam's conduct was motivated, at least in part, to serve the interest of the employer.[22] Here, Sam could be seen as serving the interest of the employer because his primary duty is to ensure the safety of patrons which may result in physical contact.[23] Drunk men trying to gain access to Midnight Madness could pose serious safety issues for other patrons.[24] As such, it is possible Sam needed to use force against the drunken men in order to protect other patrons.[25] However, it is also equally possible that Sam did not need to use excessive force against the drunken man's nose in order to ensure this safety. Further investigation into the drunken men and the circumstances surrounding the contact would be helpful to determine if Sam's conduct was motivated to benefit Midnight Madness.

COMMENTS (paragraph six)

22.   This sentence serves to link the factual analysis to the legal test and so is useful.

23.   This sentence provides an appropriate interpretation of the facts as they correlate to the legal test. This effect is achieved not through speculation, repetition or expansion of the facts but through a demonstration of legal judgment.

24.   This sentence is largely unnecessary because it focuses on supposition when the facts show actual danger to current or potential patrons.

25.   This sentence can be combined with the following two to note that a fact issue exists with respect to whether Sam's action was necessary. The analysis could be improved by noting that this question would likely lie with the jury rather than the judge, pursuant to the legal standard identified in the "R" section.

RESPONSE (paragraph seven)

Based on the foregoing, Midnight Madness is most likely not liable for Sam's actions.[26] Sam presumably used an excessive amount of force when he broke the man's nose. Unless Sam needed to break the nose of the drunken man to protect other patrons, the conduct most likely falls outside the scope of his employment. Finally, if this case were to go to trial, reasonable minds could differ on the *Birkner* test and thus the question will need to be answered by a jury.

COMMENTS (paragraph seven)

26.   This sentence is the "C" section of IRAC. The following sentences are therefore unnecessary summation and can be eliminated. The reason why the author feels the need to repeat the analysis is because the "A" section was not as tight and precise as it should have been. If the "A" section is clear, there is no need to include a lengthy conclusion.

RESPONSE (paragraph eight)

(2)   The issue is whether the above analysis would change if Carlos said, "Help me, Sam."[27] This comment would apply mostly to the scope of employment issue above.[28] Consequently, this would help bolster the plaintiff's argument and that Sam was acting within the scope of employment and "clocked back in" when he came to Carlos's aid, whose was working at the time of the incident and needed Sam's help.[29] As such, the discovery of this fact makes it more likely Sam acted within the scope of his employment, which could cause Midnight Madness to incur liability.[30]

When answering different sub-questions, consider whether any additional law can be introduced under an abbreviated "R" analysis. Often sub-questions allow authors to incorporate previous legal discussions by reference, but there typically is something new to add in terms of law.

COMMENTS (paragraph eight)

27.   This is a good "I" statement in the context of the current answer, which separates various sub-questions into different sections.

28.   The author does a good job of both identifying the key legal issue and incorporating it into the previous "R" discussion.

29.   This sentence has several grammatical errors—the "and" before "that" is unnecessary, and the sentence should probably end at "aid." Putting the notion that Carlos was on duty in a separate sentence would eliminate the incorrect use of "whose." However, the content is good and essentially reflects a short "A" analysis.

30. This sentence is a bit wordy and tries too hard to insert legal terms of art ("discovery"), but achieves the purpose of a "C" statement.

RESPONSE (paragraph nine)

(3) The issue is whether the above analysis would change if Carlos said, "It's ok, I've got this Sam."[31] This comment would also apply to the scope of employment issue above.[32] Consequently, this would help bolster Midnight Madness' argument and that Sam acted outside the scope of his employment because he intentionally inserted himself into the situation with the drunken men despite Carlos clearly telling him he did not need him.[33] As such, the discovery of this fact makes it more likely Sam did not act within the scope of his employment, alleviating Midnight Madness from liability.[34]

COMMENTS (paragraph nine)

31. This is a good "I" statement in the context of the current answer.

32. Again, the author successfully identifies the key legal issue and incorporates it into the previous "R" discussion. There is no need to try to find an "elegant variation" so that the first two sentences of this section differ from the first two sentences of the preceding section. Parallelism actually works well here, since it is both succinct and logical.

33. The author here incorrectly uses both "consequently" (there is nothing in the preceding sentence that would act as a predicate for a consequential analysis) and the "and" before "that," but these are the types of grammatical errors that tend to arise at the end of a timed essay. The gist of the argument—which is essentially a revisitation of the "A" analysis in light of new facts—makes sense.

34. Like the "C" statement in section 2, this sentence could be shorter and crisper, but it achieves its purpose, which is to identify the likely outcome of the dispute in light of the new facts.

D. Criminal Law Question

The next essay involves a criminal law question where statutory language is included as part of the prompt. This essay would likely fall in the top half of the class, largely because of the clarity with which the author lists the applicable legal rules. However, the author loses points by failing to put the legal authority in context. The author also does a good job in writing clearly and concisely, although there are some elements that could be improved upon. Nevertheless, this is a good example of how to use the IRAC method in situations where you have been given statutory language in the question prompt.

QUESTION

Claude was a horrible father and belittled his son, Brian, at every turn. Claude wasn't even proud of Brian for graduating from law school.

Brian wanted to exact some revenge on Claude and concocted a plan to steal Claude's most prized possession—his dog. On the night of the dog heist, Brian used a key his father had given him that allowed Brian to enter Claude's mansion through the basement door. Thinking the dog might be sleeping in Claude's room, Brian went upstairs and quietly entered Claude's bedroom. While tiptoeing across the floor, Brian saw a pistol resting on his father's dresser. Remembering how his father would never let him hold a gun, Brian defiantly picked up the pistol.

Suddenly, Li Wei, the butler, burst into the bedroom. Panicked, Brian fired five shots in quick succession. All five shots struck Li Wei, instantly killing him.

Discuss Brian's criminal liability for killing Li Wei, assuming that the jurisdiction in which Brian is found follows the common law approach to criminal law and includes the following statutes:

Murder defined

Murder is the unlawful killing of a human being with malice aforethought.

(a)   First degree murder: All murder which is perpetrated by means of a destructive device or explosive, poison, lying in wait, torture, or by any other kind of willful deliberate, and premeditated killing, is murder in the first degree.

(b)   Second degree murder: All murder that is not of the first degree is murder of the second degree.

Manslaughter defined

Manslaughter is the unlawful killing of a human being without malice.

(a)   Manslaughter is voluntary when it is committed upon a sudden quarrel or heat of passion.

(b)   Manslaughter is involuntary in the commission of an unlawful act, not amounting to felony; or in the commission of a lawful act which might produce death, in an unlawful manner, or without due caution and circumspection.

RESPONSE (paragraph one)

The primary issues here will be whether the killing constitutes a murder or manslaughter, and the degree of criminal liability.[1]

COMMENTS (paragraph one)

1. The author begins with a strong, straightforward presentation of the issue. In this case, the comma after "manslaughter" is discretionary. It is not absolutely necessary, but helps distinguish one sub-issue (whether the killing is murder or manslaughter) from a second sub-issue (what degree of murder or manslaughter exists).

RESPONSE (paragraph two)

First, the murder and manslaughter definitions adopted by the state represent the common law distinction between murder and manslaughter.[2] This rules out any potential use of the MPC in determining the liability of Brian in this killing.[3]

COMMENTS (paragraph two)

2. This sentence is largely unnecessary, since it simply restates information given in the exam question. While the author may have been trying to set the discussion in historical context, the effort was not successful. There are also minor issues of style. For example, the sentence begins by using the word "first," but the author never includes a "second" in the essay.

3. It is unclear what role this sentence plays. While it is true that this problem does not require application of the MPC (Model Penal Code), the question gave the applicable statute and the author is merely restating what the question already specified. The author also failed to define the MPC before using the abbreviation, which comes across as slightly unprofessional.

RESPONSE (paragraph three)

The common law provided four ways for the State to prove "malice aforethought" in order to obtain a conviction for murder: (1)An intentional killing (except those done in the heat of passion or with adequate provocation) (*State v. Guthrie* and *Giroud v. State*); (2) Performing an act with intent to inflict grievous bodily injury, and a killing results (*People v. Knoller*); (3) "depraved heart murder" (an extremely reckless act demonstrating wanton disregard for human life) (*Knoller*); or, (4) Felony murder (act with intent to commit a felony, and a killing occurs during the course of the felony) (*People v. Fuller*).[4]

COMMENTS (paragraph three)

4. Substantively this is a very strong sentence. Not only has the author provided a clear, condensed summary of the law, he or she has also provided a great deal of legal authority to support those assertions. Although it is unclear why the author is citing to *People v. Knoller*[3] for "grievous bodily injury," this kind of sweeping statement is allowable when describing a broad legal principle. Unfortunately, the author has not been as scrupulous about his or her writing style. Indeed, the sentence contains several glaring errors. For example, the author does not need to capitalize "state," nor does the author need to capitalize the first word after each enumerated definition of malice aforethought. Similarly, there are several spacing errors found in the numbered clauses. While a professor will not deduct points for these items, the author is not coming across as a cool, calm, and competent professional.

RESPONSE (paragraph four)

In order for a killing to constitute first degree murder, it must generally be an intentional, deliberate, and premeditated killing (unless the killing was perpetrated through one of the statutorily designated means) (*State v. Guthrie*).[5] A premeditated killing is one done after a period of time for prior consideration (*Guthrie*).[6] That period of time cannot be arbitrarily fixed, but instead is based on whether there was an interval of time of sufficient length, between the defendant forming an intent to kill and the execution of that intent, for the defendant to be fully conscious of his intentions (*Guthrie*).[7]

COMMENTS (paragraph four)

5. The author makes a nice transition into the "R" step, even if the text is a bit wordy. The phrase "first degree" should be hyphenated, since it is a compound adjective defining murder.

6. This sentence presents the rule for premeditation, which helps lay the groundwork for the third step in the IRAC analysis, the application.

7. Although the author has done well to include citations in this paragraph, it would be helpful to have more than just the case name. For example, the analysis would be much stronger if the author wrote: "The court in *State v. Guthrie*[4] ruled that premeditation and deliberation require 'some period' between the formation of the intent to kill and the actual killing." That approach would allow the author to introduce other cases indicating that "some period" could be no more than an instant of

---

[3]   *See* People v. Knoller, 158 P.3d 731 (Cal. 2007).

[4]   *See* State v. Guthrie, 461 S.E.2d 163 (W. Va. 1995).

reflection. Regardless, the author has identified a major case and stated its rule effectively.

RESPONSE (paragraph five)

In modern times, felony murder has often been subjected to a number of limitations.[8] These include the "inherently dangerous felony" limitation, which often requires that the underlying felony be one that is committed in an inherently dangerous manner, or that it be impossible to commit it in a completely safe manner (*People v. Howard*).[9] The "merger doctrine" limitation applies when a killing is an integral part of the underlying felony (*People v. Smith*).[10] The "killing by a non-felon" limitation ruled out any killing caused by a non-felon from being attributed to those committing the underlying felony (*Commonwealth v. Redline*).[11] Finally, the "in furtherance" doctrine requires that for a killing to constitute felony murder, the killing must occur during the attempt to commit the felony, the commission of the felony, or during the flight from the felony (*Commonwealth v. Redline*).[12]

COMMENTS (paragraph five)

8.   This sentence act as a good transition into a more nuanced discussion of felony murder.

9.   In this paragraph, the author is demonstrating a great facility with the case law in this area of law. Unfortunately, the author is not maximizing those references by putting them in context. A simple parenthetical following each case name would likely bring this essay up to one of the top scoring responses in the class.

10.   Here, a parenthetical would allow the author to better describe the merger doctrine. As it stands, the reference to the merger doctrine is so general that it is hard to tell whether the author truly understands the principles involved.

> **WRITING**
> A parenthetical is more than a memorized case holding. Instead, a parenthetical demonstrates why the case is relevant to this discussion.

11.   The author slips into writing in the past tense, which conflicts with the earlier discussion detailing the limitations of the felony murder rule, which was in the present tense. Although the essay will not be marked down for this kind of minor error, wise authors avoid these kinds of mistakes so as to look as professional as possible.

12.   This is an excellent statement of the law. However, the author might think about whether it would make more sense to include this rule as part of the definition of felony murder rather than defining it as a limitation. In these sentences, the author does an excellent job of using terms of art.

RESPONSE (paragraph six)

In order for a killing to constitute voluntary manslaughter, it must be done in a heat of passion, resulting from adequate provocation (*Giroud v. State*).[13] In order for provocation to be "adequate," it must be "calculated to inflame the passion of a reasonable man and tend to cause him to act for the moment from passion rather than reason" (*Giroud*).[14]

COMMENTS (paragraph six)

13.   A citation to authority is actually not necessary here, since the given statute defines voluntary manslaughter. However, "more is more" when it comes to legal authorities. Although the author misspells the case name (it should be *Girouard*, not *Giroud*),[5] the reference is clear enough for a timed in-class exam scenario. In a take-home essay, you must be sure to spell case names correctly.

14.   The specificity of this sentence is outstanding. Quoting judicial language and providing a source citation is precisely what you want to do to earn a top grade.

RESPONSE (paragraph seven)

Brian first shot Li Wei the butler moments after picking up the gun, in response to Li Wei rushing into the bedroom (presumably recognizing the sound of an intruder).[15] Brian shot Li Wei repeatedly, in a panicked state.[16] While this panicked state might indicate to some that Brian was firing the gun in a "heat of passion" resulting from the adequate provocation that was Li Wei rushing into the room and surprising him, the reality is that this case falls distinctly within the category of murder.[17] Malice aforethought may be proven by the state if the state can prove that the killing occurred during the course of a felony.[18] Here, Brian was still in the middle of a burglary.[19] He entered the home illegally for the purpose of stealing Claude's dog, and was still in the process of completing that act.[20] Burglary would generally be considered an inherently dangerous felony, in that it involves unlawful entry into a building.[21] There is a strong possibility that injuries to the building's occupants may result, including the high possibility of death due to the occupants defending the building.[22] Thus, this killing was a killing with malice aforethought.[23]

COMMENTS (paragraph seven)

15.   While the author has a decent handle on the law, the application section is a bit problematic, particularly with respect to organization. For example, the author begins by simply restating a fact without tying it to any of the legal authority discussed previously. The author also appears to overlook issues relating to premeditation and deliberation, although

---

     [5]   *See* Girouard v. State, 583 A.2d 718 (Md. 1991).

the discussion fortunately reverts to those points later. As a general rule, the application analysis should follow the order of the rules analysis. A number of other problems arise as a matter of style. For example, the author should put commas around "the butler," since that is a descriptive phrase. The author should also delete the parenthetical information, since at this point the reader does not know whether the phrase refers to Li Wei or Brian.

16. This sentence is unnecessary, since it simply restates a fact without applying any analysis.

17. The author is correct that the fact pattern does not likely present an example of voluntary manslaughter. However, the statement here is rather conclusory and therefore unpersuasive. The better approach would be to link the application of the facts to the law introduced in the "R" step. While the author may be correct, he or she has missed an opportunity to demonstrate legal judgment and discretion. As always, it's what's on the page, not what's in your mind that wins you points.

18. Here, the author has turned to a new topic, namely felony murder. As a result, the author should have started a new paragraph.

19. This sentence is very good structurally, since it quickly and correctly calls the burglary to the reader's attention. Although the sentence simply restates a fact that was in the question, the sentence implicitly refers to the rule identified in the previous sentence and therefore is understood as part of a several step-long analysis rather than the simple recitation of a random fact.

20. The author presumes that Brian committed burglary without giving any explanation or analysis. While Brian likely committed burglary, a professor—like a judge—would want to know how Brian (who entered using a key given to him by his father) committed a felony. The author could also note that if Brian was not in the process of committing burglary, then the proper charge would be involuntary manslaughter rather than felony murder. Stylistically, the author should remove the comma before the word "and," since the following clause is dependent rather than independent.

21. Here, the author is correct in suggesting that "[b]urglary would generally be considered an inherently dangerous felony." The author also does well to tie the facts explicitly to the law by using "inherently dangerous" as a legal term of art.

22. This sentence provides a good policy rationale for why burglary is considered a predicate felony for felony murder. The author wisely does not go any further in his or her policy discussion because there is no question about whether burglary constitutes an inherently dangerous felony.

23.   This sentence constitutes a strong, direct conclusion for the first portion of the essay.

RESPONSE (paragraph eight)

Brian could be said to have acted on reflex.[24] Li Wei rushed in, Brian felt threatened, and he instinctively shot.[25] It seems apparent in this case that Brian did not have the necessary space of time for his killing of Li Wei to be considered deliberate and premeditated.[26] He did not likely fully recognize his intentions or their consequences at the moment he pulled the trigger.[27] Therefore, this killing would properly be considered second degree murder.[28]

COMMENTS (paragraph eight)

24.   This paragraph demonstrates a number of structural problems. For example, this sentence appears to focus on whether Brian committed first- or second-degree murder, although the absence of a transition makes the author's meaning somewhat unclear. Furthermore, placing this discussion here makes little sense because the author has already concluded that Brian committed a felony murder, which constitutes second-degree murder under the statute provided in the question. As a general rule, this author would do well to have the application analysis follow the organization of the rules section, since the current structure is somewhat unclear. On a stylistic level, the phrase "could be said to have" is a bit wordy.

25.   The current sentence is a run-on, which means the author needs to place either a period or a semicolon after "Li Wei rushed in."

26.   Students (and lawyers) should avoid phrases like "[i]t seems apparent in this case," since such terms are unnecessarily wordy. Furthermore, this type of language (which may be an attempt to sound "lawyerly") makes the author appear unsure about the substance of his or her argument.

27.   The author's factual analysis is extremely strong but could be improved if the author tied the facts under discussion to the authority cited previously.

28.   The author here provides a clear conclusion for his or her analysis, which is great.

RESPONSE (paragraph nine)

Brian will be found guilty for second degree murder for the shooting death of Li Wei, because the death occurred during the commission of an inherently dangerous felony (burglary), and because the death was not committed as the result of deliberation and premeditation.[29]

COMMENTS (paragraph nine)

29.   Although the last sentence of the previous paragraph could be read as a conclusion for the second issue, the author here does an excellent job in pulling all the elements together in a single concise statement. This is an excellent way to end an essay.

This is a solid essay with some good case law. Although the strong analysis and competent use of authority will likely result in an above-average grade, the author should think about introducing more and more diverse sources so as to win more points. For example, the author might look for sub-issues involving conflicting lines of case law, since that is the best way to demonstrate a sophisticated understanding of the law. By only introducing one authority per proposition, the author misses the opportunity to discuss the fine nuances of law. When conducting this sort of analysis, it is important to link each of the cases to each other rather than just listing them seriatim; while you may know why you are naming each of these cases in this order, you must explain your rationale to your readers.

This author has done a good job of implementing a strict IRAC analysis, with separate sections regarding the rules and the application. However, the essay struggles to integrate the "R" and "A" steps. In the application analysis, an author needs to explain how the facts fit under the relevant legal standard rather than simply concluding that a particular fact leads to a particular outcome.

Sometimes students think the written word has to be formal or elevated. If you're having trouble expressing yourself, try explaining your point out loud and write down what you said. Usually you'll make your point simply and concisely when you speak.

The author could also work to improve his or her use of language. Although law professors understand that timed essays will likely have a number of minor errors, too many grammatical flaws can confuse the reader. This author obviously knows what he or she is trying to say, but that knowledge doesn't always make it onto the paper. Keeping the sentence structure simple and straightforward would serve the author better than longer, more complex sentences. Remember, persuasion involves both substance and style. You want to give the impression that you are cool, calm, collected, and capable. Appearing rushed and harried destroys the vision of you as a competent lawyer and is thus counterproductive.

E. Contract Law Question

Many students find the IRAC technique to be particularly challenging in questions involving contract law, since the concept of a cause of action is not the same as it is in tort or criminal law. Instead, when a litigator goes into court seeking to address a contract-oriented dispute, he or she is seeking either to (1) establish the existence of a contractual or quasi-contractual obligation, in which case the elements of the cause of action are the elements necessary to create a contract or quasi-contract, and/or (2) establish the breach or performance of a contractual or quasi-contractual obligation, in which case the elements of the cause of action are those necessary to establish the underlying obligation (an issue that you will dispose of quickly) and, most importantly, the standards necessary to establish breach or performance. Students answering contract questions also often need to consider the existence of relevant defenses and the calculation of damages if a breach does occur. Therefore, the "issue" from an IRAC perspective would either be whether a contract existed or whether a breach occurred, with sub-issues involving elements associated with the creation, performance and/or breach of a contract and possibly elements associated with defenses or damages. As with other types of IRAC essays, you should not seek to give a comprehensive analysis of every feature of contract law in a contract question; focus instead on what is most contentious.

TIP

Contract questions often require a few adaptations to the standard IRAC structure.

TIP

If your professor gives you special suggestions on how to approach an exam question, use them. Often the professor's approach can be combined with an IRAC analysis, as was done here with great success.

The following essay uses a modified IRAC approach that incorporates a strategy for analysis provided by the author's contracts professor.[6]

---

[6]   This student's contracts professor suggested that students approach contracts questions using the following framework:

(1)   Does this dispute fall under the Uniform Commercial Code, the common law or both?

(2)   Does the Statute of Frauds apply? If the answer is yes, then does a writing exist sufficient to satisfy the Statute of Frauds or does an exception exist to avoid application of the Statute of Frauds?

(3)   Once the Statute of Frauds issue has been addressed, is there a contract? If the answer is no, then is there another means for enforcing the promise?

(4)   If there is a contract, what are the terms?

(5)   If there is a contract, was there a breach?

Notably, this analytical technique was developed for the first half of a year-long course and therefore does not address certain elements (such as excuses or defenses to non-performance and damages associated with breach) that would

Although the essay does not follow a strict IRAC in all respects, the author incorporated IRAC into the contracts professor's analytical framework. As a result, the structure uses more of an IRACIRACIRAC approach (meaning several independent IRAC analyses on individual topics) than a strict IRAC structure. Although the adaptations are not fatal to the essay, the failure to adopt a singular IRAC approach means that the essay as a whole does not have a single overarching "I" or "C" statement, which is potentially problematic as a matter of both style and substance. Those flaws can be easily corrected, though.

This author wrote the essay halfway through a year-long contract course, which explains why certain issues (most notably, damages) are not addressed. Nevertheless, the essay manages to pack a considerable amount of content into a very small space, something that stands as a testament to the author's ability to be both concise and precise. These elements, combined with a strong, well-organized structure and a writing style that is almost entirely free of typos and grammatical errors, makes for a very persuasive and professional analysis.

The one area where the author could have improved was in the use of supporting authorities. Although the author did specifically cite the Restatement and one case, the rest of the legal authority came from relatively broad references to the common law and the Uniform Commercial Code (UCC). While much if not all of what the author says is true as a matter of law, the absence of specific authorities might have precluded sophisticated analysis of legal concepts and could put the author at a competitive disadvantage if other students in class manage to cite more authority in their essays. That would be unfortunate, since the author's overall grasp of legal principles seems quite good.

QUESTION

Two years ago, Phillip Prince bought a luxury beach house in an area prone to hurricanes. Prince hoped to use the home as a vacation getaway after his retirement. However, Prince knew that the region was experiencing a rising number of catastrophic storms capable of destroying entire beachfront communities and decided to retrofit the house to be able to endure "hundred-year storms," meaning those that come just once in a century.

Prince hired Eco-Builder Inc. to do the retrofitting, telling Ace, one of Eco-Builder's employees, that Eco-Builder should do "whatever they think is necessary" to make his home "properly equipped for future storms." Ace said, "No problem. You can rely on us to do the job right."

---

otherwise be relevant. Furthermore, other professors may have other suggestions regarding how students should approach contracts questions. This flow chart is provided only so that readers can see how the author incorporated the IRAC technique into his or her professor's individual suggestions.

Prince told Ace that he had to get back to his permanent home in London for a few months to finish up his duties with the firm, but Ace should "just do what you think is best, and I'll pay you $1.5 million when I get back." The parties did not memorialize their understanding in a written contract.

Eco-Builder decided to add premium siding, steel enforced shutters and a "breathable" roof that had been tested to withstand the extremely high wind gusts and variable air pressure associated with the most violent hurricanes that the region had experienced in the last fifty years, which was the longest period of time for which reliable data was available. Eco-Builder worked diligently to get the retrofit done before the onset of hurricane season, but they were shocked when Hurricane Elizabeth, a storm of unimaginable size, began building earlier than expected. Ace received a call from Prince, who said, "If you don't have the retrofit done by the time Hurricane Elizabeth arrives, I not only won't pay you the $1.5 million, I will sue you for any damage to the house, since I could have gotten another company to do this job properly if you hadn't promised me you could do it."

Eco-Builder called in additional workers at immense cost (since most workers were planning to evacuate with their families) and managed to complete the planned work before Hurricane Elizabeth made landfall only 100 miles to the south of Prince's house. According to Eco-Builder and its workers, who had to shelter in the house during the storm, the house was completely finished before the storm hit. However, Prince was not able to make an inspection of the property at that time, given that he was in London. Eco-Builder tried to provide Prince with a "virtual inspection tour" via property webcams, but the storm knocked out the internet connections in the region.

Unfortunately, Hurricane Elizabeth was not just a hundred-year storm, but a five-hundred-year storm, destroying the beachfront community where Prince's house was located. Although Prince's house was one of the few to remain standing due to Eco-Builder's modifications, part of the roof came off in the high winds, which led to the destruction and damage of valuable antiques in the affected part of the house.

Prince refused to pay Eco-Builder and instead brought an action for breach of contract, seeking declaratory action that he is not liable for the $1.5 million and claiming damages associated with amount needed to repair the roof and damages associated with the destruction and damage to the antiques in the affected part of the house. Eco-Builder brought a counterclaim for $1.5 million in fees and for the actual costs associated with hiring the extra workers.

What rights and remedies does Prince have (if any) against Eco-Builder? Be sure to consider Prince's possible claim(s), as well as any excuse(s), defense(s), and/or counterclaim(s) Eco-Builder may have against Prince.

RESPONSE (paragraph one)

UCC or Common Law[1]

The first issue is what law applies; UCC or common law (CL).[2] The UCC governs the sale of goods, and goods are defined as anything movable at the time of contracting.[3] The CL governs services and all other contracts.[4] Here, the predominant purpose of the contract (K) between P and D is for a service.[5] Here, P has hired D's company to retrofit P's vacation home, which is a service. Additionally, here D's company supplied materials with their service (steel enforced shutters and a "breakable" roof) which are movable goods and therefore governed by the UCC.[6] Thus, a court could find this agreement to be governed by the UCC or the CL. However, I conclude that the predominate purpose of the contract between P and D is for a service, and therefore governed by the CL.[7]

COMMENTS (paragraph one)

1.   The essay uses internal headers, which is useful to understand the structure, and tracks the analytical framework provided by the author's contracts professor, as noted in footnote 6. However, the essay would have been strengthened by a short IRAC paragraph identifying the cause of action—i.e., the establishment of a contract/quasi-contractual obligation and/or the breach or performance of that obligation. Readers— like judges—need context, even if they are the professor who set the question, since there is never any guarantee an essay will proceed in the way that the professor intended.

2.   This a good, clear issue statement with a defined term. It would be best to define UCC (Uniform Commercial Code) as well. The professor will know what the term means, but you want to show that you do, too.

3.   Although the author does not cite a section of the UCC, the standard is clear and precise. If the author wants to win more points, he or she should cite the precise section of the UCC. However, if this is a closed-book exam, that type of detail may not be possible.

4.   The author did well to distinguish the scope of the common law as compared to the UCC. Too often, students only discuss one of two options and miss out on extra points.

5.   It would be helpful if the author defined what that service was in three to four words, perhaps by combining this sentence with the next. Doing so would avoid the second "here," which is unnecessary. However, the author's use of short, direct sentences are both clear and concise, so changes to the writing style should be adopted with caution.

"P" and "D" should be defined, and it is usually better to use parties' names than their procedural status.

6.   The author could usefully omit the word "here," which is repetitive, and should use "its" rather than "their" to refer to the singular "company." The "which" clause is also misplaced (it currently refers to "service"), but these types of errors arise in timed essays, where the opportunity to proofread is often limited.

7.   The author does well to come to a preliminary conclusion, but should consider whether to analyze the problem under the UCC as well, in case he or she is wrong. This is particularly true since some aspects of the contract could be governed by one law and other aspects of the contract governed by another.

RESPONSE (paragraph two)

Statute of Frauds

The next issue is whether this contract is the type of contract that is required to be in writing, and therefore governed by the Statute of Frauds (SOF).[8] The SOF applies to the transfer of real property interests, contracts (Ks) governed by the UCC for $500 or more, Ks that by their terms cannot be performed in one year, Ks for consideration of marriage, and suretyship Ks.[9] Here, the agreement between P and D does not fit into any of the SOF categories and is therefore not required to be in writing.[10] If this case is governed by the UCC, D could argue that the SOF does apply because the agreement was for $1.5 million, which is over $500.[11] However, the court is most likely to find the SOF does not apply here.[12] Thus, P may still have a claim even though the K was not in writing.[13]

COMMENTS (paragraph two)

8.   The comma in this sentence is incorrect. Commas are not needed before "and" when combining two dependent clauses. Only in sequences of three or more dependent clauses does the "Oxford comma" arise. Commas are correct between two independent clauses joined by "and," but the author's second clause is not independent (i.e., is not a sentence that could stand on its own).

9.   Because this is an "R" statement, it would be useful to have legal authority in support, particularly given the later sentence distinguishing how the UCC and common law approach statute of fraud issues. The sentence is also slightly inelegant, in that the structure of the last item does not parallel the others, but this is a small stylistic error.

10.   This is a good, clear conclusory sentence, but somewhat premature, given the next sentence.

11. This is an "R" statement that should be combined with the earlier statement regarding the types of matters that fall within the statute of frauds. Since the author concluded earlier that the UCC applied to this matter, this provision seems very important. The author appears worried that concluding that the requirement of a writing would cut off further analysis, and that is an appropriate concern. Rather than muddying the UCC analysis, as the author does here by noting a clearly applicable provision of the UCC and then concluding, in the next sentence, that the court would simply ignore that provision, the author could carry on with a common law analysis by noting that the common law might apply to some aspects of the contract or simply saying that the subsequent analysis is being made in case the UCC does not apply.

12. As noted in the previous common, this is an odd conclusion not borne out by the law and facts identified by the author. You must be willing to live by the outcomes dictated by your reasonable analysis; not every attractive plaintiff wins in law exams or in real life.

13. Because this author has only completed half of the year-long contract exam, he or she is missing some doctrine that could help with this analysis. However, the author is doing right by continuing to discuss relevant issues in case the UCC analysis is not entirely dispositive of the dispute.

RESPONSE (paragraph three)

Is there a valid K

A valid K requires an offer, acceptance, and consideration or some type of substitute.[14] Based on the facts, a court could find that P and D have an enforceable K.[15]

COMMENTS (paragraph three)

14. This is a clear "R" statement, though it would be stronger with some supporting authority.

15. This statement is entirely conclusory, meaning it jumps straight to the "C" without going through the "A" portion of the analysis. It may be that the author is attempting to conduct a CIRAC approach, where the conclusion appears before the IRAC analysis, but that does not seem necessary. Instead, the author should move straight from the previous sentence to the sentence defining an offer.

RESPONSE (paragraph four)

Offer

The issue now is whether there is a sufficient offer.[16] An offer must be clear, definite and explicit, containing all the essential elements of the deal.[17] Additionally, an offer must be communicated to the offeree who must have a manifestation of willingness to enter an agreement.[18] An offer must also be reasonable for the other side to accept.[19] Under the CL, all essential terms (parties, subject, price, and quantity) need to be detailed in order to constitute an offer.[20] The UCC is less strict however, and usually only requires the quantity to be stated.[21] Here, the parties of this agreement are clearly communicated and agreed upon; P and D's company.[22] Additionally, here P told D's employee that D should do "whatever they think is necessary" to make the home "properly equipped for future storms."[23] P could argue that this statement detailed the subject of the K; modifications to P's vacation home.[24] However, D could argue that these terms are vague and not specific. Additionally, P told D that he would be at his permanent home for a few months and they would be paid upon his return.[25] P could argue that this informed D how long he had to complete the job. However D could argue that the statement is not specific enough because a "few months" is also very vague.[26] P told D that he would pay them $1.5 million when he returned. Here, P could argue that this term is clear and explicit, however price alone is not sufficient enough to constitute an offer under the UCC or the CL.[27] Thus, when P hired D to do the retrofitting, the offer was not sufficient [28]

COMMENTS (paragraph four)

16. The author here is trying to set up the next item for discussion by calling it an issue, but the essay would be tighter if this and the preceding sentence were deleted.

17. This is a good, clear "R" statement. However, it would be strengthened by some supporting authority.

18. Again, this shows a good clear explication of the legal rule. The word "additionally" could probably be struck, and the persuasiveness would be strengthened by supporting authority, but the author clearly knows the topic well and is using legal terms precisely and concisely.

19. This statement is somewhat unclear, in that it seems to suggest that parties can only enter into reasonable contracts, when in fact they can enter into unreasonable ones as well.

20. This is a good list of the elements that must be contained in a common law offer, although use of the word "detailed" is a little confusing, in that it suggests a degree of completeness that is not further defined in this essay. This is a minor point, though. While the author deserves points for noting that this rule comes from the common law, citing specific cases, either by name or general description, would win additional points.

21. It is good to compare the common law and UCC, although the term "usually" needs to be further explained.

22. This sentence is a bit confusing—it seems a word or phrase is left out or incorrectly included. Since this constitutes the "A" section, the author should also start a new paragraph.

23. This is good detail to support the "A" analysis, although the author should indicate how these facts meet the necessary legal standards; at this point, this is a bit of a submarine argument. The "additionally" is unclear and unnecessary, though that's a minor point.

24. This sentence, which is for the most part clear and concise, would be grammatically correct if the semicolon were changed to a colon.

25. The "they" is unclear in this context; the author should just repeat D or D's name.

26. There needs to be a comma after "However."

27. This is a run-on sentence.

28. It might be better to say "technically insufficient," since the lack of sufficiency was not fatal to the creation of a contractual relationship. However, the author does a good job in concluding the analysis of the offer.

RESPONSE (paragraph five)

Acceptance[29]

Although the offer was arguably insufficient, there is still an issue of whether D accepted P's offer.[30] Section 50 of the Second Restatement defines acceptance as manifestation of assent to the offer.[31] Additionally, Section 45 defines acceptance by performance and an offer becomes irrevocable once performance begins.[32] Here, when told D to do "whatever to make the home properly equipped for future storms," D replied and told P that he could "rely on [them] to do the job right."[33] P could argue that this statement is evidence of D's acceptance of the retrofitting job.[34] Additionally, D accepted P's offer when they began the work of the retrofit, adding premium siding, steel enforced shutters, and a breakable roof.[35]

COMMENTS (paragraph five)

29. The headers for offer, acceptance and consideration are perhaps not necessary, since the topic sentences of each section clearly identify where the reader is in the analysis, but the author is to be commended for his or her clarity.

30. This is a very clear transition statement. The author identifies the analysis as an "issue," though it's probably better termed a sub-issue or simply as one of the constituent elements of the relevant legal standard,

but the precise nomenclature is not important. What is useful is the clarity of the structure of the essay.

31. The author does very well in identifying a particular source of authority. It would probably be better to say "an offer" rather than "the offer," since we're talking about generalities rather than specifics at this point, but that is very minor correction.

32. Again, excellent reliance on specific authority; that type of detail is the gold standard in "R" analyses. The sentence has a few problems grammatically—it would likely be better to say "and <u>indicates</u> an offer"—but the sentiment is clear enough for a timed essay.

33. Good, clear citation to the facts makes for a strong "A" section. Here there is a word missing ("P" should be before the first "told"), but that is a small error.

34. The author does well to tie the facts to the law—that is the essence of the "A" analysis. You cannot assume that the reader will understand what you mean if you just list certain facts; you have to explicitly show the connection, as the author does here.

35. This concept of acceptance by performance might be improved by a reference back to section 45 of the Restatement. All the elements are there, but tying them together shows the reader that the author fully appreciates the importance of the performance aspect of the facts.

RESPONSE (paragraph six)

<u>Consideration</u>

The issue now is whether the agreement between P and D was supported by consideration.[36] All Ks have to be supported by consideration.[37] Under Sec. 71, consideration is defined as a bargained-for exchange.[38] Consideration is also defined as a benefit conferred or a legal right forfeited due to the inducement of a promise (Hamer v Sidway).[39] Inducement to the promisor is one of the keys to consideration and it's measured by the reasonable person standard.[40] Inducement consists of an act other than a promise (including money) and a promise to pay is sufficient.[41] Here, P told D that he would pay D's company $1.5 million for its service once he returned. Because this is a promise to pay, D could argue that this statement constitutes consideration.[42] Therefore, this agreement was supported by consideration.[43]

COMMENTS (paragraph six)

36. Again, the author uses the word "issue" even if consideration would be better framed as an element necessary to creation of a contract, but the terminology is not important. Structurally, this topic sentence

moves us to the next section of the analysis, which helps keep the discussion clear and concise.

37.   This statement is true and will win points, but would win more points if it included a particular source of authority.

38.   The author likely means section 71 of the Restatement, but he or she should say so to avoid confusion. Also, it would be better grammatically not to abbreviate "section" within a sentence. An abbreviation can be used in a citation, however.

39.   This is the first passive sentence structure used in the essay, so is not necessarily problematic, although a more active structure would be slightly better. The author does very well to include a case citation to support the statement and does an excellent job in using precise, legal language in the definition. This type of attention to detail goes a long way toward showing not just familiarity but mastery of the course materials, which is what you want to do.

40.   The term "keys to consideration" is a little vague and could be tightened up. Grammatically, a comma needs to be inserted before "and," since these two clauses are independent, and the contraction "it's" should be replaced with "it is." Some more detail on the reasonable person standard would be also useful.

41.   This sentence is a little vague and confusing, particularly with respect to the link between an act that is not a promise and a promise to pay. Again, the sentence needs a comma before "and," since the clauses are independent.

42.   The author does a good job in linking the relevant facts, which are briefly identified, to the relevant legal standard. That is the essence of a good "A" section.

43.   This is a good "C" statement with respect to the sub-issue of consideration.

RESPONSE (paragraph seven)

Terms of K / Modifications[44]

COMMENTS (paragraph seven)

44.   It is unclear whether the author skipped this section because of a lack of time or because of a lack of material (this essay was written halfway through a year-long course). If time was a concern, it is better to draft something in very short outline form to try to get a few points, even if a full analysis is not possible. Leaving a section entirely blank results in zero points, whereas an attempt—even an incomplete attempt—will earn something.

RESPONSE (paragraph eight)

Breach

The final issue is whether there is a breach in the agreement between P and D.[45] A breach occurs when either party fails to uphold their part of the K.[46] Under the CL, poor performance constitutes a contract, but it is also a breach.[47] The terms of the K define the duties of each party, which the court uses to determine whether there has been a breach.[48] Although the terms of this K are arguably vague, a reasonable person would conclude that D breached the K if P's vacation home was destroyed by a violent hurricane similar to what the region had experienced in years before.[49] Here, because P's home was damaged by an unforeseeable hurricane with an unimaginable size, D could argue they did not breach the K.[50]

COMMENTS (paragraph eight)

45.   This sentence is a little bit clumsy, although that is normal in a timed essay. The sentence serves its purpose, which is to switch the analysis to the question of breach.

46.   This is a clear definition of breach, which could only be improved by inclusion of a citation.

47.   Although this sentence is not as "legalistic" as others, it serves its purpose and usefully identifies the body of law that generated the legal standard.

48.   This is another good means of clarifying how breach is determined, even if the language is not extremely legalistic.

49.   The author here brings some legal terms relating to as the reasonable person standard to bear on the facts of the case, but is not quite as precise as in earlier "A" sections, likely because of time restrictions. There also may be additional law that could be used to further define reasonableness in this particular situation.

50.   The author correctly identifies the key fact, which is that this storm exceeded the standards identified in the contract, thereby eliminating the possibility of breach.

Although the essay contains various interim conclusions, there is no single "C" statement indicating whether the plaintiff or the defendant prevails. The author needs to include that sort of statement to win full points.

F. Estates and Trusts Question One

The previous samples all focused on subjects that are covered in the first year of most law school programs. However, it is helpful to include essays from upper-level courses as well.

Following is the first of two estates and trusts questions and responses. The first essay was written in the style of a timed, closed-book examination and provides an excellent example of the IRAC system at work. Although this essay does not cite many cases or statutes by name (there is only one named case and general references to the common law or statutory approach), the apparent absence of legal authority is somewhat acceptable here because estates and trusts law involves numerous detailed statutes that cannot be memorized for a closed-book exam. Furthermore, the author provides detailed analysis of several different approaches to the question at issue and therefore demonstrates a comprehensive knowledge of the law in this field.

This essay is remarkable for the clarity of its structure, even though the author does not specifically indicate which step of the IRAC analysis is underway. Instead, the author simply provides the substance of each aspect of the IRAC methodology, using clear, concise language. Each word and each thought counts. Though a few additional points or authorities might have been added if there was sufficient time, this essay has addressed all the major substantive points and would rank among the top in the class.

This essay also shows how an author can gain credibility through good writing. There are no typographical or spelling errors and only a very few grammatical errors. Although professors do not take points off for these types of mistakes, particularly in timed examinations, an essay that is full of spelling, proofreading, and similar errors does not look as polished as an essay that does not have those types of mistakes. This essay gives off an aura of calm, cool professionalism that gives the reader confidence in the author's abilities. Law is a field that relies heavily on persuasion, and students should avoid doing anything that will make their essays look frantic or labored in the eyes of the reader. Furthermore, the author is able to maintain good writing all the way through the essay, even though he or she was likely pressed for time by that point.

QUESTION

Ted the Testator has many children and wishes to benefit them at his death. His family tree is constructed as follows:

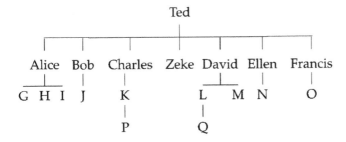

Alice, Bob, Charles and Zeke are Ted's natural (biological) children, whom he had with his first wife, now deceased. Alice has three children—G, H and I. Bob has one child—J. Charles has one child—K—and one grandchild—P. Zeke has no children.

David is the natural child of Ted's second wife, now deceased. Ted adopted David when David was ten years old. David has two children—L and M—and one grandchild—Q, who is L's child.

Ellen and Francis are the natural children of Ted's third wife, now deceased. Ted did not adopt Ellen or Francis. Ellen has one child—N—and Francis has one child—O.

Ted has created a will that states:

> I, Ted Testator, put the entirety of my estate into trust for my son, Zeke, who is developmentally disabled. After Zeke's death, the corpus of the trust should be distributed to my issue.

At the time of Zeke's death, Alice, Charles, David and Ellen, G and M had passed away. How should the residuary be distributed and why? Consider all possible alternatives.

Would your answer change if Bob and his wife were expecting another child at the time of Zeke's death? What about if Charles's widow was expecting another child at the time of Zeke's death?

RESPONSE (paragraph one)

Ted's will states that after Zeke's death, the corpus should be distributed to his "issue." Thus, the first matter to be determined is whether Ted's adopted son, David, is considered his issue.[1] The common law approach to adoption is that adopted children do not have the right to inherit from their adoptive parents.[2] Therefore, under this approach, because David was adopted by Ted, he and his children would not be permitted to inherit from Ted's estate.[3] However, under the modern majority approach, legally adopted children are permitted to inherit from their adoptive parents.[4] As a result, under the majority approach, David would be entitled to the same share of Ted's estate as Ted's natural born children.[5] Since David predeceased Zeke, his living child, L would be entitled to his entire share.[6]

COMMENTS (paragraph one)

1. Although the author does not use the traditional IRAC formula of "The issue in this case is . . . ," the result is the same. This approach is somewhat risky to the extent that it does not give the reader immediate confidence in the author's ability to progress logically through all of the relevant issues, but that fear will quickly be put to rest. However, it might be useful for the author to indicate that this question raises a number of issues, each of which will be addressed in turn. Furthermore, it would be useful early on to indicate why the author is considering various rules of intestacy when there is a will in place. Normally, rules of intestacy only apply if there is no will. However, many jurisdictions define the word "issue" by reference to the intestacy statutes, even when the word is used in a will. The author could have won more points by mentioning that element and citing any cases or statutes that included that rule.

2. This statement of the relevant rule could be improved upon by a citation to one or more cases. However, the course book used by this student did occasionally make these types of grand, sweeping statements, so the author cannot be faulted for doing the same.

3. This sentence contains both the "A" and the "C" step of the IRAC method. However, the analysis is so simple that no further discussion is necessary.

4. Here, the author is providing the alternate rule in these types of scenarios. Again, it would have been useful to cite some legal authority, but this type of sweeping statement was typical of the teaching materials used in the class, so the student is doing the best he or she can given the authorities available.

5. Again, this sentence contains both the "A" and the "C" step, which is acceptable in the circumstances.

6. This sentence contains an implicit reference to another rule in trusts and estates law, namely the rule that a person does not take through intestacy if that person's ancestor (i.e., the person through whom the prospective taker would inherit) is still alive. A minor improvement would have been to mention that rule explicitly, but the prose is straightforward enough that the author's meaning is clear. Remarkably, this one sentence manages to include the rule, the application, and the conclusion, which shows exceptional writing talent. Note that this last sentence is necessary to fully answer the question of who would take under the will.

RESPONSE (paragraph two)

Next, it must be determined whether Ellen and Francis are considered Ted's issue.[7] In the absence of a legal adoption, most states do not give stepchildren a right to inherit from stepparents. However, some states recognize "equitable adoption." The broad rule only requires a "close familial relationship" in order to acquire an equitable adoption.[8] The narrow rule, as seen in *Bean v. Ford*, requires a "strong familial relationship and clear and convincing evidence indicating that there was a legal barrier to adoption".[9] In this fact pattern, Ellen and Francis are the natural children of Ted's third wife but they were never legally adopted.[10] Therefore, we would need more facts to determine whether or not Ellen and Francis are considered to be equitably adopted. Without any further facts and considering that most states do not give stepchildren a right to inherit from stepparents, it can be assumed that Ellen and Francis (and their children) are not entitled to inherit a share of Ted's estate.[11]

COMMENTS (paragraph two)

7.   Again, the author does not explicitly say that this is a sub-issue, but the author's use of the IRAC structure is already becoming clear.

8.   These three sentences provide a very general description of the relevant rule. Although this statement is sufficient, it could be improved upon through a reference to a particular statute or case. However, the lack of detail is understandable, given the nature of a closed-book exam.

9.   This is an excellent statement of the law relating to the narrow rule of equitable adoption. To be able to quote a line from a relevant case not only demonstrates significant preparation, it also suggests that the author understands how to parse out the key language from a judicial opinion. Furthermore, the author shows good judgment in not going into great detail about the facts in *Bean v. Ford*, since the case is relevant, but not central, to the analysis of the underlying question, which has to do with the distribution of the estate. If the author had spent more time detailing everything that he or she knew about *Bean v. Ford*, there would not have been enough time to address the other issues in the question. This is an excellent example of time management.

10.   This sentence identifies the relevant facts and applies them to the rule previously identified in this paragraph. Notice how succinct this factual analysis is.

11.   These two sentences identify what further information might be useful in this analysis but do not include detailed hypothesizing about what would happen if a particular factual scenario were true. The author here does an excellent job of demonstrating the limitations on further analysis and coming to a firm conclusion on the facts provided.

RESPONSE (paragraph three)

The next matter to be determined is how the residuary of the estate should be distributed to Ted's issue.[12] According to the Strict Per Stirpes approach, the decedent's estate is distributed to the first generation of his lineage, regardless of whether any of the children are living. If the descendant closest in lineage is dead, then the interest is proportionally shared by their next descendent(s).[13] Applying this approach to this fact pattern, Ted's estate would be distributed to the first generation.[14] Therefore, the estate would be split evenly between Alice, Bob, Charles, and David and each would receive one-fourth of the estate.[15] However, because Alice is deceased, her living children H and I would proportionally split her share (one-half of one-fourth so one-eighth). Because Charles is deceased, his living child, K would receive his entire share and K's child, P would receive nothing because children of takers are not entitled to take. Because David is deceased, his living child, L would receive his entire share and L's child, Q would receive nothing. M would not be entitled to take because she predeceased Zeke and had no issue.[16]

COMMENTS (paragraph three)

12. The author here is moving on from an analysis of various preliminary issues (i.e., the status of adopted and step-children) to the primary issue, which is how the estate will be distributed pursuant to the various types of intestacy schemes. It would be useful if the author indicated that there are three major types of intestacy regimes (strict per stirpes, modern per stirpes and per capita by generation), but the clarity of the earlier discussion has given the reader sufficient confidence in the author's abilities that the reader is willing to suspend any concerns about organization and content.

13. These two sentences provide a straightforward and correct description of the strict per stirpes approach to intestacy. Although the enunciation of the rule could be improved by reference to various statutes that follow this approach (the course book did include some specific examples), the precision of the language is the most important element. The random capitalization of "strict per stirpes" is technically incorrect, but the writing has been so good up until now (no grammatical or typographical errors), that error does not detract from the credibility of the author.

14. This sentence constitutes a legal conclusion, which precedes the application of the facts to the rule identified in the previous sentences. However, this approach provides a logical and useful transition to the "A" step, so the fact that it is technically out of order is not problematic.

15. Here it would be useful to indicate why Zeke is not included in this analysis. There are two relevant points to be made here. First, Zeke has no living issue, so his share is effectively incorporated back into the

residual estate. This principle was briefly raised in the first paragraph but could have been mentioned here as well. Second, the residual estate is being distributed following a life estate in the corpus of the estate, which could give rise to a discussion of whether the takers of the residuary are to be determined by reference to the life of the testator or the life of the holder of the life estate. It is possible that the author decided not to raise this second issue because it does not affect the distribution in this case (those who are alive at the time of Ted's death are also alive at the time of Zeke's death), but a brief mention of this legal issue and the relevant legal authorities would not have gone amiss. However, the author may have been running short on time and this issue is minor enough that its omission is not problematic.

16.   These four sentences include both the "A" and "C" steps of the IRAC analysis. This approach may be easiest to adopt in a question like this, where the determinative fact (survival) is easy to state and apply, but there may be other types of questions where this technique could be used. However, combination of application and conclusion would not be appropriate in cases where the relevant facts are more complicated.

RESPONSE (paragraph four)

According to the Modern Per Stirpes approach, the decedent's estate is distributed to the first generation where there is a survivor. If the descendant closest in lineage is dead, then the interest is proportionally shared by their next descendent.[17] Applying this approach to this fact pattern, the outcome would be the same as applying the Strict Per Stirpes approach above because there are living descendants in the first generation.[18]

COMMENTS (paragraph four)

17.   The author has succinctly and clearly stated the rule relating to modern per stirpes distribution. Capitalization of the term is unnecessary and technically incorrect, but this error is not problematic given the overall quality of the writing. Although the rule is not supported by any legal authority, the author has used and defined the term of art correctly, which wins the author key points.

18.   Again, the author combines the application and conclusion in a single sentence. The author also incorporates the previous discussion by reference, which is a useful way of saving time and words. However, the author is to be commended for the precision of the cross-reference. Rather than making a vague or general reference to the previous discussion, the author says the rule is the same as in the case involving strict per stirpes, which leaves the reader in no doubt as to what is being incorporated.

RESPONSE (paragraph five)

According to the UPC Per Capita approach, the decedent's estate is distributed to the first generation where there is a survivor. Then, the estate is "repooled" and distributed equally to the next generation.[19] Applying this approach to this fact pattern, Ted's estate would be distributed to the first generation.[20] Since Bob is the only living descendent in the first generation, he would receive one-fourth of the estate. Because Alice, Charles, and David are deceased, their three-fourths are "repooled" and distributed to the next generation's living descendants. So, H, I, K, and L would split the three-fourths evenly and they would each receive one-fourth of three-fourths. Because Bob already received his share, his child J would not receive anything.[21] As one can see, the UPC Per Capita approach results in what may seem to be a more "fair" distribution in that Alice's children H and I each receive an entire share equal to K and L's share rather than splitting Alice's share as would occur under the strict and modern per stirpes approaches.[22]

COMMENTS (paragraph five)

19.   Although the author does not use a transition sentence to introduce the third method of distributing an intestate's estate, the author's meaning is clear from the structural context. In this case, the author wins points through the explicit reference to the UPC (Uniform Probate Code), which is a specific statutory scheme in the field of estates and trusts. Although the author could have alternatively referred to distribution per capita by generation, the reference to the UPC is as good as a reference to a case. Again, the author has described the rule clearly and succinctly, with no extra verbiage.

20.   This sentence works partially as a transition and partially as a conclusion. Either way, it is concise and to the point.

21.   Although law students often worry about the math that is associated with distribution under an intestacy statute, this example shows that explaining the methodology can be as effective (and is often better than) simply trying to come up with the proper number. In this case, the precise dollar figure can't be identified, since the quantum of the residuary estate is not identified in the question, but the author has done a sufficient amount of math to show how the calculations would proceed. This approach is better than simply identifying the conclusion, since you are showing rather than telling. Demonstrating why you have come to a particular conclusion is not only more persuasive than simply saying what the conclusion is, it also allows you to gain partial credit if part of your analysis is wrong.

22.   This sentence provides a bit of policy context for the discussion regarding the three types of intestacy schemes. Although the author seems well able to go into a more in-depth analysis, she is likely pressed for time. Furthermore, a lengthy discussion about policy considerations

would not be appropriate here, since the question did not ask about those types of issues. Nevertheless, this one-line reference shows a nice breadth of understanding.

RESPONSE (paragraph six)

The next issue is whether these answers would change if Bob and his wife were expecting another child at the time of Zeke's death.[23] Under the strict per stirpes, modern per stirpes, and UPC approaches, unless the potential taker dies before she becomes entitled to take, the child of such potential taker is not entitled to take.[24] As a result, because Bob is living at Zeke's death, Bob would receive his one-fourth share of the estate and his child would not be entitled to take.[25]

COMMENTS (paragraph six)

23.   Here, an explicit transition sentence is necessary because the author is shifting to the second part of the question, which involved the alternate fact scenario. This transition also serves as the "I" for the following analysis.

24.   The author does an excellent job of incorporating the previous discussion by reference even though that term is not used. Furthermore, by referring to all three intestacy schemes, the author provides a comprehensive legal analysis to the question posed.

25.   The author here combines the "A" and "C" steps, as has been done previously.

RESPONSE (paragraph seven)

The last issue is whether these answers would change if Charles's widow was expecting another child at the time of Zeke's death.[26] Under most views, because spouses are not blood relatives, they are not entitled to take.[27] However, living grandchildren are considered issue and entitled to take. Under the UPC, a child in utero at a particular time is treated as living at that time if the child lives 120 hours after birth.[28] Therefore, assuming that Charles' widow is expecting Charles' child, this child would be entitled to take part of his share if the child lives 120 hours after birth.[29] Under the strict and modern per stirpes approaches, this child would share Charles' one-fourth with his sibling, K and they would each receive one-half of one-fourth (one-eighth).[30] Under the UPC Per Capita approach, Bob would receive one-fourth and the remaining three-fourths would be "repooled" and distributed evenly between H, I, J, K, L and the new baby.[31]

COMMENTS (paragraph seven)

26.   Again, the author uses a clear transition and identifies the issue under discussion so as to situate the reader in the legal analysis.

27.   This sentence is slightly awkward, but it is still clear. The absence of legal authority for this proposition can be forgiven since the author is likely running out of time and this is a relatively minor sub-issue.

28.   The specificity of this particular legal rule is very good. Not only does the author identify the particular statutory scheme (the UPC), the author also cites the rule correctly and in detail (the 120 hour rule). Although there are other types of statutes dealing with unborn children, the author has focused on the most important and clearest of them. Again, a fuller discussion is technically possible, but time is probably an issue at this point. The author is showing good judgment in what to include and what to omit.

29.   This sentence provides a conclusion to the question of whether the unborn child will take. However, the following sentences are also necessary because they address the secondary issue, which relates to the amount that child will receive.

30.   There is a minor grammatical error in this sentence (a second comma is needed after K), but the overall quality of the writing makes this oversight negligible. It would be useful to note that the UPC approach to unborn children can be followed even in jurisdictions that do not adopt the UPC per capita by generation approach to intestacy, but the author is showing good judgment in not trying to make this one response perfect at the expense of the other questions that must be answered during the exam period. It is important to stick to a time schedule when answering exam questions so as to gain maximum points overall.

31.   Again, it is incorrect to capitalize "per capita" in this context, but the author has at least been consistent throughout the response. Furthermore, the author has done a good job in addressing all the potential issues in a comprehensive manner.

G.   Estates and Trusts Question Two

This second estates and trusts essay is also an excellent example of the IRAC method. Structurally, this essay is outstanding. Estates and trusts law (like contract law) can prove difficult for IRAC analyses, since the issue cannot always be equated with a clear cause of action, as is the case with courses like tort and criminal law, but the author here succeeds in putting the various elements together in a standard IRAC format.

The analysis is not only well-structured, it is also very well supported by authority. Not only does the author include a number of different cases and statutes, he or she does a good job of presenting conflicting authority and showing how the analysis would vary under those different legal regimes. Furthermore, the author shows how to introduce new authority in the "A" step.

The essay is at its strongest when it is tied closely to the language of the supporting statutes and cases. The author is least effective during his or her discussion of the second sub-issue, since he or she makes a number of substantive errors. However, the strong use of supporting authorities, clear structure, and concise writing, even in that problematic section, allows the author to earn a significant number of points despite those problems.

QUESTION

Teodoro and Alicia were married for over thirty years and had two children, Jack and Jill, who are twins. Before Jack and Jill were born, Teodoro and Alicia had a daughter named Hillary who survived only three days before dying. For some time after Hillary's death, Alicia was distraught and convinced that Hillary had been snatched from her hospital cot. When Alicia became pregnant with the twins, she stopped talking about Hillary and never mentioned her again.

Teodoro died several years ago. This past winter, Alicia went on an exotic holiday to Brazil, where she contracted yellow fever and died. Because Jill won the lottery a few years back and is independently wealthy, Alicia's will—which seems to be the only one made by Alicia—gives a few keepsake trinkets to Jill (i.e., some family silver and an heirloom ukulele) but gives Jack "the rest and residue of my estate."

When collecting Alicia's estate, you find a ruby necklace—valued at $30,000—located in Alicia's safety deposit box.

Along with the necklace is a short note written and signed by Alicia in her distinctive but nearly illegible script. The note stated:

When I die, I want my daughter, [the name here is not quite readable, but the last three letters look like "__ill"], to have my ruby necklace.

/s/ Alicia

The note is undated and is not signed by anyone else.

Jill has come to your law firm, asking for legal advice as to who is entitled to the ruby necklace. The senior partner on the case has asked you to draft a short memorandum outlining the various legal issues that will require further research and consideration. Include your tentative conclusions and rationales to the extent possible in the time available.

RESPONSE (paragraph one)

The question at issue is whether the note in the safety deposit box is valid.[1] The key sub-issues involve whether the note is a valid holographic will, whether the note can be admitted as extrinsic evidence of the testator's intent, and whether the note was the result of an insane delusion.[2]

COMMENTS (paragraph one)

1.   This sentence attempts to establish the issue, which can be a bit difficult in subjects where the issue is not identical to a cause of action. The author does a good job, but just needs to finish the thought by saying that validity means whether the note is valid as a testamentary document.

2.   As a matter of structure, the author does a good job identifying the sub-issues that will be discussed. There are some problems in terms of the substantive law, but those will be ignored throughout the comments, since the focus of the critique is on the structure and style of the essay.

RESPONSE (paragraph two)

In determining the validity of the note, the first sub-issue which must be addressed is whether the note is a valid holographic will.[3]

COMMENTS (paragraph two)

3.   The author here has successfully framed the first sub-issue that he or she will address, though it would be better to avoid one-sentence paragraphs.

RESPONSE (paragraph three)

According to *Zhao v. Wong*, a valid holographic will must (1) be signed by the testator, (2) contain evidence of testamentary intent, (3) be in the testator's own handwriting, and (4) be dated.[4] Unlike most wills, holographic wills do not have to be witnessed.[5] Holographic wills are recognized by approximately half of the states.[6] In states that follow the UPC, only the "material portions" of the holographic will must be in the testator's own handwriting.[7] Moreover, UPC § 2–502(b) does not require the holographic will to be dated.[8] Thus, the resolution of this sub-issue depends on the law of this particular jurisdiction.[9]

COMMENTS (paragraph three)

4.   This is a very good use of authority straight off and provides a succinct list of the elements that must be proven.

5.   This is a good comparison to other parts of the syllabus and identifies an element that does not need to be proven. Of course, the statement would be stronger if it was supported by authority.

6.   While this sentence does not add anything to the legal analysis, it provides a useful bit of background that helps reinforce the perception of the author as knowledgeable about the subject matter in general.

However, these types of statements, by themselves, will not result in a top-ranking essay.

7.   Here the author shows how to introduce competing authority. Instead of relying simply on one authority to establish the legal test, the author identifies a second. This technique not only earns additional points in those classes where exams are scored on the basis of how many cases and statutes are mentioned, it also shows that the author appreciates the reality of legal practice, i.e., that law is made up of multiple, sometimes complementary, sometimes conflicting, sources of authority.

8.   The author does a great job of remembering the precise number of the statute and in identifying one of the ways in which holographic wills differ across jurisdictional lines.

9.   This is an excellent way to conclude the "R" section. Not only has the author identified the two key authorities, he or she has identified how they differ and how that difference may affect the current analysis.

RESPONSE (paragraph four)

Here, the note in the safety deposit box meets the first three requirements of a holographic will.[10] It contains Alicia's signature, it is in Alicia's "distinctive" handwriting, and it evinces Alicia's testamentary intent ("When I die, I want my daughter ... to have my ruby necklace" expresses testamentary intent insofar as it directs the distribution of her estate upon her death).[11] However, the note is undated.[12] This is problematic because it is difficult (if not impossible) to determine when the note was written in relation to Alicia's will.[13]

COMMENTS (paragraph four)

10.   The author here clearly moves into the "A" section of the analysis.

11.   This is a good, concise illustration of how the various facts meet the legal standard at issue.

12.   Stylistically, putting a short sentence in the midst of longer sentences works well.

13.   This sentence suggests that the author may address the relationship between the note and the will. This is a useful bit of information to know, since the initial "I" paragraph did not make it clear that the author was intending to address this issue.

RESPONSE (paragraph five)

In a jurisdiction that follows *Zhao v. Wong*, the note does not meet the requirements of a holographic will.[14] In a UPC jurisdiction, the note could still be a valid holographic will even though it is undated.[15] Even if the note is deemed valid, the lack of date is still problematic because courts will not know how to define the note's temporal relationship to Alicia's will.[16] Under UPC § 2–507, a subsequent written instrument that makes a complete disposition of the testator's estate is presumed to replace (rather than supplement) any preexisting will(s).[17] UPC § 2–507 further provides that a subsequent written instrument that makes an incomplete disposition of the testator's estate is only presumed to revoke the previous will insofar as it is inconsistent.[18] If the note was written prior to the will, it could be argued that the note was revoked by the subsequent will.[19] If the note was written after the will, it could be argued that the note revoked the previous will with regard to the ruby necklace.[20] Thus, even though the note may be a valid holographic will in UPC jurisdictions, it will still be subject to significant construction issues.[21]

COMMENTS (paragraph five)

14.   This is a good, clear "C" statement.

15.   Again, this is a straightforward "C" statement.

16.   This sentence might do well as the first sentence of a new paragraph discussing the effect of the note, if the note is indeed found to be a valid testamentary document.

17.   Here the author introduces new legal authority outside the "R" section. Although it is often better to include all of the legal authorities in the "R" analysis so that the reader can understand the legal context of the "A" analysis, putting cases or statutes in the application section is acceptable. The reason the technique well works here is because the author is addressing an issue that did not arise until the validity of the holographic will had been determined.

18.   The language here is excellent. The author has drafted a precise and concise summary of the statutory language, which not only shows the author's facility with the materials but also his or her appreciation for details in legal analysis.

19.   Although this sentence is in the same paragraph as various rules, it is technically an application analysis.

20.   Again, this is an "A" analysis.

21.   Although the author chose to stop here, it might have been a good idea to continue with the analysis of the outcome of the dispute, depending on whether the note could be read to supplement the existing will. Students often need to undertake this type of judgment call in law school exams, since a question might trigger a number of potential discussion points.

RESPONSE (paragraph six)

The second issue to consider in determining the validity of the note is whether Alicia's will is ambiguous, thereby creating the possibility of admitting the note as extrinsic evidence.[22]

COMMENTS (paragraph six)

22.   Here, the author is clearly moving to a new topic that will be subject to its own IRAC analysis. Again, it often is considered improper to have a single sentence paragraph, but such niceties are often overlooked in the pressure of an exam scenario.

RESPONSE (paragraph seven)

As aforementioned, the note in the safety deposit box contains evidence of Alicia's testamentary intent.[23] The intent of the testator is a predominant policy consideration in the law of estates and trusts.[24] When a will is ambiguous, courts have two options for resolving the ambiguity in a way that honors the testator's intent.[25] Courts can look either to (1) the four corners of the will or (2) extrinsic evidence, including documents and testimony.[26]

COMMENTS (paragraph seven)

23.   This is useful incorporation by reference to an earlier discussion.

24.   This is such a general proposition in estates and trust law that a citation is unnecessary.

25.   This sentence is a bit jarring given the preceding statement—the reader is not quite sure where the author is going at this point.

26.   While this statement seems relatively basic and thus may not need any authority, it still is not quite clear where the author is going, possibly because he or she has not tied the discussion as closely to particular authorities, as was the case with the discussion about holographic wills.

RESPONSE (paragraph eight)

There are two types of ambiguities, patent and latent.[27] A latent ambiguity (such as the one at issue in *Estate of Gibbs*) exists when the will's language is facially unambiguous, but is susceptible to more than one interpretation in light of external facts.[28] A patent ambiguity (such as the one at issue in *Knupp v. D.C.*) is one that is apparent on the face of the will (e.g., failing to identify a residuary taker despite an earlier reference to one).[29] The Restatement makes no distinction between patent and latent ambiguities and allows extrinsic evidence to resolve both.[30] Under the rule announced in *Estate of Gibbs*, extrinsic evidence is permitted only where the will contains a latent ambiguity.[31] Extrinsic evidence is never allowed to cure a patent ambiguity.[32] This reflects courts' general reluctance to add — as opposed to erase — portions from a will.[33]

COMMENTS (paragraph eight)

27. This statement operates as a topic sentence.

28. This is a good definition, supported by authority. The statement is not tied as closely to the case law as some of the rules identified in the holographic will section and thus is not quite as precise, but it is sufficiently descriptive and concise.

29. Again, a good definition, supported by authority. The example is drawn from the case law discussed in class and thus shows facility with the materials.

30. This is an excellent introduction of yet another legal authority that may resolve some of the interpretive issues that arise in the "A" section.

31. Again, a relevant and concise "R" statement accompanied by authority.

32. There is case law to support this point, but the essay has already had so much authority that it is not missed here.

33. This point, which was made during class discussion, is nicely incorporated into the analysis.

RESPONSE (paragraph nine)

Alicia's will does not contain a latent ambiguity.[34] In a state that does not follow the Restatement, the court will almost certainly bar admission of the note as extrinsic evidence.[35] Based on the facts provided, Alicia's will does not contain a patent ambiguity either.[36] Thus, even in a state that does follow the Restatement, the chance of admitting the note is very low.[37]

COMMENTS (paragraph nine)

34. We have now moved to the "A" section, even though the statement appears conclusory in nature. Normally it would be useful for the author to connect the dots between the law and the facts, but the author is likely beginning to run short on time.

35. Here the author makes a mistake as a matter of substance. However, as a matter of style, the sentence seeks to connect the law and the facts in classic "application" mode.

36. This statement is somewhat conclusory and would benefit from an explanation of why a patent ambiguity does not exist. While the reader

could try to infer what the author meant, students are encouraged to avoid "submarine arguments" that put the onus of the analysis on the reader.

37.   Again, there are some errors of substance here, but structurally this statement constitutes the "C" statement for the second sub-issue in this essay.

RESPONSE (paragraph ten)

The third issue to consider in determining the validity of the note is whether it is the product of an insane delusion.[38]

COMMENTS (paragraph ten)

38.   Here we have the transition to the third issue. Again, this sentence would be better as part of a larger paragraph from a stylistic perspective.

RESPONSE (paragraph eleven)

Dougherty v. Rubenstein defines an insane delusion as a belief that is so improbable under the circumstances that no person of sound mind could give it credence.[39] The standard for establishing insane delusion is relatively high.[40] This is a relatively high standard—As long as there is any reasonable rationale for the testator's alleged insane delusion, it is not considered an insane delusion.[41] If, however, it is determined that (1) the testator was under an insane delusion and (2) the testator's will is the product of an insane delusion, then the will is invalid (see *Dougherty v. Rubenstein*).[42] An insane delusion must focus on a specific person.[43] Common examples of an insane delusion include the belief that a relative is trying to murder them, a spouse is being unfaithful, or a child was fathered by someone else.[44]

COMMENTS (paragraph eleven)

39.   As with the first sub-issue, the author starts strongly with a well-summarized proposition of law, using precise language from the case cited.

40.   Here, it appears that the author made some edits that were not corrected due to time pressures, since this sentence is repeated in the following phrase. Professors do not mark off for these kinds of errors in a timed exam situation, although such errors should be caught in papers with a longer deadline.

41.   The paraphrase may go a bit too far as a matter of substantive law, but the author is attempting to expand upon the basic test identified in the first sentence, which is a good tactic.

42.   It is acceptable to cite the same case twice, so long as both references support the proposition in question, as is true here.

43.   Often, short sentences that introduce only a single element of the legal test are problematic, since they eat up space without contributing a great deal to the substantive discussion. Instead, it is usually better to combine all of the elements of the governing legal standard into a single, densely packed sentence. However, here the author—who writes very well—uses the short sentence as means of breaking up the pacing of the paragraph.

44.   While these behaviors do not arise in the current fact pattern, they are common examples of insane delusions. The author does well to mention them here, since they may provide a useful basis for arguments by analogy during the "A" analysis.

RESPONSE (paragraph twelve)

If Alicia's note gave the ruby necklace to Hillary, then Alicia could be said to be operating under an insane delusion that Hillary was kidnapped and still alive somewhere.[45] This belief would satisfy the elements of an insane delusion because (1) Alicia's belief, which centers on a specific person, is so improbable under the circumstances that no rational person could give it credence and (2) the note in the safety deposit box is the product of the insane delusion that Hillary is not dead.[46]

COMMENTS (paragraph twelve)

45.   Although the author does not specifically state that he or she is moving into the application section of the third issue, the mention of the facts, combined with reference to the legal standard at issue, demonstrates that beautifully. This transition shows that you do not always need a transition sentence, per se, to move between sections of the IRAC analysis.

46.   This is a very nice way of combining the "C" step with the "A" step. This technique allows the author to pack a great deal of information into a very small space.

RESPONSE (paragraph thirteen)

Insane delusion is a question of fact to be decided by a jury, thus the outcome in this case is more difficult to predict.[47] If the note gave the necklace to Hillary, it would be invalid as the result of an insane delusion and the necklace would pass to Jack (as part of the residuary estate).[48] If the necklace was not left to Hillary, then the court would likely inquire into Alicia's intent as to who the necklace should go to.[49]

COMMENTS (paragraph thirteen)

47.   The author has included one final "R"-type element, thus showing the reader that he or she has legal authorities and propositions to spare—a phenomenon that professors always like to see.

48.   The "it" in this sentence refers to an incorrect antecedent (the necklace as opposed to the note), but the author is obviously seeking to tie the three sub-issues together in a single "C" statement. This technique is critical, given the multiplicity of sub-issues discussed in this essay.

49.   It is perfectly acceptable to provide an alternative outcome, as is done here, provided that it is not done simply to avoid making a difficult judgment call. Notably, the author was quite clear in the earlier analysis, avoiding the type of wishy-washiness professors dread, so an alternative outcome is not a problem. Furthermore, it is useful to discuss the various alternatives here, since the disposition of the necklace requires an understanding of estates and trusts law. There is a grammatical error—it should be "to whom" not "to who"—but that is a minor point.

Index

References are to Pages

249